Hardcore, Punk   Junk

Hardcore, Punk, and Other Junk

Aggressive Sounds in Contemporary Music

Edited by Eric James Abbey and Colin Helb

LEXINGTON BOOKS
Lanham • Boulder • New York • Toronto • Plymouth, UK

Published by Lexington Books
A wholly owned subsidary of Rowman & Littlefield
4501 Forbes Boulevard, Suite 200, Lanham, Maryland 20706
www.rowman.com

10 Thornbury Road, Plymouth PL6 7PP, United Kingdom

Amorphis. All Amorphis lyrics used with permission courtesy of Nuclear Blast Records and
Amorphis.

Eluveitie. All Eluveitie lyrics used with permission courtesy of Nuclear Blast Records and Eluveitie.

Korpiklaani. All Korpiklanni lyrics used with permission courtesy of Nuclear Blast Records and
Korpiklanni.

Stone Vengeance Lyrics. All lyrics used with permission courtesy of Michael Coffey.

Stone Vengeance Epigraph. All lyrics used with permission courtesy of Michael Coffey.

Hellmouth. All lyrics used with permission courtesy of Jay Navarro and Hellmouth.

British Library Cataloguing in Publication Information Available

Library of Congress Cataloging-in-Publication Data

Hardcore, punk, and other junk : aggressive sounds in contemporary music / edited by
Eric James Abbey and Colin Helb.
     pages cm
   Includes bibliographical references and index.
   ISBN 978-1-4985-3231-0 (pbk : alk paper)
   ISBN 978-0-7391-7605-4 (cloth : alk. paper) -- ISBN 978-0-7391-7606-1 (electronic)
 1. Hardcore (Music)--History and criticism. 2. Punk rock music--History and criticism.
 3. Heavy metal (Music)--History and criticism. 4. Noise music--History and criticism. 5.
Popular music--Philosophy and aesthetics. 6. Popular music--Social aspects. I. Abbey,
Eric James, 1976- editor of compilation. II. Helb, Colin, editor of compilation.
   ML3534.H373 2014
   781.66--dc23
                                 2013050231

Printed in the United States of America

For those who struggle with aggression.

Contents

Foreword
Jeremy Wallach

Aggressive music was not supposed to change the world. At the outset it was imagined more as a rearguard action, a cathartic outlet. It was what frustrated young men and women turned to when the world didn't go their way, when it instead attacked them from all sides. Loud guitars and forceful drums drove back the all-out assault on one's humanity, on dignity, on the right to have a good time. Aggressive music in all its stripes, from the most hedonistic heavy metal to the most politically strident grindcore to the most orthodox punk, is what Lester Bangs called "unarguable affirmation." It exhorts its listeners to claim their essential humanity in the face of the dehumanizing forces—deindustrialization, dictatorship, deindividuation, whatever—that threaten to overwhelm them on a daily basis. We can add the searing pain of imperialism, racism, sexism, and homophobia to that list, for as improbable as it may seem to those who adhere to stereotypical notions of rock as the exclusive domain of straight white, Western males, the weight of the empirical evidence collected by the authors of the following essays as well as a whole host of other ethnographers, sociologists, and other qualitative researchers over the last decade is undeniable. This is a party to which everyone is invited.

All over the world, the musics aggression gave kids a way to say to themselves: we've got a right to be angry, we've been lied to, it's not us, it's *them*. The list of *them*s is extensive and, as my co-editors and I found out in our global metal study, varies considerably across time and place. It ranges from the timeless—lousy, booze-addled parents—to the timely—the latest corrupt, hypocritical politician or cleric to scapegoat young people for social ills created and perpetrated by adults. If all the music did was help people survive adolescence, that would be no mean feat, but in certain times and places it did much more. Aggressive music has played a role in some of the most dramatic social uprisings of the last quarter century, from the 1990s democratic revolutions in the former Soviet bloc to the Indonesian overthrow of the Soeharto regime in 1998 to the 2011–13 Arab Spring. Aggressive music was not supposed to change the world, but by stubbornly insisting on the importance of never surrendering humanity, it has.

The essays in this volume run the gamut from an ethnographic study of a contemporary heavy metal scene in Puerto Rico (by Nelson Varas-Diaz and Eliut Rivera-Segarra) to an analysis of Sid Vicious's vicious cover of Frank Sinatra's "My Way" (by Evan Ware). Race and metal are discussed with the band Stone Vengeance (Kevin Fellezs) as well. The art of Throbbing Gristle (Brian Cogan) is also considered. Within the book's rubric of aggressive music, punk and metal are considered together, so we also look at heavy metal lyrics (Mika Elovaara), vocal techniques (Marcus Erbe), and rituals along with more esoteric musical oddities such as Krishnacore (Colin Helb) and avant-garde noise (Ross Hagen). The volume is rounded out with Sean Ahern's discussion of the popular band the Dropkick Murphys and their articulations of Irish - American identity and Eric Abbey's discussion of the cult of Hellmouth. Most of these chapters share a focus on the last century, a time when rock music enjoyed a greater market share in the United States, but a smaller one in many other parts of the world. This was also the time of the formative years for hardcore, punk and metal. These years, perhaps rendered safer through temporal distance, have become the focus of greater scholarly scrutiny, but this is not in itself a bad thing. Appreciation of great art is better late than never. The essays in this volume narrate chapters in the ongoing story of amplifiers and throats, of drums and guts, of one of the greatest art forms of twentieth-century global culture.

Acknowledgments

Eric Abbey would like to first and foremost thank Ann, Owen and Brendan for being a part of everything that I do and for the space to write. This collection would not have been possible without my co-editor Colin Helb and his dedicated work. To Tom Kitts for mentorship and being a great friend, thank you. To everyone involved with the PCA/ACA organizations around the world, thank you as well for continuing to inspire people to research and write on topics that they love. For the contributors to this collection, it was great to work with so many different and exciting viewpoints from around the world. Thank you for your work and for putting up with us throughout the process. To Emily Natsios, Eric Wrona, and everyone at Lexington Books for seeing the potential in this collection and seeing it through to completion, thank you as well. Thank you to Maggie Lin for her extremely hard work on indexing and finishing up the book. Lastly, to everyone that loves aggressive music and the feeling they get from being in a pit, enjoy.

Colin Helb would like to thank Carolyn and a baby to be named later for putting up with sporadic hours, caffeine-induced all-nighters, and occasional rants. A huge thank-you is reserved for Eric Abbey for inviting me into this project and for being a friend and colleague. Thank you to the faculty, staff, and students of Elizabethtown College, specifically the Department of Communications, for allowing me the opportunity to do what I get to do. Thank you to the membership of the Popular Culture Association/American Culture Association and the Mid-Atlantic Popular & American Culture Association for the inspiration to study popular music, media, and culture. Finally, thank you to all the contributors to *Hardcore, Punk, and Other Junk* (especially my mentor, Dr. Jeremy Wallach); the wonderful people at Lexington; and all the musicians, authors, and fans who came before us and those who will follow us.

All effort was made to contact the rights holders for lyric permission for: the Dropkick Murphy's "The Fields of Athenry," "Caps and Bottles," "Time to Go" and "Going out in Style," Amon Amarth's "With Oden on our Side" and "War of the Gods," Frank Sinatra/Paul Anka's "My Way" and Sid Vicious's "My Way."

Introduction
Eric James Abbey

The concept of aggression in society is often viewed with disdain. This collection of writings challenges the notion that aggression in society is something to be shied away from. The chapters that form this collection demonstrate that aggression is a positive and necessary thing in music and in life. Without it, people repress emotion and become withdrawn and possibly violent and depressed. There is a distinct difference between violence and aggression and, through music, this difference is brought out and displayed with force. At this time in society there are many avenues to vent frustration. Music channels this frustration in positive ways and allows for growth of the listener and performer. While other forms of music create scenes, there is something about aggressive music that bonds people together. From the use of the past to reconfigure a classic song to the contemporary sounds of hardcore in America, this collection brings together the diverse sounds that form aggressive music. This is in no way the end of this discussion and the hope of this collection is to further the conversation about aggression in our society and the way that music is used in aggressive ways. Our hope is that you will find your own version of aggressive music represented in this collection and that it will possibly make you go back through your record collection in search of those songs that made you feel.

What does it mean to be aggressive in music? Is it something that is found in the lyrical content, the performance of the musicians, the chord structure? This collection demonstrates that it is all of these things and more. While focusing on any form of music that could be asserted as aggressive and not simply one genre, this book contains chapters on punk, metal, noise, hardcore, and anything that could be called aggressive. *Hardcore, Punk and Other Junk: Aggressive sounds in Contemporary Music* brings these genres together in an effort to share a commonality of aggression.

The questions then are what does it mean to be aggressive and how does this differ from violence or destructive tendencies? The answer lies within these chapters and this book is an effort to begin the conversation of the importance of aggression within contemporary society. What is sometimes viewed with a lack of understanding or a feeling of fear is oftentimes used by performers and participants to expel anger, vent frustration, or to come to a sense of internal peace.

Although the term aggressive music can mean a variety of different things, this collection strives to bring different forms of music under a similar moniker. The intent is to find the similarities in diverse forms of music from noise to metal, punk to hardcore, and many things in - between. This similarity, as evidenced in the following chapters, is the way that these forms bring people together and allow for people to express an emotion that is usually not accepted within society.

Our contemporary world has become one in which people are angry at the government, the established rules, and society in general. While this is not different from the past, it has taken a much broader feel. Aggressive music, whatever the intent, gives people a way to express this anger. The importance lies in this expression. It is not simply a way to release emotion but the coming together of people in unity to express a disdain for society in whatever way they choose.

The foundational view of this book works with the concept of aggression that was proposed by Konrad Lorenz in 1966. In his view of aggression the human body consistently builds up aggressive energy and must release it somewhere. This has oftentimes been called the steam-boiler model. The importance here is that Lorenz's discussion suggests that we all have to deal with our own aggression in some way. "According to this model, aggressive behavior is the inevitable of the continuous production of aggressive energy. Even if it were possible to remove all instigating stimuli, this would not abolish aggressive behavior."[1] This ethological model is what this book attempts to build upon. Aggressive music allows for this release and for the formation of collective identity.

An important distinction in this book is how the definition of aggression varies within our society. Social psychologists consistently view aggression as a negative response to stimuli of some sort. "Most social psychologists have focused on aggression as a negative form of social behavior that causes problems between individuals, groups, and societies."[2] This viewpoint may be correct from the standpoint of observing and studying negative aggressive behavior in our society, but what of the needed release that Lorenz and many others have discovered? The need to release aggression in some form is the focus of this book.

Through hardcore, punk, and other junk, performers and participants in the music come to a commonality of aggressive release through listening to the music, going to concerts, and becoming a part of something that they find greater than themselves. The concept of what some say is junk is also an important issue within this book. Many listeners and the "general" public would consider some of these styles of music junk and not worth creating or listening too.

It is this throw away mentality that aggressive music is vying against. The way that society rejects or wishes to move away from harsh feelings of aggression is what this form of music thrives on. Joe Strummer stated in an interview for *Sniffin Glue*, "We deal in junk, you know, I just realized that the other day. We deal in junk. We deal in . . . the rubbish bin."[3] The aspect of junk and trash continues and in some ways, listeners to this type of aggressive music find a type of transcendence. In many of the following chapters, there is a sense of something greater being obtained through listening or following a group. Is this really a type of transcendence?

Any music can bring the listener to a different state of being; happy, sad, and full of love and joy, whatever. It is with aggressive music that the feeling of release is the focal point. As with music labeled as trash or garbage and thrown away by critics and pop music fans, "everyday people (and every day, people) talk about rock 'n' roll music in terms of salvation, transcendence, and lest we forget, trash"[4] The discussion of finding something greater in relation to musicians flows throughout this collection. The chapters were not specifically chosen for this, but somehow, all of them mention a feeling of togetherness that comes from just knowing about the music, as if listening to aggressive music in any form makes you part of something.

To be a part of something through the encouragement of musicians playing music that is meant to repel or to antagonize you is the reason that this book, and others like it, exist. The people who listen to aggressive music all begin with the basic premise that they need to release some form of negative thought or that there is something that they cling to that they feel is missing in their lives. This is the reason that musicians continue to perform types of music like hardcore, death, metal, noise, and punk; to release aggression in a nonviolent way.

What may appear as violent to outsiders is an aggressive trope that binds all of the mentioned musicians together. A sense of the vulgar and needed appellations of society being reflected through music is the key to this collection. This is inherently different from violence and aggression that is negative within our society. The distinction is not always clear and, even to members within these scenes, cause conflict and derision. The World Health Organization's definition of violence is "The intentional use of physical force or power, threatened or actual, against oneself, another person, or against a group or community that either results in, or has a high likelihood of resulting in injury, death, psychological harm, maldevelopment or deprivation."[5] Violence then is specifically aligned with intent to do harm. These musicians and participants in these scenes are not intending to harm others. They are intending to release negative emotions and to perpetuate an understanding between performers and listeners.

Even in scenes where the aggression leads to a pit or to a feeling of dread, participants revolt against people who "take it too far" or cross the line into actual violence. Within a mosh or circle pit, members who fall are often helped up or given a way out of the chaos. At a noise show, when performers actually become violent they are vilified and removed from the scene. This distinctive reaction is one that defines the line between aggressive release and violence at shows. Participants in the scene may appear violent or thuggish in nature or in their political views; however they are there for release of aggression, not to commit violent acts. This does not preclude exceptions, but when these exceptions occur at a show or performance the majority of people stand together to remove the violent person and to continue the show.

Contemporary examples of this abound. At a March 13, 2013 Dropkick Murphys show, an audience member was on stage dancing and started to give the Nazi salute.[6] The Murphys singer/bass player, Ken Casey stopped playing and dragged the audience member off of the stage while the rest of the audience and band kept the show going. After the incident the band members spoke to the audience about having a good time and that they would not put up with something like that. Examples continue in more localized shows as well.

If you are ever at a performance where a pit begins, all you need to do is watch what happens to people who fall. They are helped up and the "dancing" continues. This may be after eyes are blackened, legs are bruised, and ribs are smashed. The difference here is in the intent. It is the release of aggression through music and dancing that allows for these forms of music to affect participants and to succeed. This collection offers a view of many forms of aggressive music and challenges the notion that these forms are violent. They may be harsh and abrasive, but that is why they are essential to our contemporary world.

From the Sex Pistols to Hellmouth and every chapter between, *Hardcore, Punk, and other Junk: Aggressive Sounds in Contemporary Music* discusses the important need of aggressive release in our world. Through music, performers and participants share a commonality of release and form bonds within a community that accepts this aggression. The contributors to this volume have all felt this commonality and release in different ways, but through their writings we hope that you can see the similarities of listening to aggressive music within the contemporary world. So, sit back and enjoy the way that people from various parts of the world interpret, analyze, define, and have fun with the aggressive output of musicians who have become a part of them.

Notes

1. Krahé Barbara, *The Social Psychology of Aggression*: 2nd Edition (New York: Psychology Press, 2013), 35.
2. Krahé, 2
3. Hamelman, Steven L. *But is it Garbage? On Rock and Trash.* (Atlanta: University of Georgia Press, 2004), 61.
4. Hamelman, 213.
5. WHO global consultation on violence and health. *Violence: a public health priority (WHO/EHA/SPI.POA.2)*World Health Organization, Geneva (1996) 1.
6. For video please see http://www.youtube.com/watch?v=OsdQc2r7TPE

Chapter 1
Food for Thought: On Sid Vicious's Cannibalization of "My Way"
Evan Ware

"As an indicator of difference, as a way of dominating, stigmatizing and dehumanizing the other, food—or what is designated 'food'—has served as a powerful political tool. In fact, the degree to which one feels superior to another people might be gauged by the degree of one's repugnance to their diet. Like all such imprisoned fictions, this one gave rise to a reality (i.e., haute cuisine), and to an abiding cultural principle: 'Tell me what thou eatest, and I will tell thee what thou art.'"

Sherod Santos[1]

"Speculating irreverently on the qualities he would acquire after eating 'a little bit of Elvis,' Bangs, while punk's fire still glowed in 1980, has the chaos of Sid Vicious supplant the malaise of Presley: '. . . At least Sid Vicious got to walk onstage with 'GIMME A FIX' written in blood on his chest and bash people in the first row over the head with his bass if he didn't approve of the brand of beer can they were throwing at him. Sid got to have all the fun.'"

Neil Nehring quoting Lester Bangs[2]

I. Apéritif

We live in a world suffused with cover songs. This is not just the case of the playlists on Top 40 radio, but also in karaoke bars, and on nightly television where we witness strings of newly deemed pop classics sung by reality-show contestants, all oozing sincerity, all keeping an eye on the prize. In what George Plasketes has called the "cover age," it is an understandable mistake to think of cover songs as necessarily paying tribute to their forebears, since this would seem to be the dominant paradigm; it may be just as accurate to say we live in an age of homage.[3] But, although many cover songs are indeed reverent of their originals in some ways, others have more complex interrelations, and these—to

1

say nothing of the enterprise of studying cover songs in general—have received surprisingly scant scholarly attention.[4]

Philosopher Kurt Mosser has suggested that one of the problems current scholarship faces is a lack of vocabulary for accurately discussing cover songs. If we speak only of imitation, and do not pause to consider the difference between the kinds of imitation that are vehicled—servile tributes or radical departures—then we are collapsing the meaning of "covering" completely. To rectify this, Mosser has proposed a typology along an axis of decreasing veneration toward the original so that the reduplicative cover gives way to minor, and then major interpretations, send-ups, and finally parodies. He considers parodies to be the antipodes of reduplications or tributes, that they have only a minimal connection to the original.[5]

But what about covers that are *aggressive* toward their originals? It's not clear where in his typology these would fit in. Are they major interpretations? What if an aggressive cover contains elements of parody? What specific aspects of the song need to be changed and how extensively for the interpretation to qualify as "major"? Also, Mosser's categories belie an important conceptual inconsistency: terms like "minor/major interpretation" speak to a *quantity* of change, while labels such as "comic" or "parodic" speak to a *quality* of change. Though I think his terms are a useful beginning, their ambiguities make them too problematic to use exclusively. Moreover, given that musical performance is a dynamic reality that exists in time, I am reticent to ascribe labels that fix the process in a kind of categorical amber. In my experience boundaries are more fluid, so it might be more productive to speak of *processes* of covering rather than types of cover, and to examine the specific musical and performative ways these processes are enacted. This would have the advantage of considering both the quantity and quality of changes in describing how a song's interpretation unfolds.

In this chapter, I will examine how Sid Vicious's cover of Frank Sinatra's classic "My Way," as performed in Julien Temple's film *The Great Rock'n'Roll Swindle* (1980), embodies an aggressive covering process.[6] Punk is clearly not a genre in which praise is a strong element, and Sinatra's original, with its suave sophistication, its classy and urbane manner, was in many ways anathema to the blue-collar punk aesthetic of raw emotion and "authentic"—that is to say anti-virtuosic—musical performance. Yet Vicious sinks his teeth into "My Way" so deeply that it is not an exaggeration to say that he doesn't just cover it, he cannibalizes it. Explaining how Vicious devours Sinatra and therefore creates what could be called a hyper-aggressive cover, therefore, is the main course I am tempting you with here. Before that, I will be serving a soup to whet your palates, a way of framing and understanding the changes from one song to the next. I will do so by proposing that both songs are considered simultaneously and that one is considered the standard to which the other responds. I will then serve up an extensive platter of appetizers, analyzing how the qualities of changes from one song to the next manifest through quantities of such changes in the lyrics, physical gestures, vocal performance, music, and form. Then, the cannibalism, and after it's all over, there will be a digestif to cap off the meal.

And now, shall we begin? Perhaps you would like to look at a wine list? I'd recommend the house red. . .

II. Soupé du Jour—Stereophonically Listening to Strategies and Tactics

Michel de Certeau's "theory of practice," a view of the way consumers act in society, sees somewhat antagonistic forces called *strategies* and *tactics* attempting to each establish a way of being in the world. Strategies represent institutional or organizing forces that create spaces in which they relate to exterior agents, while tactics are the responses of these external agents, found in their decisions and, most specifically in their small-scale subversions of the institutional strategies.[7] Likewise, this frame can be applied to an analysis of cover songs in which the original is ostensibly the strategy and the cover a collection of tactics applied to create—to some extent—a new song. Seeing Sinatra's recording of "My Way" as a strategy is not a problem. It can be easily considered the most influential version of the song in existence. Immediately subsumed into the narrative of Sinatra's career and life, it became synonymous with him, and a staple of most of his concerts after 1969. I think that today, due to its incredible global influence, it would be unlikely for the average popular music listener or performer to be unaware of it. Performers in particular must contend with it and its meanings in the creation of their own way of performing it. Thus it is impossible to fully divorce the song from the man, or his image at any rate. This is the situation Sid Vicious faced in performing "My Way."

But the analyst is also faced with a similar issue, described by sociologist Deena Weinstein as "stereophonic listening," wherein a listener will hear both original and cover simultaneously, constantly comparing one to the other.[8] In this sense, the cover is never divorced completely from the original either in the ears of the listener or, presumably, in those of the cover performer. This is advantageous for the analyst. With constant direct comparison it becomes possible to point out very specific aspects of the performance that have changed. The degree to which the alterations contrast with the original can then be discussed, evaluated, and interpreted in order to come to some understanding of how these alterations change the song; how they reveal the cover's process of creation. Thus a major part of the intertextual framework of this cover is already a given and, taken with an understanding of Sinatra's version as strategy, so is the framework of influence. To be clear, my analysis is not an interpretation of Sid Vicious's intention, which is mostly unknowable. Rather, I want to examine how Sid Vicious's tactical responses give rise to analyzable musical aggression of such magnitude that it can be discussed as cannibalization.

In the following analysis, I will be looking at Sid Vicious's "My Way" in dialogue with Sinatra's. I will treat the latter's as a baseline against which the former's performative and expressive divergences can be made clearly audible and visible through lyric comparisons, physical gesture photos, and musical examples. But Sinatra's will also serve as a baseline for understanding how Vicious's meanings deviate from the "expected" or "normal." It is therefore important to acknowledge the work of music theorist Lori Burns, who has made specific musical arguments for how singers have changed the meanings of songs they cover.[9] In all of these cases, Burns has endeavored to link the material elements of music to social ideas through concrete analytical examples. Many of my analytical approaches draw from her methods.[10]

III. Entrée—Analysis

In covering "My Way," Vicious responds to the original's strategies by using two tactical modes that initially may seem at odds with each other. On the one hand, he injects artifice into the song by changing the lyrics at certain moments, by using body language to reinforce or otherwise comment on the song, and by using a vocal performance style quite different from its crooning beginnings. On the other, Vicious's version strips away artifice: vocal rhythms are squared and regularized, bass lines (and thus the harmonies) are simplified, and the vocal register is made importantly less expansive. The reason for this two-pronged assault is, actually, fairly understandable. Since Sinatra's performances tend to rely heavily on vocal delivery and musicianship, his physical performance is often rather muted, usually limited to a few gestures with the free hand while the hand holding the microphone stays very still.[11] In cooking up the song his way, Vicious has, therefore, two good points of entry to make changes: by seasoning the physical and vocal performance with his own material, and by trimming away excess bits of the music not essential to the song. In this manner he reverses the original's emphasis on music and musicianship in favor of body and vocal performance. The following analysis dissects how Vicious uses tactics to recast "My Way" in his own image.

Lyrics

Table 1 below illustrates all of the lyric changes Vicious makes. There are fifteen in total, divided up into "major" changes—in which significant words or entire passages are replaced with new material or omitted completely, resulting in change of semantic meaning—and "minor" changes—in which expressions are simplified or slightly changed without their overall meaning being affected. This chart quickly illustrates their effects. Of the twelve major changes, the vast majority directly subvert the triumphalism expressed in the original. Seven of the changes are related to issues of homosexuality and explicit violence, and two deal with powerlessness of personal expression. In this context, references to homosexuality are not made in a positive light; it is something to be denied ("I'm not a queer," "not in a gay way"), or sexually violent ("I fucked a bloke, and did it my way").

Table 1 Lyric Changes in Sid Vicious's "My Way" (Minor changes in italics)

Vicious Lyric	Original Lyric	New Meaning Category	Major/Minor
Ha, ha! You cunt, I'm not a queer	My friend, I'll say it clear	Homosexuality	Major
along the highway	*upon the byway*		*Minor*
There were times	*Yes, there were times*		*Minor*
when there was fuck-, bugger-all else to do	when I bit off more than I could chew	Homosexuality	Major
I shot it up, I kicked it out	I ate it up and spit it out	Violence	Major
I faced the wall -----(omitted)------	I faced it all, and I stood tall	Violence	Major
I've been a snide	I've laughed and cried		Major
To think I killed a cat	To think I did all that	Violence	Major
And might I say, not in a gay way	And might I say, not in a shy way	Homosexuality	Major
For what is a brat?	For what is a man?	Inside Reference	Major
When he wears hats, then he cannot	If not himself, then he has naught	Inside Reference /Powerlessness	Major
say the things	*to say the things*		*Minor*
but only the words (of one who kneels)	and not the words	Powerlessness	Major
I fucked a bloke	I took the blows	Homosexuality	Major
--------------(omitted)--------------	Yes it was my way		Major

Either way, when homosexuality is invoked in the song, it is threatening and disturbing. The violent images, of killing cats, of hard drug abuse (a kind of self-directed violence), and execution (facing a wall), also cast the song lyrics into bleak and nihilistic territory invoking psychopathy, substance abuse, and death.[12]

Arguably, the dark turn of the lyrics is mixed with a certain playfulness, one that delights in tearing down the banal monumentality of lines like "I took the blows" by making it about what was, in 1979, still popularly seen as a transgressive form of sex, "blokes fucking blokes."

The lyrical changes, then, while keeping the overall frame of the song intact, provoke surprise in a first-time listener familiar with the original. Whether that surprise turns to laughter, revulsion, or possibly both clearly depends on the listener, but it also has to do with the musical and performative context the words are found in. Sid Vicious singing these words in a punk take on "My Way" is less surprising than it would be hearing Sinatra use the same words in the original setting.

Physical Gestures

The film integrates Vicious's physical performance directly. Set in a French theatre, the illusion of a taped live event is given when an emcee gives Vicious an introduction in French to an enthusiastic audience that figures in several cutaway scenes during the segment. As the music starts, Vicious descends a long staircase—the only set on the stage—and begins to sing—the only human actor on the stage. In this way, all of the viewer's attention is focused on Vicious, who capitalizes on this by using physical gestures to spread his own meanings over the song unopposed. Interestingly, with only a few spectacular exceptions, these are not used to reinforce the lyric changes discussed above. Instead, Vicious "fills in the gaps" as it were, redefining the meanings of unchanged lyrics in the context of his own physicality. This is particularly relevant to the opening (0' 00" – 1' 15"), in which he directly mocks the crooner musical style and claim to authenticity. Using a combination of eye-rolling and knowing eyebrow raises, Vicious rends the fourth wall and communicates a certain disbelief in his own performance. Certainly, none are signs of homage or of sincerity. The "gay" limp wrist at (0' 36") also references his own performance in the sense that he is critiquing what he is doing as "gay," a concept that is treated disparagingly by lyrics, as we have already seen. This gesture is also likely aimed at the viewer of the video, not the in situ concert audience who cheer the sign of homosexuality, blithely ignorant to the gesture's disparagement of the song and of themselves.

When the "crooner" section ends and the overdriven electric guitar comes in at 1' 15", Vicious's demeanor changes from one of false pomposity to what appears to be for him a more comfortable—he smiles for the first time—sneering punk rocker persona.

The gestures that Vicious uses most frequently in the subsequent "punk" section of the song: the pursed-lip sneer, the teeth ripping head shake (like a dog ripping a piece of meat), the defiant fist shake, and falsely innocent looks ("Oh, no, not me!") are punk gems. These gestures are all slathered onto unchanged lyrics from the original, taking them out of their confessional and intimate context and placing them into one of defiance and aggression. The only exception to this is the look Vicious gives with the line "when there was fuck-, bugger-all else to do." Here we have both a changed line and a physical gesture, one that reinforces the mocking nature of the words.

There are, however, five moments when gesture and word changes combine, and these all revolve around the miming of lyrics: "I shot it up" (2'19"), "I kicked it out" (2' 22"), ". . . as tears subside" (2'49"), "I killed a cat" (3'00"), and ". . . when he wears hats" (3' 22"). These moments represent some of the most potent tactics present in the song. In each case but one, the physical acts performed by Vicious reinforce lyric changes, drawing attention to them, but also displacing their expressivity from music—where expressivity is mostly found in Sinatra's performances—into the body. The only exception, when he sings "as tears subside" and indicates tears with his finger, has the effect of over-determining the meaning, making it ironic, distanced, and insincere. In the rest of the cases, Vicious is explaining the lyrics with his actions, emphasizing the passages and their transgressive natures. This corporealization is taken further in Vicious's vocal tactics.

Vocal Performance

Much like his physical gestures, Vicious's vocal performance is a layer that is added onto the song without fundamentally changing its musical components. His performance works on one level, I believe, because the original is never totally obscured through the various interpretive tactics. Vicious uses his voice as yet another way of either distancing himself from the original lyrics or emphasizing word changes or gestures, sometimes both at once.

At first, in the "crooner" section, Vicious sings in what is obviously a put-on chest voice, mocking the typical crooner baritone. While the voice does have a parametric aspect, structuring the song into "crooner" and "punk" sections, for now, I will treat it as a kind of baseline from which Vicious diverges for expressive effect.

Ex. 1 (all transcriptions by the author)

Example 1 above shows how Vicious performs the changed lyrics "Ha ha! You cunt/I'm not a queer/I'll state my case/Of which I'm certain" (0'39" – 0'50"). The words "cunt" and "queer" are sung on notes that are decidedly flat of a tempered A (illustrated above by a backward flat sign). Also, in both cases Vicious pushes to raise the pitch to a normal A without success; on "cunt" he causes his voice to break high, and on "queer" the upward pressure is unremitting but never brings the note into tune. Since he sings normally tuned pitches on "not" and "state," this is clearly not an issue of competence but of deliberate emphasis on two key words. As these words recall "others"—women and homosexuals—they inhabit an "other" world, and they are set to resemble but not belong with the surrounding music. With the word "case," Vicious's voice wavers so much as to become a trill, rapidly alternating with the in-tune A and a nondescript higher pitch. The now normalized A is simultaneously combined with the "othered" pitch world.

By the turn to a clearly punk-rock genre at 1' 15", Vicious adopts a nasal head voice.

Ex. 2 a)   *b)*

c)   *d)*

He thereafter rhythmically and performatively distorts words in the first half of certain measures. Examples 2 a through d illustrate these moments compared to their analogues in Sinatra (Vicious is the upper example of each letter). Where Sinatra tends to be freer with the upbeat (beat 4 in a 4/4 bar), Vicious's upbeats are mechanical 3 quarter-note patterns (2a and c), sometimes slightly syncopated (2b and d). He does, however, replace Sinatra's mostly unadorned beats 1 and 2 with more elaborate gestures, usually coming from his idiosyncratic—and certainly not "correct"—pronunciation.

Vicious also chews up the words using a few different techniques. Speech-song is one in which the singer approximates pitches but really delivers the line as a kind of heavily inflected speaking voice (inflections are notated with "x" noteheads approximating pitches).[13] Other techniques he uses are scoops (rising into a note), falls (a drop from a note), and glissandi ("swooping" from one note to another without articulation). These tend to obscure the sung pitches, all the more when used in conjunction with speechsong. As "My Way" develops, Vicious uses these tactics more frequently and for longer time spans, but also increasingly in moments where the lyrics have been changed. The passage in Ex. 3 demonstrates how Vicious ultimately saturates the music with his various vocal tactics, moving from scooping and falling to speechsong to out of tune notes (the D# on "way" is actually ¼ tone higher) to altered downbeat rhythms. But this passage also links the three analytical lenses used thus far—lyric changes, physical gestures, and vocal performance—showing their overlapping and intensification

Ex. 3

and thus the degree to which Vicious is changing—it is tempting to say digesting—the song.

Melody, Harmony, and Form

If Sinatra's restrained performance represented an opening for Vicious to take a bite out of "My Way," elaborating meanings vocally and physically over original and modified lyrics, then the musical materials of the song represented a different kind of opportunity: the chance to simplify, break down, and trim the fat. Paring down the musical artifice of the song, therefore, becomes a powerful tactic for asserting his expression within preexisting musical context.

Despite the vocal performance tactics noted above, the melody of "My Way" as it is manifest in Sinatra's and Vicious's versions is remarkably similar. The most notable change is certainly the increasing *lack* of it as Vicious's version progresses, the pitches being replaced by speechsong approximations and eventually even shouting. As noted above, the rhythms that Vicious employs tend to be much squarer than Sinatra, who maintains a fairly consistent triplet feel and frequently holds notes over strong beats, singing "between" beats as it were. Such subtlety and sophistication of rhythm is nowhere present in Vicious's performance, though his distortions of words on the downbeat are occasionally quite intricate in their mastication of the original setting. But there is another element of Sinatra's performance that Vicious strips away that is even more telling. At first blush it is not an overtly obvious change, but it is nevertheless one that I think has strong implications for the musical expressivity of the melodic line.

One of the principal ways that melodies get stretched out in Western music is through the ornamentation of a fixed tone, usually the third or fifth note of the scale (in this case G#, the third note of E major).[14] Part of what creates a sense of phrase and section endings is how this pitch moves down by step to the tonic of the scale (G#-F#-E). A common way to ornament or prolong this "head" tone is to shift it up an octave. This can be done by a single leap or by step over time. In Sinatra's recording exactly this happens (see Ex. 4a).

Ex. 4 a) Sinatra

b) Vicious

It is therefore interesting to note that Vicious's version does *not* do this. Yes, the musical line rises in the analogous moments (see Ex. 4b), but it stops short of reaching the higher G#. This has the effect of dislocating the essential melodic motion G#-F#-E, of reaching for something never achieved, of denying an expectation (because it is, after all a very common move), and thus removing some of the punch from Vicious's phrase endings.

This does not happen in isolation, of course. The passages in Sinatra's version in which the G# is transferred up an octave are more fully orchestrated, and thus much louder and more dramatic than their surrounding verses. Vicious's version does not achieve climax in this fashion. I suggest that this is because the climax in Vicious is not musical, but performative: the catastrophic moment when Vicious literally draws his gun and fires on the concert audience in the film. The end is arrived at, not by musical buildup as in Sinatra, but by increasingly intense *performance*, perhaps a kind of foil to "deficient" melodic unfolding.

Similarly, the harmonies used in Vicious's "My Way," while they are mostly the same chords, are presented in a much less elaborate way. The bass lines in each version, which give definition to the harmonies above them, stand apart despite their similarities. The principle difference between them is the level of counterpoint, or interaction of melodic and nonmelodic musical voices (in this case notes played by the guitars and bass).

Ex. 5
a) Vicious intro

b) Sinatra intro

The bassline that descends in half steps in Sinatra's is present in Vicious's but as a voice above the bass. This simplifies the harmony to E major for the first few measures instead of the more convoluted progression in Sinatra. Moreover, two moments of disconnect occur in the musical semantics. First is the F#m/E chord moving to the B chord (a). The common progression would be to resolve the E (the 7th of the chord) by step in the bass to Bmaj/D#. By moving directly to B, the seventh (a common dissonance) is left unresolved. Secondly, the F#/A to E maj move (b) is, in the original a move to B with the E chord notes moving to the B chord notes over a stable bass. In Vicious, this does not happen; the E chord simply stands in and interrupts the move to B (the goal of the harmonic motion). It is a small rupture, but one at a harmonically important and quite conventional moment. The overall effect is to defuse the force with which the B chord is arrived at, making the ending sound less conclusive.

In example 6 below, both bass lines from the "Yes, there were times" section are compared. It is easily observable that the bass line in Sinatra's is much more active and complex than the one in Vicious's. Indeed, the overall musical

Ex. 6 (note that Sinatra's version is ½ the speed, so each of his measures equals two of Vicious's)
a) Vicious

b) Sinatra

texture in Sinatra's is busier and more intense. The harmonies are an integral part of this activity and the intensity that arises from it. Again, the same passage in Sinatra's is a climax that in Vicious's is not significantly more musically intense than the verse before it. True, the harmonies are changed more frequently, but the texture and level of musical activity remain otherwise constant. The fundamental reason for this divergence is the very different core idea behind each song's development.

Whereas Sinatra's "My Way" is built up along a traditional Tin Pan Alley format (AABA, but in this case slightly modified to AABAB), Vicious's is more through-composed, that is to say continuous from beginning to end. There is a definite break between the "crooner" and "punk rock" sections at 1' 15" as observed in both vocal performance style and the sudden more than doubling of the tempo, but the subsequent sections do not share as much differentiation as Sinatra's. This "flatness" of musical profile—the same instrumentation, the same dynamics, the same or slower rate of chord changes, the voice's incomplete melodic rise—neutralizes the climactic profile of the original, leaving the real work of intensification to Vicious's performance. Thus he acts out more, changes more lyrics, and uses more elaborate vocal interpretations more frequently as the song continues. The images of violence in the lyrics as well as in his body and voice all proliferate gradually over the various musical sections until the final "my way" results in Vicious not even singing the tonic (E), but screaming and then throwing down the microphone, drawing a gun, and shooting into the audience seven times before flipping everyone off and walking away. The violence that was hitherto an artifact of performance and musical interpretation transgresses the fourth wall and becomes real.

IV. Plat du Jour—Cannibalism as an Interpretive Framework

Vicious's approach to covering "My Way" is directly aggressive to its subject. By changing the lyrics to include violent imagery, by adding bodily enactments of this violence in performance, by distorting words and melody, by denying the melody its climactic high note, by denying the harmonies their climactic contrasting loudness and contrapuntal activity, and by ultimately performing a physical act of violence toward the audience in the video, Vicious runs contrary in almost every way to Sinatra's polished, performatively restrained, and musically sophisticated—and conservative—original. Where Sinatra is sober, Vicious is dynamic. Where Sinatra is subtle, Vicious is in your face. Where Sinatra is aiming for sincerity, Vicious is aiming to trash it. The extent to which the song is wrenched from its original context—a context directly alluded to in the actual song during the "crooner" section—and how we are made to witness this wrenching as it unfolds, pushing the song further and further beyond its original meanings, makes a description of it in static terms like Mosser's "parodic cover" seem inadequate. While there are undeniable elements of parody in the performance, parody is only a beginning point for the interpretation, which grows and changes as the song goes on. The emergent quality of Vicious's interpretation leads me to argue that this song is best discussed in terms of process rather than message, *cannibalizing* rather than parody.

As a transgressive trope, cannibalism is particularly savory since it activates not only the revulsion of a broken taboo, but also a whole host of "other" associations, particularly ones stemming from the ignominy of colonial rule and the fear of the human beast. Much has been made in the anthropological community over the past thirty years about the actual existence of cannibalistic practices, with some arguing that cannibalism is a colonial fiction created to ease the domination of indigenous cultures.[15] It is not my intention to contribute to that debate here. Instead my interest is in the very idea the controversy brings up: that there is a received view of cannibalism in the West, one that comes in part from an agenda of colonial imperialism, one that would have been available to British youths in the 1970s as it still is available to youths today.

Surveying the current state of anthropological research on cannibalism, Shirley Lindenbaum has noted that "cannibalism"—the colonial trope—is dependent upon the binary opposition of "savage other" versus "civilized self."[16] It is thus a strategy of exclusion, of othering and difference-making so as to be able to feel no human relationship to those to whom the term is ascribed.[17] In fact, Margaret Kilgour has argued that this trope was a projection of Western imperialist appetites onto those they sought to dominate so that they may have good reason to dominate them; the cannibalistic savage must be subjugated.[18] Writers have often used it as a metaphor, Swift (1729) as political criticism, Defoe (1719) as ambiguous desire, de Sade (1797) as a critique of colonialism, and Flaubert (1862) as a critique of the bourgeoisie.[19] In all cases, it is a matter of "transgressive consumption" and a part of the Enlightenment split of the "noble savage" trope into either the "beautiful siren" or the "bestial cannibal."[20] That as late as 1986, anthropologist William Arens called the word "cannibal" the "ultimate derogatory comment" attests to its enduring cultural potency as a nexus of "otherness."[21]

This "otherness" is often observed as a kind of "other world," a world in which cannibalistic practice turns a society into a kind of unregenerative anti-society. In his survey of Scandinavian folk stories, John Lindow has discussed this aspect in relation to the folk legend "The Outlaws that Kidnapped the Girl" collected in 1915.[22] In most versions of this tale, a girl is kidnapped and held in the outlaws' village, where they rape, impregnate her, and proceed to eat each baby after its birth.[23] The outlaw society, therefore, cannot grow since it eats its offspring, and thus becomes an "other," a gruesome anti-society that is then contrasted to the girl's home village where normal relations prevail and to which she ultimately escapes.[24] Far from an isolated story, Lindow says, the idea of taboo food as a marker of passing into an "other world" is quite common in rural legendry in general.[25]

Another aspect of cannibalism as nonregenerative social practice, as Kevin Ohi argues with reference to the film *Suddenly, Last Summer* (1959), is its longstanding tropological association with gay sex.[26] Here the inability to create offspring and the resulting futility of the gay man's mother's role in bringing a nonreproducing child into the world are equated to social self-consumption of cannibalism; and of course sexual otherness also conjures images of "other worlds" in which the familiar is—for some—shockingly deterritorialized.[27] Thus the trope of cannibalism—be it cannibalism, homosexuality, or colonial relations—is fundamentally a trope about othering, about making the other bestial, savage, and nonhuman.

Anthropologists recognize three distinct categories of cannibalism: endo-cannibalism, in which the people eat the dead of their own culture/group; exo-cannibalism, in which the people eat the dead of their enemies; and pathological cannibalism, often the result of serious mental disorders. The exocannibal is of particular interest to me here, as it is this practice that is born of anger and aggression. The cannibal finds their own selves through the process of ingesting that which is most hated, the enemy.[28] I think that understanding Sid Vicious's interpretation of "My Way" as a kind of exocannibilistic practice, wherein he consumes something anathema to punk—Sinatra's version is quite ripe with meaning because I believe that Vicious is in fact inverting the trope. Rather than using it to dehumanize and "other," he is in fact othering *himself*.

As we have seen, what lyrical changes he made to the song have the effect, for the most part, of drawing in issues of gay sex ("I fucked a bloke"), violent and self-destructive actions ("I shot it up, I kicked it out"), and the trappings of antisocial personalities ("I killed a cat"). All of these issues construct his persona as "other" and even as a part of an "anti-society" as described above. To emphasize his otherness, he relies on a repertoire of physical gestures that contrast markedly with Sinatra's staid physicality. Teeth ripping and defiant fist shaking are frequently recurring actions, homosexuality is referenced with a "gay" limp wrist, and some of the more violent images in the changed lyrics are mimed (shooting up, killing cats).[29] This kinetic, dynamic performance adds layers of meaning to the song far beyond the boundaries of the original. There is none of Sinatra's triumph or self-satisfaction to be found here, there is no consolation.

Thus not only is Vicious "othering" himself by changing the words to those of an "anti-society" or "other world," but he is acting them out bodily in the video, making his *performance* "other" with respect to Sinatra.

The theme of otherness runs through the music as well. Vicious's vocal performance runs against Sinatra's bel canto smoothness and technical proficiency. Instead, Vicious distorts the original words by missing the pitches or bending them beyond recognition, by staking out the liminal space between song and speech, and by removing the stylized and subtle rhythmic inflections of the original in favor of square rhythms that sound so oddly unfitting in comparison. Vicious's melodic line in the two meatier verses ("There were times/I'm sure you knew" and "For what is a brat?"), just like in Sinatra, ascends from a low G# up toward the G# an octave above, but unlike Sinatra, he never makes it, the highest note of the song is never sung—so to speak—the goal is never reached. Taken with the chord progressions that defuse the sense of intensity and goal-directedness present in the earlier version, the melody and harmonies work to *deaden* a sense of closure. The instrumental changes between verses are negligible as well, producing a flatness of texture along with the weakened phrase endings that give the song a feel of continuity whose only strong articulation of "ending" is Vicious's screaming "my way" over the din. These considerations also run against the Sinatra version, and indeed certain conventions in Western musical practice. The music—just like the performance and the words—is othered.

The markers of otherness I have identified in the filmed performance of "My Way," while they certainly set it apart from the original, and possibly from "civilized" society in some kind of "other" musical and performative world, set the stage for but do not in and of themselves refer to cannibalism. As I indicated above, a good interpretive frame for this song has to be one that takes into account its dynamic processes, and cannibalization was the lens through which I wanted to look. This process, I think is made quite explicit in the form of the song. "My Way" starts in the world fairly close to that of Sinatra, the world of showbiz, of big useless stage staircases and crooning but with a number of interpretations that make this showbiz world an "other world." As the song progresses, however, the genre of punk, which was always present in the background, asserts itself fully and in increasing intensity, with vocal techniques gradually suffusing the melody and trying to overpower the climax-resistant musical texture. Throughout, the singer's homosexuality is vehemently denied but just before the climactic vocal utterance of "my way" that loses all sense of pitch in its shouted utterance, Vicious declares that he "fucked a bloke." The music misses its climactic note (the high G#), and then Vicious throws down the microphone, draws his gun and opens fire. This moment, when the violence alluded to, talked about, and mimed in the song crosses the threshold from performance to reality (at least in the context of the film's narrative world) is also the moment when the othering becomes absolute, when Vicious becomes a monster, an uncivilized beast murdering innocent people. Thus the process of the song takes the listener into increasingly othered territory, territory that is more and more remote from

Sinatra. Vicious eats up Sinatra's suave and civilized song and spits it out transformed beyond all recognition into a savage act of mass murder.

V. Digestif

Cannibalizing a song is not without its corollaries in the reception of punk music in general and Sid Vicious in particular. Certainly, there is no lack of identifying punks as "others." Lawrence Chua called the Sex Pistol's music "profoundly non-human," and the punks themselves supposedly thought they were "niggers of the world."[30] Most of the British punks came of age in the UK at a time of widespread youth unemployment and ineffectual government initiatives to deal with this reality, many also failing out of school.[31] Sheldon Schiffer's account of punks as outsiders looking for inclusion is ápropos, but the relationship is apparently a bit more complicated.[32] In his review of the film *Sid and Nancy*, Maurizio Viano discusses how Vicious's cover of "My Way" is somewhat of a paradox: in seeking success, Vicious engages with the music that the Sex Pistols were attacking.[33] Through my analysis, I aimed to demonstrate how Vicious's "My Way" was such an extreme cover that it could be thought a kind of aggressive cannibalization of a song, a case of exocannibalism. But in the end, isn't covering a song also making a statement that the song is worth being reheard? Doesn't the cover implicitly value the original? Perhaps in some way Vicious's cover could be thought of as a kind of endocannibalism as well, in which he was eating that which he desired for himself, or what he considered part of his "tribe." Complicating this situation is another form of cannibalism:

> For decades, pulp rock novels had ended with a scene out of The Golden Bough, with the ritual devouring of the star by his followers, and Sid Vicious was begging for it: for the absolute confirmation that he was a star.[34]

Maybe these distinctions are ultimately unimportant. In the midst of such intensity, all three realities may exist simultaneously in an ambiguous relation with each other: Vicious swallowed a famous song and in doing so revealed the savage beast that was in turn the wellspring of his own fame and ultimate consumption.

* * *

The endpoint of this analysis then is in identifying, through the matrix of cannibalism, a hyper-aggressive process of covering a song. It is not my intention to suggest that cannibalization is a fixed category of cover that can be applied as a label, but rather that it is a tantalizing way of serving up an explanation—at least for Sid Vicious's "My Way"—of the dynamic relation of the performer to the cover song, and ultimately to the original. Because, in this case,

"tell me what thou eatest, and I'll tell thee what thou art" has a certain applicability. . . but so does "tell me *how* thou eatest . . ."

And now that we have finished with this matter for the time being, would
you care to see a dessert menu?

Notes

1. My deepest gratitude to my wife Megan Hill for her sharp editorial eye, patience,
and love. The quotation is from Sherod Santos, "Divine Hunger: A Poetics of Cannibalism," *The Kenyon Review* 22, no. 1, New Series (January 1, 2000): 55.

2. Neil Nehring, "Rock Around the Academy," *American Literary History* 5, no. 4
(December 1, 1993): 785.

3. George Plasketes, "Further Re-flections on 'The Cover Age': A Collage Chronicle," in *Play It Again: Cover Songs in Popular Music,* George Plasketes, ed., (Burlington,
VT: Ashgate, 2010): 29.

4. This observation was made by Plasketes in the introduction to his book (Plasketes, "Introduction," 2). In fact, Plasketes's volume is probably the first to be devoted to
critical approaches to cover songs. The only other full-length book on the subject, to my
knowledge, is Thomas Schneider's dissertation on blues covers, Thomas A. Schneider,
*Blues Cover Songs: The Intersection of Blues and Rock on the Popular Music Charts
(1955–1995)* (Memphis: Dissertation, University of Memphis, 2001).

5. Kurt Mosser, "'Cover Songs': Ambiguity, Multivalence, Polysemy," *Popular
Musicology Online* 2008,
http://www.popular-musicology-online.com/issues/02/mosser.html. (Accessed on 1 August 2012)

6. The movie was assembled out of Temple's live footage of the Sex Pistols in addition to material shot specifically for the film. The recording of "My Way" is detailed in
Géant-Vert, "Sid Vicious—My Way: The true story of the recording of My Way in Par-
is," http://www.philjens.plus.com/pistols/pistols/pistols_sid_myway.htm (accessed 1
August 2012) and seems to be in March–April 1978 (though the source appears a bit
apocryphal). For the purposes of this analysis I am using the unabridged video, found on
Youtube at "Sid Vicious—My Way," http://www.youtube.com/watch?v=HD0eb0tDjlk
(Accessed 1 August 2012).

7. Michel de Certeau, *The Practice of Everyday Life*, (Berkeley: University of California Press, 1984): xviii-xix.

8. Deena Weinstein, "Appreciating Covers," *Play It Again: Cover Songs in Popular
Music* George Plasketes, ed. (Burlington, VT: Ashgate, 2010): 246.

9. See Lori Burns, "'Joanie' Get Angry" in *Understanding Rock: Essays in Musical
Analysis,* John Rudolph Covach and Graeme M. Boone, eds. (New York: Oxford University Press, 1997); Lori Burns and Alyssa Woods, "Authenticity, Appropriation, Signification: Tori Amos on Gender, Race, and Violence in Covers of Billie Holiday and
Eminem," *Music Theory Online* 10, no.2 (June2004),
http://www.mtosmt.org/issues/mto.04.10.2/mto.04.10.2.burns_woods.html (accessed 1
August 2012); Lori Burns et al., "Cotextuality in Music Video: Covering and Sampling in
the *Cover Art* Video of "Umbrella" in Nicole Biamonte, ed., *Pop-Culture Pedagogy in
the Music Classroom: Teaching Tools from American Idol to YouTube* (Lanham, Md.:
Scarecrow Press, 2011).

10. For instance, she demonstrates how Bilie Holliday's melodic economy hearkens to Toni Morrison's descriptions of understatement as a narrative strategy for survivors of the trauma of slavery, Burns and Woods, "Authenticity, Appropriation, Signification," 17–18, 24.

11. Sinatra's performance style is clearly demonstrated in his 1971 performance in London "Frank Sinatra – My Way (Frank Sinatra Live in London 1971)" and "http://www.youtube.com/watch?v=dqBlIyFcjXs (accessed 1 August 2012) and his October 1974 performance at Madison Square Gardens, "My way (Subtitulada) Madison Square Garden, New York 1974, http://www.youtube.com/watch?v=vQRSIUNeZTI (accessed 1 August 2012).

12. Domestic animal cruelty is considered to be an early indicator of antisocial personality disorder. See Roman Gleyzer, MD, Allen R. Felthous, MD, and Charles E. Holzer III, PhD, "Animal Cruelty and Psychiatric Disorders," *Journal of the American Academy of Psychiatry and the Law*, vol. 30, no. 2 (2002): 257–265

13. I am adapting this from Arnold Schoenberg's notated speechsong, or *Sprechstimme*, first used in his work *Pierrot Lunaire* (1912). *Sprechstimme* has been discussed as a punk technique in Caroline O'Meara, "The Raincoats: Breaking down Punk Rock's Masculinities," *Popular Music* 22, no. 3 (October 1, 2003): 309.

14. This and what follows is a very short summary of some of the melodic theories of Austrian music theorist Heinrich Schenker. These can be found in Heinrich Schenker, Ernst. Oster, and Oswald. Jonas, *Free Composition = (Der Freie Satz): Volume III of New Musical Theories and Fantasies*, Longman Music Series (New York: Longman, 1979).

15. The controversy was started by William Arens's book *The Man-eating Myth: Anthropology & Anthropophagy* (New York: Oxford University Press, 1979). Although it fostered a host of widely varying reviews, it was by 2004 accepted as an important contribution to the field, a wake–up call for anthropologists to remember that they are subject to their own blinding cultural biases, see Shirley Lindenbaum, "Thinking About Cannibalism," *Annual Review of Anthropology* 33 (January 1, 2004): 475–6.

16. Lindenbaum, "Thinking about Cannibalism," 477.

17. Lindenbaum, "Thinking about Cannibalism," 476.

18. M. Kilgour (2001) cited in Lindenbaum, "Thinking about Cannibalism," 476.

19. Lindenbaum, "Thinking about Cannibalism," 486–7.

20. Lindenbaum, "Thinking about Cannibalism," 485, 488.

21. Arens is quoted in Gina Kolata, "Anthropologists Suggest Cannibalism Is a Myth," *Science* 232, no. 4757, New Series (June 20, 1986): 1500.

22. John Lindow, "Kidnapping, Infanticide, Cannibalism: A Legend from Swedish Finland," *Western Folklore* 57, no. 2/3 (April 1, 1998): 103–117.

23. Lindow, "Kidnapping, Infanticide, Cannibalism," 103–105

24. Lindow, "Kidnapping, Infanticide, Cannibalism," 111

25. Lindow, "Kidnapping, Infanticide, Cannibalism," 112.

26. Kevin Ohi, "Devouring Creation: Cannibalism, Sodomy, and the Scene of Analysis in 'Suddenly, Last Summer'" *Cinema Journal* 38, no. 3 (April 1, 1999): 39.

27. Ohi, "Devouring Creation," 40. Also see David Bergman, *Gaiety Transfigured: Gay Self-Representation in American Literature* (Madison: University of Wisconsin Press, 1991), 142 referenced in Ohi, "Devouring Creation," footnote 15 for an appraisal of the history of cannibalism as a trope for homosexual sex. Beth A. Conklin has also linked cannibalism with sex, though not specifically homosexual sex, in "Consuming Images: Representations of Cannibalism on the Amazonian Frontier," *Anthropological Quarterly* 70, no. 2 (April 1, 1997): 70.

28. J. M. Blanchard, "Of Cannibalism and Autobiography," *MLN* 93, no. 4 (May 1, 1978): 667.

29. It is interesting to note, however, that the cat killing mime looks suspiciously like he's slitting his own wrists, making this, along with the fact that he murders his "girl-friend" in the final shooting sequence, somewhat ominously prescient; Vicious would attempt suicide by slitting his wrists while awaiting trial for Nancy Spungeon's murder only a few months after this video was made in 1978.

30. Lawrence Chua and Julien Temple, "Julien Temple," *BOMB*, no. 72 (July 1, 2000): 43. Maurizio Viano, "Sid and Nancy," *Film Quarterly* 40, no. 3 (Spring 1987): 37. For more on the issue, see Dick Hebdige, *Subculture, the Meaning of Style* (London: Methuen, 1979), particularly chapters 2–4.

31. Kathleen McDermott, "'All Dressed Up And Nowhere To Go': Youth Unemployment And State Policy In Britain," *Urban Anthropology and Studies of Cultural Systems and World Economic Development* 14, no. 1/3 (April 1, 1985): 94–97; Eric Bryant Rhodes, "The Filth and the Fury," *Film Quarterly* 54, no. 3 (March 1, 2001): 58.

32. Sheldon Schiffer, "The Cover Song as Historiography, Marker of Ideological Transformation," *Play It Again: Cover Songs in Popular Music*, George Plasketes, ed. (Burlington, VT: Ashgate, 2010): 85.

33. Viano, 36.

34. Greil Marcus, "Martian Genes," *The Threepenny Review*, no. 26 (July 1, 1986):

Chapter 2
Let the Shillelagh Fly:
The Dropkick Murphys and Irish American Hybridity
Sean Ahern

Celtic punkers the Dropkick Murphys cover Irish folk songs alongside gruffy, angry working-class tirades from the heart of Boston. As punks, they breathe new life into Irish folk songs made popular in the United States by the Clancy Brothers and the Dubliners. Possessing a "full range of characterization"[1] of the Irish that is present within punk mainstays the Pogues, the Murphys apply popular Irish folk songs and stereotypes within the space of the American punk and hardcore scenes to connect with an imagined homeland.

The Dropkick Murphys use the cultural stereotypes of the Irish American to create a new cultural space within punk rock and national identity. With bagpipes, tin whistles, and banjos that sanctify Irish labels in the states the Murphys have defined what it means to be Irish American through specific cultural texts, sounds, and codes. This chapter discusses the ability to create hybrid cultures through appropriation and association of real hometowns and fantasized homelands. Using the theories discussed by Ien Ang in *On Not Speaking Chinese* as a starting point, I will analyze the works of the Dropkick Murphys as an Irish American hybrid that uses cultural patterns as fuel for self-othering, self-discovery and community maintenance. To illustrate my points I will look at three Murphy songs—"The Fields of Athenry" and "Time to Go" off their fourth album *Blackout* (2003) and "Going Out in Style" off *Going Out in Style* (2011). Each of these songs connects the band to their hometown of Boston while simultaneously connecting them to the struggles of Irish immigrants to the United States and the geographic space of Ireland.

The New American Way: Irish Folk and its Influence on Celtic Punk

The relationship with an imagined homeland for the Dropkick Murphys is reminiscent of reggae, its appropriation by London punks in the late 1970s, and the creation of oppositional discourses through the application of past struggles. Sarah Daynes writes about the idealized image of Africa in "The Musical consumption of Diaspora: the case of Reggae and Rastafari." The power of a "special elsewhere" helps to link those abroad back to a reinvented homeland (in this case, an idealized Africa of the past) with various levels of identification through shared symbols. These symbols come from past experiences but help to collapse temporal and special boundaries into a fictional "elsewhere" experienced by fans (and the displaced descendants) abroad.[2] In the 1970s the struggles of reggae and Rastafarianism would be applied to the emerging punk movement in the United Kingdom as the black, West Indian style was appropriated by bands like the Clash and the Slits to make them oppositional to modern British society through the application of reggae anthems alongside the calls for anarchy.[3] Reggae would help to bring in outside influences to the movement while creating a political and cultural edge that was lacking within a movement started within the chic fashion boutiques of Kings Cross.

Alongside Daynes and Dick Hebdige, using Ang's ideas on national culture versus national identity, Ang argues that self-identification with a specific culture creates a sense of belonging to a real or imagined place of birth, however those same feelings marginalize those abroad.[4]

> It is clear that many members of ethnic minorities derive a sense of joy and dignity, as well as a sense of (vicarious) belonging from their identification with a "homeland" which is elsewhere. But this very identification with an imagined "where you're from" is also often a sign of, and surrender to, a condition of actual marginalization in the place "where you're at."[5]

I would argue, in relation to the Irish abroad in America, then, that bands like the Dropkick Murphys or Flogging Molly create a new hybrid sound with their appropriation of traditional folk songs, creating a new fusion between Irish American culture, punk rock, and the displaced, diasporic longing for a homeland. Ang goes on to talk about the linkage of international viewpoints of the minority group abroad to the local, the past image of a homeland and the present situation in the country, and the conceptions of national culture and national identity which are based largely on the geography and the history of the culture. She states that diasporic cultures should let go of a national culture in favor of a hybrid between "where you're from" and "where you're at." She explains the idea of "biculturality" but states that this type of branding does not do justice to the creation of a culture out of a hybrid of the two.[6]

Divorcing oneself from a culture through self–othering may remove the individual from national discourses and further marginalize them, but it also creates a hybrid culture where one balances his/her birth home with an imagined ancestral land. A band like the Pogues speaks to the Irish abroad in England as much as the fans of the punk rock genre through their use of Irish folk songs and traditional Irish instrumentation.

Alongside Ang, Simon Frith's *Sound Effects: Youth, Leisure, and the Politics of Rock 'N' Roll* and *Performing Rites* helps to explain personal engagement with popular music texts. Frith argues that popular music helps to elevate common, everyday language past the mundane, with individualized responses to mass texts.[7] In *Performing Rites* he explains how popular music can change temporal and geographical boundaries as the experience of listening leads to extraordinary experiences.[8] Finally, Peter Doyle's *Echo and Reverb* discusses distinct images of specific locations important to the musician created by blues artists at the Chess and Sun Studios in the 1940s and 1950s that act as reference points for the audience.[9] The ever-present image of a landscape and/or personal identity within a presumed nationality appears within rock music and helps to associate past forms with new audiences. It creates a picturesque setting to connect an audience with the performer and other concertgoers. Both of these authors point out that it is not only about the mass text but also the personal connection that one may (or may not) make with the text when listening to and reacting to popular music.

Since the 1970s, popular music acts from Ireland have ran the gamut from rock acts like Van Morrison, Thin Lizzy, U2, and Sinead O'Conner, punk bands Stiff Little Fingers and the aforementioned Pogues, and pop acts like Westlife and B*Witched in the 1990s. While Bono and company remain the blueprint of rock bands to emerge from Ireland over four decades later, influences from Irish - folk bands like the Clancy Brothers have been covered and released by contemporary Celtic rock/Celtic punk bands. Two of the best known bands—the Dropkick Murphys and Flogging Molly—routinely cover Irish folk songs on albums and in concert. Unlike Flogging Molly, whose lead singer Dave King is from Dublin, the Murphys are Irish American, rather than simply an Irish touring rock band. Since 1996, the Dropkick Murphys have played a brand of punk rock that promotes local roots, familial bonds, and working–class heroism behind a veil of Celtic instrumentation: notably tin whistles, banjos and the bagpipes of Robbie "Spicy McHaggis" Medenos or Josh "Scruffy" Wallace. Alongside original songs, the band have recorded renditions of "The Wild Rover," "Courtin' in The Kitchen," "The Fields of Athenry" and "The Rocky Road to Dublin." Since their 2003 release *Blackout* the band has included an expanding arsenal of instruments. The application of folk instruments to later albums shows a desire to experiment and create a balance between Boston punk and the Irish culture of New England.

In 2005 the band released *The Warrior's Code* as a follow up to *Blackout*. On their 2007 release *The Meanest of Times* the band further plays up local roots, Catholicism, and records the folk songs "(F)lanagans Ball" and "Johnny, I Hardly Knew Ya." In 2011, the band released *Goin Out in Style*, a concept album that intertwines familial stories with fiction to create the tale of Cornelius Larkin. The album includes a cover of "The Irish Rover." There is, as Ang states, a mixture of "where you are from" and "where you're at" within the music of the Murphys as these songs are reinvented and reinterpreted through a punk lens.[10] This balance between new and old allows for the discovery of cultural roots by fans that can act out what they believe it means to be "Irish." The songs simultaneously connect the band to Boston while at the same time retell the struggles of earlier generations.

"It's so lonely 'round the fields of Athenry:" The Irish Diaspora of Irish —American Punks

The Dropkick Murphys, cover of "The Fields of Athenry" retells the tale of a man sent to Australia for stealing to feed his pregnant wife and family during the Irish famine of the mid-1800s. The song is filled with bagpipes and heavy guitar riffs that bring new life to the folk song. A listener does not need to be aware of the laissez-faire politics of the 1800s or the work of Sir Charles Trevelyan during the famine to understand the underlying fear of leaving one's homeland for the last time.

> By a lonely prison wall
> I heard a young girl calling
> Michael, they have taken you away,
> For you stole Trevelyan's corn
> So the young might see the morn
> Now a prison ship lies waiting in the bay
> Low lie the field of Athenry
> Where once we watched the small free birds fly
> Our love was on the wing, we had dreams and songs to sing
> It's so lonely 'round the fields of Athenry [. . .][11]

Ken Casey's delivery of the song retains the traditional lyrics of a man forcibly removed from his family and homeland. As Casey sings about "raising her child with dignity" now that Michael has been sent away the woman becomes the embodiment of Ireland and her child its people. There is longing to come home to the family, safe with one's family, but circumstances have divided them (most likely, with his exile to Australia) for generations to come. The singer of the song is an outsider relaying the message back to an audience as he watches the two lovers part for the last time as Michael is sent from Ireland for what many could say are unjust reasons.

While "Athenry" is a cover of a traditional Irish ballad, it falls in line with original songs written by the band that remind the listener to stand up for their hometown, family, region, and nationality. While there is a plentitude of songs by the Murphys that associate with this idea (including the pro–mining union "Which Side are You on?" and "10 Years of Service") they can be sublimated into one lyric from "Caps and Bottles:" "Protect your friends and family name" (*Sing Loud, Sing Proud!*).[12] Even though the members of the Dropkick Murphys are Irish *Americans*, unlike bands such as House of Pain, who, as Noel McLaughlin and Martin McLoone point out, were less acceptable within Ireland because "they self-consciously parody aspects of Irish 'authenticity,'"[13] they are accepted. While Irish stereotypes are present within the Murphys songs (one only needs to look to "Kiss me I'm Shitfaced" off *Blackout* for instance), they are re-imagined or "rearticulated" in new ways, much like McLaughlin and McLoone state about The Pogues:

> In music and performance, the nostalgic associations are wrenched out of their context both by the irreverent way that folk forms are played (and played with) and in the lyrical associations that are attached to them. The Pogues parody and interrogate aspects of Irishness in complex and confusing ways, and to see in them only a lack of positive stereotyping is to miss the point. What is interesting about them is the full characterization present—drunken Paddies, sentimental Paddies, homesick Paddies, pathetic and nostalgic Paddies in tandem with representations of Ireland collapsing under the weight of tradition and economic peripherality.[14]

The Dropkick Murphys use a spectrum of images from their own lives as a way to present a characterization of what it means to be Irish American in the punk scene. On the 1998 release *Do or Die*, for instance, the band begins the album with "Cadence to Arms," a traditional bagpipe-laden track that leads into the title track "Do or Die," in which former lead singer Mike McColgan belts out pro–union laden verses of rising up against the powers that be. Later on the album, song such as "Caught in a Jar" and "Far Away Coast" start off with traditional guitar riffs and tin whistles that are reminiscent of traditional folk acts like the Clancy Brothers and Tommy Makem.[15] On *Sing Loud, Sing Proud!*, the band covers traditional Irish folk songs "The Wild Rover" and "The Rocky Road to Dublin" while also making references to other parts of Irish tradition with "The Legend of Finn MaCumhail."

The songs by the Murphys are patriotic—oscillating from the U.S. to Ireland—but remain within the confines of middle-class/working-class Irish Americans. Early outings in the band's career dealt with unions, working-class heroes, and regional sports fandom. The application of bagpipes and working-class gruff also act as symbols of Celtic roots and underdog status. While the cover of "The Fields of Athenry" can stir up longing for an ancestral homeland or familial ties, songs like "Time to Go" relate the Murphys back to Boston and the sporting community of New England.

Take the Red to the Orange Line: Sports as a Community Builder

Bassist/vocalist Ken Casey has owned local Boston sports bar McGreevy's since 2008—a reference to Michael "Nuf Ced" McGreevy who started the local baseball fanbase the Royal Rooters in 1910.[16] McGreevy is also immortalized in the Murphy song "Tessie" in 2004, after the Boston Red Sox won the World Series that year. The music of the Murphys is filled with local sports symbolism that graft the punkers to local fanbases in New England—most visibly in song format those of the Boston Red Sox and the Boston Bruins. "Time to Go" ties the band to Boston through the use of sports as a communal activity for the denizens of Boston. Where "The Fields of Athenry" shows the influence of Irish themes on the Dropkick Murphys, "Time to Go" balances the ancestral leanings of the band with local loyalties to the Boston Bruins of the National Hockey League. While the Murphys have written songs that associate the act with the Red Sox and boxing legend Micky Ward, "Time to Go" connects hardcore punk to the fast and physical game of hockey. "Time to Go" is filled with images of Boston and Bruins hockey that creates an image in the listener's mind of a specific destination and specific fanbase.

> GO! GO! Black and Gold!
> Old time hockey, bar the door
> Clear the track, it's all out war
> Light the lamp, throw a hit, black and gold never quit
> The barn is full, our teams in town
> Put 'em up boys, knock 'em down
> Drop the puck, it's time to go!
> Bust out of work, it's a quarter-past five
> Time to round up the gang and take the Red to the Orange Line
> Head to the street and the Causeway crowd
> You can feel it in the air when the team's in town[17]

Sports allegiances and songs devoted to the Boston Bruins connect the Murphys to a hometown as much as their folk-centered covers connect them back to Irish American heritage. Both "Fields of Athenry" and "Time to Go" from *Blackout* illustrate the hybridity that Ang writes about. It is not only about a specific region but where your parents, grandparents, and extended family came from. In the same way as "Fields of Athenry," "Time to Go" acts as a centralizing force to ground the band within a specific region while also tailoring their message through the use of regional symbols. References to two Boston Transit Lines (the Red and Orange Lines) map out how to quickly get to TD Bank North Garden while the chorus revolves around the colors of the Bruins (black and gold). The "Causeway crowd" (fans of the Bruins) are mentioned in the first verse while Rene Rancourt (who sings the national anthems at Bruins home games) is mentioned in the final verse. Like their New Jersey contemporaries the Bouncing Souls or Pennsylvania's the Menzingers who reference local celebrities, bars, and hangouts in their respective states, the Murphys make a concentrated effort in their songs to cement themselves as hometown bards. The difference between the Dropkick Murphys and the Bouncing Souls or the Metzingers is that the Murphys are balancing two different sets of symbols. Both Celtic symbols and spaces are explored alongside Boston-based hangouts and sports teams. In the same way Doyle writes about the distinct images created by blues artists in the Chess and Sun Recording studios, the Murphys add Boston references in an autobiographical style. As Doyle states about Muddy Waters and his inwardness in writing about Chicago, there is a connection to his own life in the locations that are cited in his music.

> Just as Jon Lee Hooker in his "Boogie Chillin" (1948) referred by name to Henry's Swing Club (a Detroit bar frequented by Hooker), Waters refers to locations specific to his own life, with little apparent concern for whether his listeners will "get" the reference. Stovall's Plantation is mentioned, his home town of Rolling Fork, and so on [. . .]The effortless inclusion of such personal references in music that was produced for local and, it was hoped, national markets shows the extent of this new type of inwardness in recorded music. It would be difficult to imagine Frank Sinatra or Nat King Cole singing about their respective New Jersey or Chicago homes with the same degree of autobiographical specificity.[18]

The image of Ireland that they present in their folk song covers may be read as preconceived and based upon a shared image of Ireland—much like Daynes speaks of in relation to reggae and Jamaicans abroad. With that said, their specific image of Boston and Irish America speak not only to a particular group in New England, but are nationally (or globally) recognized for their specific, autobiographical nature. The songs reflect their own world experiences and build upon the various locations (or sporting franchises) of the Boston area. From their 2007 release, *The Meanest of Times*, the song "Famous For Nothing" talks about, "[G]rowing up in a neighborhood trying to avoid drug pushers, the police, your parents and other unsavory characters, blowing up police cars, and street politics," while their cover "(F)lannigan's Ball" includes, "lots of shoutouts to friends and relations,"[19] On "Caps and Bottles," on *Sing Loud, Sing Proud!*, the band makes reference to "The Rathskeller," (more commonly referred to as "The Rat") a famous (and former) punk rock venue in Boston: "When I was thirteen I bought a scally cap/Looked up to the older guys that drank at the Rat/ Couldn't wait to grow up just to drink with the crew/put my name on the map and have a social few."[20] The addition of local scene references helps to authenticate the Murphys as symbols of their hometown who idealize both Ireland and highlight the best of what Boston has to offer. At the same time, many lyrics can be interpreted to other locales. As stated on their website, the note that goes along with the lyrics for "Famous for Nothing," cited above could well relate to Boston's South Side as much as it could relate to the poor neighborhoods of Detroit, Los Angeles, and New York City.

While the references may be lost on some not familiar with the New England area, the images that they portray can be made secondary to the music itself—or relate to other images in the listeners own world. As Stuart Hall wrote in "Encoding/Decoding" in relation to the transmission and consumption or reception of messages in television newscasts, the encoded meanings of communicated information changes as it becomes "meaningful" discourse. The consumers, the listeners in this situation, can then apply the ideas of the music in their own new ways.[21] Those who are of Irish descent but not in Boston may relate to one aspect of the Dropkick Murphys' music, while those who are from Boston (or in the immediate New England area) may relate to the local references but not the Irish imagery. Each listener of the Murphys then creates his/her own idea of what the music means to them (rebellion, Irish tradition, hometown pride, working–class woes, etc.). Each idea is transformative on a larger scale and can relate to different locales out of the coded areas of Boston and Ireland. The heavy use of Celtic symbols post–*Sing Loud, Sing Proud!* in song lyrics and album art is stereotypical but appropriates Irish American culture as a part of the hardcore punk/rock scene. While the Murphys may not have the shocking fashion sense of the first wave English punks that Hebdige writes about-using "'Cheap' trashy fabrics" such as PVC, latex and animal print materials that questioned both conventional ideas of fashion but what was acceptable in society—the use of stereotypical Irish images in a subversive context uses images and products in society for new, subversive reasons much like those early punks. While the products and images from society may involve Guinness, skeletons, kilts, bagpipes, and shamrocks rather than safety pins, studs, fetish wear, and piercings their use within the subculture of punk rock creates a new meaning for them outside their original or traditional use.[22] *Blackout*'s use of Irish culture not only for covers of songs but for album art sets a tone that the band has used to their advantage since 2003. On their most recent release, *Going Out in Style*, the title track combines the images of a stereotypical Irish wake with a slew of Boston landmarks.

"Going Out in Style:" Ashes, Fenway, and Localized Hybrids

Going Out in Style is a concept album that tells the tale of Cornelius Larkin, a fictionalized hero whose life story is told through the songs on the album. Larkin is a combination of fiction and family folklore from the members of the Murphys, whose story is told through the album by either the first-person Larkin or the band members.[23] The title track, "Going Out in Style" tells the story of an Irish wake and the type of people who show up to pay their respects to Larkin. The song is rife with shout-outs to local celebrities and punk acts as Ken Casey sings about one final party.

I've seen a lot of sights and traveled many miles
Shook a thousand hands and seen my share of smiles
I've caused some great concern and told one too many lies
And now I see the world through these sad, old eyes

So what if I throw a party and all my friends were there?
Acquaintances, relatives, the girls who never cared
You'll have a host of rowdy hooligans in a big line out the door
Side by side with Sister Barbara, Chief Wells, and Bobby Orr
I'd invite the Flannigans
Replace the window you smashed out
I'd apologize to Sluggo for pissing on his couch
I'll see Mrs. McAulille and so many others soon
Then I'll say I'm sorry for what I did sleepwalking in her room

So what if I threw a party and invited Mayor Menino?
He'd tell you get a permit
Well this time I don't think so
It's a neighborhood reunion
But now we'd get along
Van Morrison would be there and he'd sing me one last song
With a backup band of bass players to keep us up all night
Three handsome four-string troubadours
Newton's own Fat Mike
[Fat Mike:] I'll be in the can having a smoke with Gary and Johnny Fitz
But there's a backup in the bathroom
Cause the Badger's got the shits

Chorus:
You may bury me with an enemy on Mount Calvary
You can stack me on a pyre and soak me down with whiskey
Roast me to a blackened crisp and thrown me in a pile

I could really give a shit—I'm going out in style
You can take my urn to Fenway spread my ashes all about
Or you can bring me down to Wolly Beach
And dump the sucker out
Burn me to a rotten crisp and toast me for a while
I could really give a shit, I'm going out in style.[24]

The song is filled with off-color humor and a plethora of instruments including prominent use of bagpipes and drums. Casey lists local heroes (former
Bruin Bobby Orr, Boston Mayor Thomas Menino), punk rockers (Fat Mike of
NOFX) and locales around the greater Boston area (Wolly Beach, Fenway Park,
McGreevy's Pub,[25] Mount Calvary Cemetery). Casey mentions Irish singer-
songwriter Van Morrison in passing as a part of the wake's guest list that has
come to pay their respects. In "Going Out in Style" the band pours on stereotypical Irish American culture but applies punk rock flair to the festivities. It is a
final homage to a dead friend (as portrayed in the accompanying music video for
the single) but not an elegant one. Lines about broken toilets, busted windows,
and soiled furniture stand next to Catholic imagery of nuns, cemeteries, and last
rites.
    As a song "Going Out in Style" combines the many different cultural identi-
ties of the Murphys under one banner to create a hybrid culture that is not just of
Bostonians, drunk punks, or Irish Americans from "Southie" but all these things
at once. They run the gamut of Paddies described by McLaughlin and McLoone
in regards to the Pogues. It is less about the positivity or negativity in the stereotypes present within their songs but about how these range of symbols resonate
in the communities the Dropkick Murphys are a part of and combine to create a
new cultural text.

Conclusion—Which Side Are You On?

In the wake of the Boston marathon bombings of 2013, the Dropkick Murphys
set up a benefit concert on April 28. The money raised from the concert would
be combined with the already over $150,000 collected from selling "For Bos-
ton" T-shirts—a nod to their cover of the Boston College fight song—in the
wake of the tragedy.[26] The money that was raised from the shirts and the concert
went towards those affected by the bombings through The Claddagh Fund, the
501(c)3 charity founded by Ken Casey in 2009.[27] The connections to popular
Irish culture and its symbols are intertwined in the music of the punk band, but
are also a part of how they interact with their surroundings in the everyday.
Sighting "the three attributes of the Claddagh Ring—Friendship, Love and Loyalty," the foundation works with local hospitals, veteran's charities, and alcohol
and drug recovery charities in the Boston area while a Philadelphia chapter was
opened in 2011 working to benefit the City of Brotherly Love.[28] The Dropkick
Murphys have worked to not only present themselves as an integral part of their

community as rockers as well as a band that, after making it big, has worked to engage the needs of their hometown through direct community action. The Dropkick Murphys as a punk band have found a way to combine their hometown with an imagined homeland while as a band from the city of Boston they worked to become the musical embodiment of a hardworking community— displaying regional loyalties through sports and community action.

The Dropkick Murphys have created a style of punk rock that began as angry tirades from Boston that backed unions and Irish roots that has evolved to represent a specific community and their heritage. The Murphys walk between different aspects of Boston and Irish American life and use cultural stereotypes as fuel to further hone their message and gain further prominence. While the band may not be "authentic" in their presentation of Irish culture or Boston-based musicians, they do create a new hybrid of what it means to be Irish American when one is three or four generations removed from a familial homeland. The use and application of Irish stereotypes and local sports teams connects tradition, family, and local athletics to subversion—creating personal meaning from mass texts. While other bands and performers have used their local roots as fuel for songs (and to build a fanbase) the Murphys cast a wide net with the relationships to both Boston and Ireland. It is a mixture of experiences built within popular culture texts from two cultures that simultaneously occupy the same space. While it is a merging of cultures it is a specific image of Irish American culture that resides in working-class family values. While the images that the Dropkick Murphys muster within their songs may not always based in a diaspora, if at all, the use of Boston alongside an Ireland of the past highlights the ways images can be redistributed and reinterpreted in the present. The synchronized use of both cultures within their songs solidifies the historical connection of New England, Boston, Ireland, and the Irish abroad for a new generation that claim ancestry to Erin. Not only is it important to look at the power of punk music to create a community of like-minded fans, but also how it reflects upon where the band originates. For the Murphys, that origination does not end at Boston but also the familial roots in both story and song that define and develop a new understanding of cultural texts and global boundaries.

Notes

1. Noel McLaughlin and Martin McLoone. "Hybridity and National Musics: the Case of Irish Rock Music." *Popular Music* 19, no. 2 (April 1, 2000): 191.

2. Sarah Daynes. "The musical construction of diaspora: the case of reggae and Rastafari." *Music, Space and Place: Popular Music and Cultural Identity*, Ashgate Popular and Folk Music Series (Aldershot; Burlington, VT: Ashgate, 2004), 25–27.

3. Dick Hebdige, *Subculture: The Meaning of Style* (Methuen & Co, 1980), 39.

4. Ien Ang, *On Not Speaking Chinese: Living Between Asia and the West* (London; New York: Routledge, 2001), 34.

5. Ibid.

6. Ibid., 35.

7. Simon Frith, *Sound Effects: Youth, Leisure, and the Politics of Rock'n'roll*, 1st American ed (New York: Pantheon Books, 1981), 37–38.

8. Simon Frith, *Performing Rites: On the Value of Popular Music* (Cambridge, Mass: Harvard University Press, 1996), 152–157.

9. Peter Doyle, *Echo and Reverb: Fabricating Space in Popular Music, 1900-1960*, 1st ed, Music/culture (Middletown, Conn: Wesleyan University Press, 2005), 176–177.

10. Ang, *On Not Speaking Chinese*, 34.

11. Dropkick Murphys (Musical Group), "The Fields of Athenry." *Blackout* (Los Angeles, CA: Hellcat Records, 2003), liner notes.

12. Dropkick Murphys (Musical group), "Caps and Bottles." *Sing Loud, Sing Proud!* (Los Angeles: Hellcat Records 2001).

13. Noel McLaughlin and Martin McLoone, "Hybridity and National Musics: The Case of Irish Rock Music," *Popular Music* 19, no. 2 (April 1, 2000): 194.

14. Ibid., 191.

15. Dropkick Murphys (Musical group), *Do or Die* (Los Angeles: Hellcat, 1998).

16. Carol Beggy and March Shanahan, "The Adams Family, revisited," *The Adams family, revisited—The Boston Globe*, April 23, 2008, http://www.boston.com/lifestyle/food/articles/2008/04/23/the_adams_family_revisited/.

17. Dropkick Murphys (Musical Group), "Time to Go." *Blackout,* liner notes.

18. Doyle, *Echo and Reverb*, 176–177.

19. Dropkick Murphys, "The Meanest of Times," Band Website—Music Page, *Meanest of Times<<Dropkick Murphys*, 2011, http://www.dropkickmurphys.com/music/albums/the-meanest-of-times/.

20. Dropkick Murphys (Musical group), *Sing Loud, Sing Proud* (Los Angeles: Hellcat, 2001).

21. Stuart Hall. "Encoding and Decoding." *Media and Cultural Studies: Keyworks*, Rev. ed., Keyworks in Cultural Studies 2 (Malden, MA: Blackwell, 2006), 165–166.

22. D. Hebdige, *Subculture: The Meaning of Style* (Methuen & Co, 1980), 107.

23. Dropkick Murphys (Musical group), "Going Out in Style." *Going Out in Style* (Boston, Mass.: Born & Bred Records, 2011), liner notes.

24. Dropkick Murphys (Musical group), "Going Out in Style." *Going Out in Style* (Boston, Mass.: Born & Bred Records, 2011), liner notes.

25. Carol Beggy and Mark Shanahan, "The Adams Family, revisited," *The Adams family, revisited—The Boston Globe*, April 23, 2008, http://www.boston.com/lifestyle/food/articles/2008/04/23/the_adams_family_revisited/.

26. "Dropkick Murphys Announce Benefit Concert In Boston This Sunday, April 28," accessed May 13, 2013, http://www.dropkickmurphys.com/2013/04/24/for-boston-benefit-concert/.

27. "'About the Claddagh Fund' The Claddagh Fund," *The Claddagh Fund*, 2011, http://www.claddaghfund.org/cf/index.php?option=com_content&view=article&id=170&Itemid=54.

28. "'About the Claddagh Fund' The Claddagh Fund." *The Claddagh Fund*, 2011, http://www.claddaghfund.org/cf/index.php?option=com_content&view=article&id=236&Itemid=219.

Chapter 3
Am I Evil?
The Meaning of Metal Lyrics to Its Fans
Mika Elovaara

Not unlike rock 'n' roll when it burst into contemporary culture in the 1950s, Metal has faced strong criticism since its first beats, chords, screams, and growls hit the airwaves. Various groups of people, including politicians and musicologists, have tirelessly called into question the musical quality, morality, and propriety of the genre; the negative image the musical genre and its culture have long had in the public eye is globally known. As acclaimed metal sociologist Deena Weinstein notes in her groundbreaking monograph *Heavy Metal: The Music and Its Culture,* rock critics, Baptist ministers, and professors of music as well as politicians and members of the mass media all have historically denounced any possible merits metal music might have and pointed out numerous negative aspects about it—whether musically or socially.[1] Weinstein's observations have also been noted by numerous other scholars who have studied metal exclusively or as part of wider studies on popular music, including Shuker, who notes that metal "is frequently criticized as incorporating the worst excess of popular music, notably its perceived narcissism and sexism, and it is also often musically dismissed."[2] Both Weinstein and Shuker make note of the fact that even Lester Bangs, "the only noted rock critic who had anything favorable to say about heavy metal at its inception," publicly scorned the genre.[3] Throughout the 30+-year history of heavy metal, or simply "metal" as it is nowadays commonly called by academics and lay audiences alike, several meanings have been associated with the music and the culture directly related to it. Challenging some of the more common demographical assumptions and findings about metal audiences and offering an examination into the meaning of metal lyrics to its fans, this chapter briefly introduces a new path for further exploration in the study of metal in contemporary culture as it discusses the potential meanings of the much-criticized genre to its fans and artists alike, thereby providing further depth to explaining the different potential meanings metal music can have to its audience and thus further demonstrate that indeed, metal "values and symbols have multiple, ambiguous, and undecidable interpretations."[4]

35

Broadly speaking, one could argue that metal in the twenty-first century is a large cultural phenomenon: the once marginal subculture seems to have become a cultural scene for masses, an important form of cultural export, and even a source of national pride. There are many forms of evidence of the diffusion of metal music and its culture to contemporary global culture. On the one hand, there are the numerous festivals of metal music in major cities worldwide, the prevalence of metal artists' concerts on the schedules of rock clubs around the world, and the metal tourists from Japan, Australia, Central Europe, and North America, for example, who travel to Scandinavia simply because some Scandinavian metal bands never tour elsewhere. On the other hand, "metal" has penetrated the North American culture and consumer culture in a variety of ways as well. Consider, for example, the likes of the two people I met randomly in a school event in Wilmington, North Carolina—an Argentine young man and an American sales assistant—both of whom had started to study Finnish on their own, so that they could understand the lyrics of their favorite Finnish folk metal band, Korpiklaani, which sings in Finnish. Walking in the malls of America, you will find that there is the plethora of metal merchandise sold in Hot Topic (a franchise specialized in selling metal, punk, and Goth clothes and accessories). As a related example, not too long ago, there was a customer competition at Spencer's Gifts—another nationwide mall franchise in the United States—the main prize of which was a trip to Finland to meet HIM. Then there's the success of Paganfest—a folk metal tour with Scandinavian bands on the bill around the United States in 2008—and the numerous other successful tour of metal bands regularly on the calendar around the United States and Canada. These examples add further evidence to the suggestion that the significance and meaning of metal seems to be much more than simply spending time listening to music; participation in metal culture includes active concert attendance, cultural tourism, fashion, and self-education, among others. The meaning of metal seems to be more diverse than has previously been noted, and the effects of direct participation in the metal scene or subculture seem to be far from the much publicized suicidal behavior, violence, and chaos metal supposedly causes in its listeners according to some scholars, parishioners, and politicians.[5]

Whereas the early portion of the study presented in this chapter relies on a look at a few examples of metal lyrics, the empirical data for this study consists of participant observations at numerous metal shows and several rock festivals in Europe and in the United States between June 2007 and July 2011, the first 500 responses to a semi-structured questionnaire gathered via anonymous online submissions through www.metalculture.net between June 15, 2008 and November 15, 2011, and dozens of artist interviews conducted during the same time period. The demographic statistics of the respondents in the 500 responses used in this study are as follows: 380 (76%) of the respondents were males, 93 (18.6%) were females—27 (5.6%) respondents chose not to answer the question. The average age of respondents was 23.4, ranging from 13 to 55. There were 55 countries represented in the responses, and the respondents' occupation could be grouped in three main categories: 35 percent of the respondents were students (26.9% of whom were under the age of 20), 30.6 percent of the respondents were white-collar workers, and 17 percent blue-collar workers.

Metal Under the Microscope—A Look into Theory and Public Prejudice

As Shuker notes, despite the fact that metal has long enjoyed mass appeal, has a large fan base, and some of its subgenres have enjoyed commercial success, there were few attempts to discuss metal seriously before Weinstein[6] and Walser[7] conducted their comprehensive studies on metal.[8] Kahn-Harris's monograph on extreme metal[9] in 2007 can now be added alongside Weinstein and Walser, and the last few years have witnessed a surge in the academic interest in metal, resulting in post-doctoral research and even the first ever scholarly conference on metal music, held in Salzburg, Austria, in November 2008. When discussing previous studies on rock music in general and metal in particular, it is important to recognize that most studies thus far, including Weinstein's pioneering work, tend to treat metal as a youth subculture. Shuker[10] is one scholar who recognizes that rock may once have been youth culture only, but this is no longer the case. Quoting Dave Marsh, who says that "rock and soul-based music has become more sustaining, not less, as I've aged. It may be true that young people were the first to realize that rock and soul had a serious message to convey, but that message has little or nothing to do with youth per se," Shuker seeks to demonstrate that "attempts to locate the audience for popular music primarily among 'youth'" no longer applies.[11]

As Weinstein and Shuker, among others, clearly demonstrate, metal music has been under continuous attack for the past thirty-five years. The debate over the lyrical contents and their potential to cause action in listeners has caused controversy since the earliest days of rock 'n' roll. For decades, discussion of censoring of music has revolved around the free speech rights of artists and public debates on "obscene" material. As a result of the founding of The Parents Music Resource Center in 1985, the "Parental Advisory: Explicit Lyrics" sticker has become a familiar addition to album covers in the United States. Around the time of the PMRC founding, many metal bands were publicly criticized for their lyrical content. Among them, Judas Priest was accused in a court of law of having subliminal messages on their album *Stained Class*, causing two young men, James Vance and Raymond Belknap, to attempt suicide. The boys' parents' case relied on their argument about the existence of instigative, pro-suicide subliminal messages on the album. However, District Judge Jerry Whitehead, who heard the case after the lawyers agreed not to have the civil suit decided by a jury, ruled that there was no conclusive evidence of subliminal messages on the album and dismissed the case against Judas Priest and its record company, CBS.

While scientific research on subliminal messages contends that people's "hearing" subliminal messages is most likely a function of active construction on the
part of listeners based on something they have been told to listen to, and there
haven't been court cases of subliminal messages since the Judas Priest trial,
musicians—especially rappers, punk rockers and Metal bands continue to face
strong public scrutiny and criticism of their lyrics and their potentially inciting
contents.[12]

In the 1980s, leading to the foundation of PMRC, Twisted Sister (for their song
"Under the Blade") and Ozzy Osbourne (for his song "Suicide Solution"),
among others, were taken to court because of the supposedly controversial
themes and topics of their music. Despite the fact that already in the 1980s,
those lawsuits regarding a cause-effect relationship between lyrical contents of
popular music and criminal behavior did not result in convictions, various genres of popular music continue to draw sensational headlines, accusations, and
negative stereotyping. One of the reasons why the accusations and speculations
continue to resurface is the fact that some

> Academics who have studied adolescents and music have expressed concerns
> about the possible effects on children who already have psychological prob-
> lems. Professor Don Roberts of Stanford University thinks that perhaps the
> children who are already violent or depressed are the people who should be
> kept away from death metal. "What the music may well be doing is simply re-
> inforcing beliefs that they might have started with in the first place."[13]

At the turn of the millennium, one of the most vocally criticized musicians in the
United States was Marilyn Manson. Among the numerous things Manson was
criticized for, he was accused of inspiring the Columbine school shootings in
1999. In one of the earliest news reports of the shooting, the two high school
shooters were stated to have been "fans of the Goth look as well as Marilyn
Manson's music"[14] Immediately, "Hilary Rosen, president and CEO of the music
industry trade organization, the Recording Industry Association of America,
[commented]: "In the coming days, we may find out more about the cause of
this tragedy, but we do know that music does not drive teenagers to violent des-
pair, nor does it put guns and weapons in the hands of children. It's too easy to
make music a scapegoat"[15] Manson himself responded to the accusations with
his own discussion of music, its impact on listeners, and the values of American
culture in general in *Rolling Stone*, in an article entitled "Columbine: Whose
Fault is it?"[16] Starting his essay with a perhaps expectedly provocative approach—a discussion of the contents and lessons of the Bible—Manson stated,

> It is sad to think that the first few people on earth needed no books, movies,
> games or music to inspire cold-blooded murder. The day that Cain bashed his
> brother Abel's brains in, the only motivation he needed was his own human
> disposition to violence. Whether you interpret the Bible as literature or as the
> final word of whatever God may be, Christianity has given us an image of
> death and sexuality that we have based our culture around [17]

He described the publicity about him after Columbine as a "witch hunt," and said, in an interestingly similar fashion to Elvis Presley in June, 1956, that the "speculation snowballed into making [him] the poster boy for everything that is bad in the world."[18] In the end, Manson was not put to trial regarding the accusations of his inspiring the Columbine shootings, but he does remain a controversial artist, not the least because, as he said it himself, he "dares to have an opinion and bothers to create music and videos that challenge people's ideas," examining "the America we live in" in his music.[19]

As the aforementioned examples illustrate, most often the object of scrutiny and criticism in metal is the song lyrics, as profoundly demonstrated by the PMRC hearings and the consequential implementation of the Parental Advisory sticker on album covers in the mid-1980s. In academia, studies on the negative effects of metal on its participants have often been conducted through psychological experiments (with music but no lyrics), through textual analyses of lyrics, and through focus-group sociological and ethnographic studies. Studies on metal often work from a hypothesis about the supposed effects the music has on the behavior and/or attitudes of the listeners. Weinstein's observations in her groundbreaking and exhaustive and yet somewhat subjective and narrow study conclude that "no single lyrical theme dominates the [metal] genre [and] the themes of heavy metal song lyrics span a wide range, 'from Christian salvation to oral sex," excluding, however, optimism and hope, and primarily forming "two [thematic] clusters defined by a binary opposition: Dionysian and Chaotic"?[20] The following sections suggest an alternative conclusion, based on both lyrics themselves as well as empirical research.

The Meaning(s) of Lyrics—Decoding the Code

A holistic examination of metal lyrics would warrant a book of its own, but for the purposes of examining themes in metal lyrics, we will focus on the lyrics of one globally popular subgenre: folk metal. As a genre that is deeply rooted in specific local traditions while attracting a global fan base, folk metal is an appropriate choice for an examination of themes in metal. At least hypothetically, a look at the lyrics of folk metal more closely could work as an illustrative example of how there may be important themes in contemporary Metal beyond the realms of Dionysian and chaotic clusters. Broadly speaking, lyrics in folk metal often deal with nature, pre-modern themes, pre-Christian themes, fantasy, mythology, and historical events. Echoing Weinstein's conclusion that there is no single dominant theme in metal, this disparate topical range suggests that it is difficult, if not impossible to exhaustively and conclusively explain what folk metal songs are about lyrically. So let us look at a few examples.

Proud Mythological Pasts, Nature, Creation

Albeit only a few lines from two songs, the following lyrics from the Swedish Amon Amarth work to illustrate that their lyrics deal with the Norse and Viking mythology, as demonstrated by the Viking soldier's proud proclamation in "With Oden on Our Side:" "Under the winter skies / We stand glorious! / And with Oden on our side / We are victorious!"[21] As further evidenced in the detailed mythological storytelling of Norse gods and their adversaries in "War of the Gods," themes in Amon Amarth's songs include glory, death, honor, pride, afterlife, pride in one's heritage, Norse mythology, and Norse gods: "The Vanir felt deceived / Höne was a fool / without Mímir at his side / Höne could not rule / In a fit of violent rage / Mímir's blood was shed / and to Odin's court they sent Mímir's severed head."[22]

Moving on from the death/folk metal of Amon Amarth, the following lyrics of Korpiklaani are also very illustrative of the discography of the band: "Growing up with the wild bears / Breathing the smell of burning wood / Rain and clouds my only friends / Sun and moon and stars and light / Now it's time of a midnight sun / The eternal light and a breathing night."[23] The band's name in their native Finnish means "The Clan of the (Deep)Wood" and their lyrics most often deal with nature, the primal nature of man, man's relationship to nature, and other premodern, or "un-modern" topics, thematically implying a longing for a simpler and different life, perhaps a more authentic life.

Finally, Amorphis, the Finnish progressive melodic death metal band has almost a whole catalogue of songs inspired and derived from the storytelling of *The Kalevala*, the national folk epic of Finland. *The New York Times* explains that "Vainamoinen [is] a shaman and sorcerer who can charm wild beasts with his kantele and use words as weapons. He is the Gandalf-like 'eternal sage' who establishes the land of Kaleva and leads and teaches its people."[24] This example from their latest album, *The Beginning of Times*, offers an explicit but not isolated example of the strong presence of Vainamoinen in Amorphis's catalogue: "No man nor a god, with a sword he carved / With a feather he conjured / An instrument from the bone of fish / A kantele from the jaws of a pike / Sat on a golden rock, on a bank of a golden river / By the brink of golden falls, under the golden sun."[25] The song is completely about Vainamoinen, the Creator in *The Kalevala*, and in the lyrics of "Song of the Sage," we not only hear the story of Vainamoinen's song, or his call to all creatures through the national folk instrument of kantele which he made of the jaws of a pike, but we also hear elements of the Kalevala-typical reversed syntax and even remains of the Kalevala-meter, the trochaic tetrameter, both of which further illustrate the homage the contemporary metal rockers are paying to their national heritage, in topic and form.

When asked about the prominent role of *The Kalevala* in their lyrics, members of Amorphis commented in a following manner,

> We never set out to "do" *Kalevala*, but rather, came across it and then it stuck with us. That we are identified with our national epic is something we are

proud of and feel comfortable with. In the earliest years of the band, before we had *The Kalevala* themes in our music, we couldn't really relate to themes of murder and brutality, but it feels quite natural for us to draw inspiration from our own literary heritage. *The Kalevala* is a part of our identity as a band, and we do realize that even though we did not plan for it, we now play a role in making our national epic better known around the world. We even have fans around the world who want us to sign a copy of *The Kalevala* in their native language, even though everyone obviously knows that we did not write the book.[26]

The band collaborates with a lyricist outside the band in writing the lyrics for their music, which is another sign that the authenticity of themes in their lyrics is important to them, and once again, works to demonstrate that the themes of Amorphis could hardly be grouped under Dionysian and Chaotic.

"Folk" as the Language of Performance—What Meaning Lies within?

Obviously, with more bands and examples, a more holistic understanding of the topics and themes in metal lyrics would be achieved, but suffice it to say that the aforementioned four songs do work as representatives of major thematic issues in metal, offering a broader range for lyrical themes than those that fall under "Dionysian" or "Chaotic." When considering the meanings of lyrics to metal fans, one other key area of distinction is the language of the songs. The examples we have looked at thus far have been from bands who sing in English. However, within the metal scene in general, and folk metal in particular, even though English seems to be the most popular language of metal worldwide, there are numerous major bands who sing in their native languages, most often other than English. Let us now look at a few examples of non-English songs. Eluveitie, a Swiss band, sings in both English and Gaulish. Here is an example of Gaulish lyrics: "Immi daga uimpi geneta, / lana beððos et' iouintutos. / Blatus ceti, cantla carami. / Aia gnata uimpi iouinca, / pid in cete tu toue suoine, / pid uregisi peli doniobi? / Aia gnata uimpi iouinca, / pid in cete tu toue suoine."[27] Finntroll, a Finnish band, sings in Swedish, the other official language of their homeland: "Svartkonst och magiska krafter. / I natt jag tar den som en tid var min. / Jag suger livet ut. / Blåsa till urgammal asken. . . /. . . urgammal asken! / Jag är världens mörkret. / Jag är det dödande vattnet. / Jag är livets blod. / Du ska bli pinad för dina brott."[28] Reading these lyrics, it becomes clear to English speakers that unless you know the language, you do not know what the songs are about, and therefore, the meaning of the lyrics remains enigmatic.

Crowd Response

Having been in the audience of both bands both in Europe and in the United States, it is difficult for me to say which concert experiences were more intensive, which fans (those of kin in Europe or those of further or no relation in the United States) were more "into" these songs and others sung in these languages other than English. If I were really pushed on it and had to say either or, I would vote for the American audiences. Witnessing a capacity crowd in Raleigh, North Carolina, cheer when the lead singer of Finntroll shouted "Jag ar Varlden's Morkret" in Swedish and then seeing how the crowd of the headlining band sung along to Nattfodd, in Swedish of course, was almost an otherworldly experience. I thought to myself: how can this fifteen-year-old stereotypical metal-head next to me and the paralegal, forty two-year-old mom of three next to him both be into the same, peculiar music so intensively that they sing along in a language neither of them speak? Well, this chapter cannot offer an all-conclusive answer, of course, but I'm sure many of us are already onto it. Similarly, the other experience, seeing a capacity crowd in Charlotte, North Carolina, erupt when Eluveitie started "Omnos" and how passionately the American audience of all ages, genders, and ethnicities sung along in the ancient Gaulish language, celebrating this very specific folk heritage with the band, left me awestruck, in a very positive way, of course. Given the enthusiasm of the crowds of folk metal bands, regardless of, or maybe *because* of the foreign language, it is amusing and discouraging that the industry is trying to take away that authenticity, but it does seem to be the case. As "Tundra" of Finntroll explained it to me, they have been asked to start recording and singing in English numerous times, so that they would sell more records, but the band consistently shoots down such crazy ideas. In Tundra's own words: "how can we be true to ourselves and celebrate our folk heritage and sing in English? Our heritage is Finnish/Swedish, and therefore it is the only way for us to go."[29] This example is not an isolated one for folk metal bands, but fortunately for their global fans, folk metal bands truly seem to be about their art, authenticity, and passion, not about the money or the industry's standards.

A Norwegian folk metal artist, who wished to retain his anonymity for the purposes of the research, illustrates the meaning of folk elements to the bands and fans alike

> I feel that it is important that people understand why they have been born and that other people fought for our well-being and to preserve our culture and society. Our cultural heritage is going to die because people ignore it or do not even realize its significance. Vikings and Norse mythology have been described as something evil and distant, but in reality, it is close to home and not necessarily evil at all. That it is not Christian does not mean it is evil. I use the mythology to describe situations in the world and politics, actual topics that were part of our lives a thousand years ago just as they are today. One can be proud of one's heritage and identity without any racist or nationalistic tendency. And Satanism is quite outside of all of this.[30]

This last comment warrants another important topic for a closer look: the pagan elements of folk metal have often been misconstrued as Satanic or anti-Christian, whereas in reality, they often simply represent narratives of a time period before Christianity and arouse questions about the entrance of Christianity, through crusades, to the Central European and Nordic countries, among others. In a *Decibel Magazine* interview, "Big Boss" of the Czech Black Metal band Root, explained the complexity of cultural heritage, stating

> In the old days dozens of different nations and tribes passed through the territory where Bohemia and Moravia lie. Root is from Moravia. They left their traces of various pagan rituals and customs, and magic here. These people have lived here for a while, leaving followers, and departed. And as we live here, we have inherited all from them. And because we are musicians we feel it even more. And that's what makes our music so different.[31]

The complexity he is alluding to in his interview suggests that even though he is a Satanist himself, his music, in itself, should not be seen as such; that pagan themes and elements in a band's music and lyrics can be merely "folk" rather than "Satanic." Explaining the same issue further when he explains the forming of his band, Johan Hegg, lead singer of Amon Amarth, explained in a recent interview with *Metal Hammer* that

> We didn't feel a connection with the Satanism in Black Metal, so the Viking mythology and culture appeared to be very open, flexible system to work within, as a system for personal philosophy and musically, artistically, and conceptually, too. It was a stark opposite to the monotheistic or political world we see around us. . . . a lot of people are interested in that [Viking] part of our history and I think that's because it's very mysterious in lots of ways but I is also very interesting culturally. Vikings are our ancestors and they were not just brutal savages. They were skilled craftsmen and artists and poets and everything. There's so many different aspects to it that people are beginning to discover and it appeals to a lot of people.[32]

And indeed, that is exactly what is happening. Folk metal, or metal with various folk elements depending on the band, is becoming one of the most popular genres in the increasing global metal community, and the lyrics of the genre have various meanings to artists and fans alike. Speaking of fans, let's look at what some of the first five hundred survey respondents state their favorite music means to them.

So what do the songs really mean? Let the fans speak!

As the British pioneer of cultural studies, Stuart Hall, famously posited, cultural objects most often gain a new meaning during the process of consumption. Whereas the artist encodes a certain meaning into his product while creating it, in the act of consumption, the fan decodes the object and the product can gain a meaning quite independent from the meaning encoded by the artist. Therefore, in a thorough examination of what lyrics in music mean, mere textual analysis is only a part of the process; data from empirical research facilitates access to the fans' perspective on the music they like. Here are some excerpts of representative responses from the five hundred survey respondents to the "Meaning of Metal" questionnaire.

Representing a significant number of survey respondents with her statement, one respondent states

> It means everything basically. As cheesy as it sounds, I live for music and I really don't have any other interest at all. There's something about the art of it that transcends worldly association but still feels rooted and accessible. In my opinion metal is really the most superior form of popular music as it lacks boundaries. It can be minimalistic, bombastic, symphonic, progressive, pompous or just downright dirty. Its diversity is its strong point.[33]

Echoing similar sentiments, and representing very common answers among the first five hundred respondents in the survey data, another, male respondent reflects

> Metal is a form of music that can take many different shapes and forms. Metal bands can make use of pianos, synthesizers, keyboards, or folk instruments, but still keep in touch with their metal roots. I love metal because it's so diverse and because the music and the aggression inherent in it speaks [sic] to me. But at the same time, metal ballads also sometimes appeal to my softer sides. There's a metal song for every moment. Plain and simple.[34]

Finally, the following two statements demonstrate yet another common theme in the survey responses, summarizing the meaning of metal into something concise, yet immensely powerful and definitive, if not conclusive: "It means freedom, life, love and eternity. It describes me better than I could. When I feel bad, good, or undecided it always makes me feel good" (male respondent).[35] "Mirror to my soul. I'm a shy person otherwise, but Metal helps me deal with a range of emotions, it liberates!" (male respondent).[36]

Now these statements, while they are mere extracts of a larger corpus of empirical data gathered in the survey, are very representative of how people feel about metal and their participation in the culture. As Lawson writes in his article,

> One common misconception about heavy metal is that it is entirely founded on a need for escapism and fantasy. Grandiloquent narratives detailing the adventures of marauding Vikings on the stormy seas certainly serves that purpose as well, but there is also plenty within those tales that exhibits a sharp and poignant relevance to the real life experience of many metalheads. Notions of community, solidarity, battling against the trials of life and the everlasting search for meaning and purpose all have been integral tenets of metallic expression from the early works of Sabbath through to the present day. . . . There is clearly something going on here, something that transcends music and reaches deep into the heart of our entire culture as fans of heavy music and members of a worldwide community of like-minded individuals.[37]

In conclusion of the examination of the meaning of metal lyrics, holistically looking, it seems legitimate to suggest that unlike what Weinstein claims, the primary themes of metal music could not be categorized into the binary opposition between Dionysian and Chaotic themes, and there is, indeed, a variety of themes in the music, whether explicitly in the lyrics or implicitly decoded from the songs.

Music or Lyrics, or Both?

In addition to considering lyrical contents, another key area to examine when we study the meaning of music to the fans of any genre of music is to try to discover whether the fans even care for the lyrics that much. Despite her weaknesses in her discussion of the essence of metal lyrics overall, in this area, Weinstein does recognize that too much emphasis on lyrics ignores essential aspects of the music, which is dissimilar from the majority of politicians and parents who often criticize the music primarily because of its lyrical content. As the fact that bands who sing in their native language, unintelligible to most fans, become and remain globally popular suggests, the significance of lyrics is nowhere near the level to which it has been raised by scholars and detractors unfamiliar with the music and its subculture/scene. Furthermore, when asked about it, fans and artists alike consider melody and rhythm far more important and meaningful than lyrics.

Looking at statistical evidence from the empirical data gathered through the multiyear study, the numbers suggest a conclusion that may seem obvious to many: that music is, by far, more important to both artists and fans of Metal than the lyrics. Based on the fifty two artist interviews conducted for this study, the uninitiated consensus among the artists seems to be that the lyrics do mean something, for we are not dealing with an instrumental genre, but that the meaning of lyrics is far more personal to both the artists and the fans than the detractors seem to understand. While punk bands often do hope to inspire or cause action for good causes, metal bands seem to wish their music would make the listeners think critically. Question #18 in the Meaning of Metal research survey asks, "Which one means more to you in a song, melody/rhythm or lyrics? Why?" Of the 500 responses analyzed for this chapter, 81.5 percent of the respondents answered "Melody," 10.5 percent of the respondents answered "Both/Can't Say," only 7 percent of the respondents answered "Lyrics" and 1% of the responses were blank. For the explanatory part, here are some representatives of common responses.

A significant number of responses followed along the same lines as this male respondent's statement: "Melody. Not even good lyrics can save a song that has no interesting melodies or riffs. But if a song has good melody and it 'works' otherwise, too, the lyrics can be totally meaningless and the song still brilliant."[38] A statement such as this one was also very common: "Melody. More often than not, I cannot make out the lyrics when listening, and I'm not bothered to read lyrics in the CD jacket."[39] These statements downplaying the significance of lyrical themes are further supported by the following statistic: when asked what the lyrics of the listener's favorite music means to him/her, 31.5 percent of the respondents said "nothing" or "nothing much" etc. Of those who said they mean at least "something," here are some sample responses representing fairly broad and yet uniform categories of responses.

One group of responses agreed with the statement that "The power to continue when all seems to fall apart. It gives you strength. If you, the reader of this, are a religious person, you may understand that listening to good music gives the same thrill as praying,"[40] or that "They make me forget about a bad day."[41] Many fans also feel that "many of [their] favorite bands have lyrics that speak directly to [them]. Often some song comes to [their] mind[s] at a particular moment in a particular state of mind and the lyrics suit the occasion perfectly. It gives [them] strength to think that maybe someone else, many people probably, have thought the same way and gone through similar emotions."[42] Finally, even though very short and simple responses, the following statements by female fans illustrate very common perceptions among metal fans, and also quite effectively call into question the perception of metal fans as a sheepishly behaving herd, following the evil messages of the music: "They mean critical thinking and encourage independent thinking"[43] and ""They are a complete mystery to me. And that's OK."[44] When one combines these statements with the fact that the statistics in response to a question about the explicit/implicit balance between metal lyrics suggests that most fans deem that most songs require interpretation, that the lyrics are not straightforward, the empirical research seems to suggest that regardless of the level of depth and meaning the lyrics have to their writers, to many fans, the lyrics of metal may be insignificant, and the fans' attitude toward the lyrics indifferent.

Discussion and Conclusion

Going back to the objectives set out at the outset of this research, it seems legitimate to suggest the following findings in conclusion of this chapter. The statistics of the respondents' demographics challenge the view that metal is youth subculture. An average age of 23.4 means that for every fifteen-year-old fan that Weinstein, among others, claims to primarily populate the metal audience, there is a thirty one-year-old counterpart. The occupational statistics also suggest that metal is no longer—if it ever truly was—a scene for blue-collar men only. Though the statistics show that a significant number of fans seem to be students or blue collar workers, there is no data on what students the respondents are, which means that they could just as well be students of medicine as students of carpentry. Moreover, my participant observations show that a metal audience often consists of a group of people with a variety of occupations—including physicians, lawyers, professional athletes, and teachers. The fact that metal bands consistently tour in rock clubs where no minors are allowed further works to demonstrate that metal is no longer a youth scene or subculture.

The statistics and summaries of qualitative responses to question #18 ("Which one means more to you in a song, melody/rhythm or lyrics? Why?") in the Meaning of Metal research survey suggest that the significance of lyrics is nowhere near the level to which they have been raised by scholars unfamiliar with the music and its subculture/scene. Fans and artists alike consider melody and rhythm far more important and meaningful than lyrics. The statistics show that emphasis on lyrics in vain.

Even when the lyrics are considered important, the thematic diversity is far wider than what Weinstein claims it to be, and unlike the detractors of metal persistently claim, the themes are not always, or even often, anything offensive or inappropriate. Moreover, unlike what Weinstein claims, themes in metal lyrics no longer can be categorized with the binary opposition between Dionysian and Chaotic themes. The respondents' elaborate explanations to what the music means to them also suggests that fans find a lot of hope and optimism through their relationship to the music and its scene. Even if the themes of metal lyrics were categorized through some method of textual analysis, the fans still seem to think that the majority of lyrics are susceptible to individual interpretation depending on numerous variables directly related to each listener's individuality.

Answers to question #30 ("Finally, please explain, in your own words, what your favorite music means to you and why") show the wide range of views of what the music means to the fans. Indeed, many of them offer further proof of Weinstein's notion that "at its best [metal] is rebellion against inauthentic culture, an attempt of life to raise itself above the herd. In heavy metal the transvaluation of religious symbols joins with the sound of the music, which is inherently vitalizing, to tweak a devitalizing, bureaucratic, inauthentic, iron-caged, and unfair world."[45] However, the elaborate and profound explanations the fans and the artists give for the meaning of the music also add much more depth and range to the meanings listed by Weinstein. The broad groupings of the qualitative responses I have made demonstrate there are a lot of fans who, among others, feel that metal gives them positive emotions, makes them happy when they are sad, picks them up when life has kicked them down, if you will, and in general, provides "the soundtrack for their lives," whether they be male or female, teenagers or middle agers, plumbers or physicians.

Finally, then, the results of this study suggest that participants in metal culture cannot be categorized as one group of people because of the diversity in age and profession, among others. Challenging the most common demographics in studies on metal music which tend to find that metal fans form a homogenous group of young blue collar males, the diversity in "metal demographics" is so vast that one should conclude, instead, that both local and global metal scenes bring together people from all walks of life who might have nothing in common except for their participation in metal culture, and who otherwise might not be associated with each other at all if it weren't for the shared interest in (and often passion for) the music and its culture. While it is true that none of the survey responses nor interviews necessarily overrule the possibility of metal as a cause of violent, suicidal, or otherwise inappropriate behavior, as they provide data on the subjective views of the participants in the scene, this study shows that the essence and effects of metal are more diverse than many previous studies recognize, and introduces the fans' voice on the issues their favorite music has been long criticized about, allowing them to explain and in some cases, speak in defense of their music and their own attraction to it. These first results of a much larger study suggest that something that seems so extreme and threatening on the surface is, in fact, a global cultural phenomenon that seems to have a lot of positive meanings to the individuals participating in the scene on an individual level as well as promoting unity and loyalty to an increasing global fan base of youth and grown-ups alike. This chapter has been a mere run-through of the first findings in a large corpus of empirical data. To reach more conclusive results in the future, the areas for study briefly introduced today must be examined in more detail and in greater extent in order to really discover and explain the hues and colors of the formerly black-and-white face of metal.

Notes

1. Deena Weinstein, *Heavy Metal: The Music and Its Culture* (New York, NY: Da Capo Press 2000), 1–5.
2. Roy Shuker, *Understanding Popular Music* (New York, NY: Taylor & Francis 2008),127
3. Shuker, *Understanding*, 121
4. Weinstein: *Heavy Metal*, 275.
5. Christine Hall Hansen and Ranald D. Hansen R, *Schematic Information Processing of Heavy Metal Lyrics*. Communication Research 18 (1991): 373-411.
6. Deena Weinstein, *Heavy Metal– A Cultural Sociology* (New York, NY: Lexington 1991).
7. Robert Walser, *Running with the Devil: Power, Gender, and Madness in Heavy Metal Music* (Middletown, CT: Wesleyan University Press 1993).
8. Shuker, *Understanding*, 127.
9. Keith Kahn-Harris, *Extreme Metal, Music and Culture on the Edge* (Oxford, UK: Berg Publishers).
10. Shuker, *Understanding*, 127.
11. Shuker, *Understanding*, 177.
12. Mika Elovaara, "Controversies in Music" in *Music in American Life: An Encyclopedia of the Songs, Styles, Stars and Stories that Shaped Our Culture*, ed Jacqueline Edmondson (Santa Barbara, CA: ABC-CLIO Press, in press, 2013).
13. Sam Bagnall. "Investigating the 'death Metal' Murders." BBCNews.co.uk. British Broadcasting Company,http://news.bbc.co.uk/2/hi/programmes/thisworld/4446342.stm>.(Accessed 13 Sept. 2011).
14. Eric Boehlert, "An Old Debate Emerges in Wake of Shooting." RollingStone.com. <http://www.rollingstone.com/music/news/an-old-debate-emerges-in-wake-of-shooting-19990422?print=true>. (Accessed 13 Sept. 2011).

15. Boehlert, "Debate."

16. Marilyn Manson, "Columbine: Whose fault is it?." *Rolling Stone* 815 (1999): 23.

17.Manson, "Columbine."

18. Manson, "Columbine."

19. Manson, "Columbine."

20. Weinstein: *Heavy Metal*, 34-35.

21. Johan Hegg / Amon Amarth, "With Oden on Our Side" in *With Oden on Our Side* (Orebro, Sweden: Metal Blade, 2006).

22. Johan Hegg / Amon Amarth, "War of the Gods" in *Surtur Rising* (Orebro, Sweden: Metal Blade, 2011).

23. Jonne Jarvela / Korpiklaani "Midsummer Night" in *Tales Along this Road* (Helsinki, Finland: Napalm Records, 2006).

24. Cori Ellison, "An Epic Gave Finns a Lot to Sing About" *New York Times*, January 7, 2005, www.nytimes.com <http://www.nytimes.com/2005/ 01/07/arts/music/07 scan.html?pagewanted=print&position=> (Accessed March 20, 2012).

25. Tomi Koivusaari and Esa Holopainen, "Song of the Sage" in *The Beginning of Times* (Helsinki, Finland: Nuclear Blast, 2011).

26. Niclas Etelavuori, Esa Holopainen, Tomi Koivusaari (Amorphis members) interviews by Mika Elovaara, July 2008 and July 2011.

27. Eluveitie, "Omnos" in *Evocation I: The Arcane Dominion* (Helsinki, Finland: Nuclear Blast, 2009).

28. Trollhorn, "Nattfödd" in *Nattfödd* (Helsinki, Finland: Century Media, 2004).

29. Tundra (Finntroll member) interview by Mika Elovaara, March 5 2011.

30. Norwegian Interviewee (Folk/Black Metal musician) interview by Mika Elovaara, June 2009.

31. Chris D, "Big Boss (Root) Interviewed" in Decibel Magazine. www.decibelmagazine.com   .<http://www.decibelmagazine.com/interviews/big-boss-root-interviewed/> (accessed March 20, 2012).

32. Johan Hegg in "Amon Amarth - the untold history of viking metal" Metal Hammer, March 12, 2012: 72.

33. Respondent # 1 in the Meaning of Metal Research Corpus, accessed May 2012.

34. Respondent # 2 in the Meaning of Metal Research Corpus, accessed May 2012.

35. Respondent # 3 in the Meaning of Metal Research Corpus, accessed May 2012.

36. Respondent # 4 in the Meaning of Metal Research Corpus, accessed May 2012.

37. Dom Lawson in "Amon Amarth - the untold history of viking metal" *Metal Hammer*, March 12, 2012.

38. Respondent # 5 in the Meaning of Metal Research Corpus, accessed May 2012.

39. Respondent # 6 in the Meaning of Metal Research Corpus, accessed May 2012.

40.Respondent # 7 in the Meaning of Metal Research Corpus, accessed May 2012.

41. Respondent # 8 in the Meaning of Metal Research Corpus, accessed May 2012.

42. Respondent # 9 in the Meaning of Metal Research Corpus, accessed May 2012.

43. Respondent # 10 in the Meaning of Metal Research Corpus, accessed May 2012.

44. Respondent #11 in the Meaning of Metal Research Corpus, accessed May 2012.

45. Weinstein: *Heavy Metal*, 263.

All Korpiklanni lyrics used with permission courtesy of Nuclear Blast Records and Korpiklanni.

All Amorphis lyrics used with permission courtesy of Nuclear Blast Records and Amorphis.

All Eluveitie lyrics used with permission courtesy of Nuclear Blast Records and Eluveitie.

Chapter 4
By Demons Be Driven? Scanning "Monstrous" Voices
Marcus Erbe

To say it upfront: there is no definitive answer to the question of why the vocal utterances heard in extreme metal bring about notions of monstrosity and demonic possession with almost all people who come in contact with this kind of music for the first time. It seems, however, that the continuity with which such reactions occur perfectly lends itself to mass media exploitation. I shall clarify this observation immediately by discussing a recent case from Peruvian television: In the second season of the talent show *Yo soy* [I am], in which the contestants are invited to impersonate their favorite singer, Napoleón Ochoa, a young metal musician from the province Camaná, performed a vocal cover version of Satyricon's "Mother North." Ochoa's interpretation served as the backdrop for a series of ludicrous audiovisual comments. From the very first second of the song's recital the two show hosts vied with each other for the most hair-raising displays of horror, as their spectacle encompassed acts like sending up a hurried prayer, turning into a zombie, or uttering cries of anguish and dread. To make this burlesque complete, some wildly exaggerated jingles were played, including the chattering of teeth and a Theremin-like melodic figure, both of which can be regarded as highly conventionalized sonic icons[1] for the uncanny.

Despite their flamboyant production (and despite the fact that candidates in casting shows constantly run the risk of being ridiculed irrespective of the musical genre in which they choose to perform), all these efforts aimed at identifying a certain type of vocalization as evil incarnate. One could of course object that the responses to Ochoa's presentation stemmed first and foremost from the diabolical aura that surrounds the metal genre in general and black metal in particular, and that the vocal rendition had been of secondary importance for the public dismantling of his performance. It would go beyond the limits of this chapter to enumerate the countless occasions on which media executives have chosen to associate metal music with positive values after all. What is crucial for our example is to note that the contestant's version of *Mother North* differed significantly from the original recording. First, in order to meet the requirements of the show's audition phase, the song was only allowed to be accompanied by the piano. Because of this reduced instrumentation the voice in itself attracted more attention than it probably would have within a full metal ensemble. Second, Ochoa's attempt at portraying the band's vocalist Sigurd Wongraven resulted in a singing style which, compared to the hoarse rasp of his idol, had to it a deeper, much "grislier" quality. Various remarks to that effect were made by the members of the jury. After comparing the contestant to the giant monster Godzilla and imitating his growls (backed up by yet another sonic icon, namely a few chords of eerie organ music), one of the judges went on to describe Ochoa's voice as the manifestation of an evil spirit, whereas his outward appearance, especially the fact that he was wearing corpse paint, sparked little to no interest. Why am I stressing this particular detail? It is altogether hardly surprising that the voice should become the central point of reference in a singing competition. However, the degree to which the entire event reveals itself as being profoundly staged around a certain type of voice—with all the pre-calculated effects and subsidiary gestures exposed throughout the show—reinforces the impression that there must be a specific cultural prototype underlying the perception of vocal monstrosity.

Before further exploring this thought, it seems to me worth involving in the discussion a distinctive mechanism behind the introduction of exceptional cases and sensational novelties within the media. In an analysis of modern-day newspaper articles about outstandingly horrific criminal offences, Christina Bartz (2006) arrives at the conclusion that there is a strong leaning toward the amalgamation of normality and abnormality. Drawing upon press coverage of crimes committed by individuals with no prior history of violence, she points out the reiteration of a narrative in which the unthinkable deed is contrasted with ordinary occurrences from the perpetrator's biography, often followed by proclamations of amazement over the fact that people leading inconspicuous lives may actually be monsters. According to Bartz, the incidence of such narratives can only be explained insufficiently by previous theories of mass media normalization, at the heart of which lies the assumption that extreme or abnormal acts are generally being reported as sudden leaps from a moral middle ground. In contrast, she reasons that the politics of news production require a permanent inclusion of the sensational within the ordinary (or vice versa), as both the experiences of everyday life and events possessing a rarity or shock value are major selection criteria with regard to the relevance of any potential news item. Apparently, mass media audiences are on the one hand conditioned to perceive deviance from the norm as a threat to social stability, while on the other hand it is not uncommon among journalists to showcase wickedness as, so to speak, an extreme instance of normalcy. This particular newsroom strategy can already be witnessed at the level of the headline, when, for instance, a phrase along the lines of "Monstress: the diary of a child murderer" (Goc 2007, 157) slyly merges the unscrupulous incident with the widespread social practice of writing down one's innermost thoughts.

One would assume that the relatively harmless emergence of black metal on a popular TV show has no connection with news reports on acts of transgression whatsoever. But on closer inspection, there is indeed a common ground on which deviators in both the news and the entertainment sector are being portrayed. Only by joining together the ordinary and the extraordinary can a universal human activity like singing become a sensation. The procedure as such is essentially Janus-faced. Should the display of vocal eccentricity occur within the boundaries of a generally accepted tolerance zone, it may give rise to the medial fostering of prodigies (like Susan Boyle or Paul Potts). On the other end of the spectrum we are presented with the atrocious vocal freak. In this regard, Ochoa's case is certainly not an isolated one. As a result of the global installation of various so-called reality talent formats one does not need look far to discover similar auditions with aspiring extreme metal vocalists. Needless to say, these candidates never get to the next round, let alone the finals.

A further explanatory model that may throw light on the subject becomes apparent in Theodor W. Adorno's writings on popular music and the culture industry. While Adorno's theories have, with some justification, often been criticized for their polemic character and anti-American sentiment, the immediacy of at least some of his ideas is not to be easily refuted. Pondering over the personality projections of jazz musicians, he notes that the entertainment business, since it relies on the reoccurrence of the spectacle as an effective means of masking the uniformity of its products, readily embraces individual displays of eccentricity and rebelliousness, but only insofar as to integrate them with a predetermined set of (pop) cultural norms. In this process of domestication, the once probably unsettling artist becomes no more than a court jester, serving publicly as an object for the audience's own fantasies of deviation (see Adorno 1953, 133–37). Or as Jeffrey Jerome Cohen would have it

> The monster is continually linked to forbidden practices, in order to normalize and to enforce. The monster also attracts. The same creatures who terrify and interdict can evoke potent escapist fantasies; the linking of monstrosity with the forbidden makes the monster all the more appealing as a temporary egress from constraint. [. . .] We distrust and loathe the monster at the same time we envy its freedom, and perhaps its sublime despair. [. . .] The co-optation of the monster into a symbol of the desirable is often accomplished through the neutralization of potentially threatening aspects with a liberal dose of comedy: the thundering giant becomes the bumbling giant. (Cohen 1996, 16–18)

Granting all of this, it stands to reason that the bigger the gap between the expected and the unexpected, between a cultural norm and the violation thereof, the bigger the potential for having one's target audiences simmer with excitement. One noteworthy example in this respect is the appearance of the twenty four-year-old female vocalist Rachel Aspe on *La France a un incroyable talent*[3] (the French implementation of the UK *Got Talent* franchise), as it adds to the prearranged media shock of the monstrous voice the problem of gender. To fully comprehend the impact of her performance, it is necessary to stress a few important details. Contrary to the case of Ochoa, or rather the case of any other metalhead entering these kinds of competitions, Aspe (whether voluntarily or on somebody's advice remains an open question) refrained from outwardly displaying even the slightest hint of metal-ness. Instead, she was wearing a festive evening dress, complete with a pair of elegant shoes, a black Alice band, modest makeup, and fashionable silver jewelry, that is to say an outfit more suitable for a sophisticated concertgoer than a female rock star. Appropriately enough, she behaved in a friendly, well-mannered way and was received in just as friendly fashion by the jury. When asked beforehand about her particular talent, Aspe replied with a winning smile: "le chant" (meaning "singing" in the most traditional sense of the word). All this preliminary chitchat ought not to obscure the subtlety with which the contestant's vocal demonstration has been used by design for its shock value.[4] From an objective point of view, Aspe delivered a well-rehearsed and proficiently executed version of the Sybreed song *Emma-0*, following meticulously the original (male) singer's transitions between screaming and a mid-range growl. The rhythms as well as the phrasing of the words did not differ in the least from traditional singing, as is, mind you, the case with many realizations of extreme metal vocals. The chief differ-ence between the two lies in the absence of musical pitch, seeing that in extreme metal, vocal pitch gives way to various sorts of noisy tone produc-tion. This is not to say that the vocal contour becomes flat, since it is possi-ble to identify in growled or screamed lyrics successions of timbre. But as opposed to conventional vocal melodies, the relative positions of those sounds have more to do with the internal organization of complex spectra than with the perception of fundamental frequencies. I shall take up that point later in the text. Returning to the subject at hand, it may, however, help us understand that what accounts for the abnormal effect is not so much the musical context framing the extreme voice as is the voice's sheer mate-riality, or, to be more precise, the supposed incongruity between a human body and a seemingly inhuman voice. And it would appear that in our (pop-ular) culture the said incongruity is felt most fiercely when the "abnormal" voice emanates from a female body. During Aspe's performance this was expressed visually by means of overemphasized cross-cuts between the nu-merous puzzled expressions in both the audience and the jury, while simul-taneously a couple of lurid shouts from the hosts—perhaps the most predict-able (and also telling) of which had been the call for an exorcist—added to the outrageousness of the spectacle. The same applies to the subsequent, all-too-emphatic jury statements about the stark contrast between the young woman's physique and her voice, which we can regard as a further example of how the unimaginable is medially constructed through the lens of normal-ity.

This twofold issue of normalization and gender becomes even more pressing when we take into account the online circulation of the event in question. With millions of views across different social networking services and video-sharing websites, Aspe's audition attracted far more attention on the Internet than did any previous prime time television display of growling and-or screaming skills. Given the sheer quantity of user comments, it is virtually impossible to keep track of all the conceptions and preconceptions about this particular performance. However, the persistence with which many users, among them professed metal fans, continue to update "reactionary gender values" so as to defend a virile understanding of metal musicianship (Waksman 2009, 195) is fairly remarkable. With this in mind, even a well-intentioned observation along the lines of, "But she's great [. . .] There are not many women who can sing like this for longer than a few seconds,"[5] betrays the widespread belief that growling and other male dominated modes of vocal expression—despite the ever-increasing number of female fronted or all-female extreme metal bands[6]—are subject to biological constraints. As opposed to this generally accepted view, the composer and film theorist Michel Chion paints a different picture (and we would just have to replace the word "speaking" with "singing" in the following quotation to get a first idea of the essentially gender-neutral potentialities of the extreme metal voice)

> [T]he human voice has no organ. We humans forget that our speech results from the deployment of a whole assortment of bodily parts, none of which, including what are wrongly called the vocal cords, is principally and solely an organ of phonation: the pharynx, lungs, jaw, lips, tongue, teeth. As Roman Jakobson showed, if an individual can no longer form a given phoneme with the part of the mouth or body normally mobilized for its production, she or he will with surprising quickness mobilize other muscles to produce it. For example, if you voluntarily block your tongue and prevent yourself from using it, your mouth will make a detour and immediately find other movements that allow you to produce the same phonemes. Elocution will be altered, certainly, and it would take some time to master this new way of speaking, but through concentrated effort it would come rather quickly, and you could manage to make yourself understood. The principal problem would be the possibly embarrassing sound of this new voice and putting up with the possible irritation of its new timbre. At any rate, this example serves to show that anything can be used for speaking, so long as it can be articulated. The speaking body is not the physical body; or put another way, our visible physical body is itself the mask of our invisible speaking body. (Chion 2009, 336–37)

From what has been said thus far, we might conclude that in contemporary Western (or Westernized) musical cultures the singing voice splits up into two distinct vocal spheres. Simply speaking, the first of the two is based on what phoneticians call the modal voice or on any other vocal register, as for example the falsetto, in which regular vibrations of the vocal folds generate harmonic spectra. Within this first sphere we come across all instances of conventional singing, be it historical forms such as plainchant and bel canto or the more recent vocal styles associated with all kinds of melody-based popular music. Vocals in the second sphere display, by contrast, a high degree of roughness and noise. Here, the modal voice is either absent or appears only conditionally as a part of other uncommon phonation types, that is, types of voice production (see Figure 1). All these unusual phonatory modes combined account for the various manifestations of metal growling, squealing, shouting, and screaming. They are also to be found, as I can note merely in passing, over the entire spectrum of avant-garde composition and sound poetry.[7]

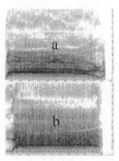

Figure 1: Comparison between a voiced and an unvoiced scream. Whereas the voiced variant (a) displays both harmonic (regular) and inharmonic (irregular) frequency components, the turbulent airflow underlying the unvoiced scream (b) generates noise

The two vocal spheres are prone to overlap at times. This happens not just in the modern sound arts, but in the repertoires of blues, jazz, rock, and pop as well. The latter becomes particularly apparent when we think of such renowned singers as Cab Calloway, Louis Armstrong, Little Richard, Janis Joplin, Robert Plant, James Brown, Tom Waits, and Screamin' Jay Hawkins, whose performances are imbued with shouts and screams, occasionally even with growls, groans, and grunts. The incidence of these sounds is nevertheless fundamentally different when it comes to extreme metal, for there they are no by-product of an otherwise melodic singing but rather the primary means of vocal expression. Consequently, it is not metal per se that causes a stir in mass culture contexts. The music of bands like Iron Maiden or Nightwish, in which the "beautiful" singing voice is still given priority, may very well serve as a template for widely accepted performances on talent shows, whereas all styles of metal (or punk, for that matter) revolving around extremely harsh and thus seemingly abnormal modes of vocal production—regardless of how good or bad their rendition—will most likely continue to eke out a miserable existence.

Although I addressed at the beginning the impossibility of putting one's finger on the exact spot where a) the mere perception of the vocals in question and b) the attribution of monstrosity converge, there is good reason to believe that due to audiovisual training people build up mental representations of what a monstrous voice should sound like. As a matter of fact, our world is filled with monstrous voices. We encounter them on a regular basis while watching movies and cartoons, playing video games, or listening to radio dramas. And it would seem safe to conclude that people are inclined to transfer their individual experience with suchlike vocalities also to the realm of music. In the next section, I will thus ask about the medial prerequisites of the monstrous voice. What are the features that set apart monstrous from human voices? Which strategies have been employed by, for instance, horror cinema in the construction of vocal monstrosity? Are there any similarities to be found between voice acting for film or video games and the vocal practices that are characteristic of extreme metal? Here, I shall draw upon a number of relevant field observations that I made during my research with metal and hardcore vocalists in Germany. Bearing in mind that the phenomenon of extreme vocal techniques has been widely neglected in academic studies, this will give me the opportunity to draw attention to the conditions under which the singers themselves master and carry out their art. I will close the chapter by presenting additional data regarding the physical processes that underlie different realizations of growling and screaming.

Monstrosity and the Monstrous Voice: Theory Versus Practice

Given how many ways and by how many thinkers monstrosity has been defined throughout the ages, it would be more than bold to try to combine the various implications of this cultural concept into an all-encompassing frame of reference. As with every discursive universe that is simply too complex to be tackled in a straightforward manner, one can either explore certain concrete manifestations of the phenomenon at hand[8] or find criteria under which to determine some relevant aspects of its meaning. One such typology has been put forth by Rasmus Overthun (2009, 52–76), whose aim was to outline the esthetic fascination with the monstrous in poetry, prose, the theatre, and the visual arts by comparing the writings of Mikhail Bakhtin, Jorge Luis Borges, Jacques Derrida, Michel Foucault, Peter Handke, Franz Kafka, Immanuel Kant, Jacques Lacan, Arthur Rimbaud, Karl Rosenkranz, Friedrich Schlegel, Horace, and the Marquis de Sade. In so doing, Overthun identified four major categories of artistically cultivated monstrosity, which I shall recapitulate to provide a basis for discussing further the aspect of the monstrous voice:

1. Bodily monsters (the alien body) ["Körpermonster (Der fremde Körper)"]. This first category encompasses deviations from or fragmentations of the classical/neoclassical ideal of the smooth and unscathed human body. It relates to physical mutilations of all sorts as much as to the display of primal corporality in the form of body hair, genitals, excretory organs, grimaces, or any other physical feature that is closely associated with the animal kingdom. The prospect of a real amalgamation of man and beast takes on even greater threatening dimensions, since the monstrous crossbreed symbolizes not just a potential transformation of the rational being into a creature solely driven by its physical urges, but (as with Kafka's zoomorphic entities) hints at the hybrid and thus frail nature of the human psyche.

2. Moral monsters (the great outlaw) ["Sittenmonster (Der große Gesetzlose"]. Here we arrive at a type of monstrous delinquency that has al-

ready been mentioned in connection with the study undertaken by Christina Bartz and that continues to fascinate journalists and artists alike. The category of the moral monster shows a tendency to overwrite the time-honored, originally mythical category of the body monster, as from the late eighteenth century onward monstrosity becomes more and more associated with human acts of transgression (i.e., the breaking of taboos such as incest, buggery, cannibalism, necrophilia, and infanticide), while at the same time the growing scientification of society takes away the fear of the monstrous body and exiles it almost completely to the realm of fiction where it still may serve as a metaphor for atrocities inflicted by man.

3. Subjective monsters (the alter ego) ["Subjektmonster (Das andere Ich)"]. Propelled by Cartesian dualism and, thereafter, by Enlightenment thought and the ideas of psychoanalysis, the notion of the disordered or even divided self, along with its various manifestations of madness and schizophrenia, turned out to be one of the most trusted symbols of the de-ontologicalization of the subject in romantic and postromantic narratives. In Overthun's view, the existence of an alter ego transcends the categories of both the bodily and the moral monster, for the interchangeability of a person's identity implies not so much a sudden transformation into a monstrous other, but rather the gradual fading of self.

4. Monstrous orders (the almost impossible representation) ["Monströse An-Ordnungen (Die fast unmögliche Darstellung)"]. This last category is introduced to stress that all the available variations on monstrosity are, in a sense, unwieldy when it comes to taxonomy and theory formation. Since art production can be described as a kind of esthetic sandbox, with the possibility of constantly putting to the test and readjusting the boundaries of norms and normality, it tends to spawn very "flexible monsterizations" (76) which sometimes might be hard to grasp. This notwithstanding, Overthun concludes that one of the fundamental conceptions behind the esthetics of the monstrous is the preference of fragmented representations over the representation of an integrated whole, of stable and thus meaningful contexts. This is not to say that suchlike disruptions of clarity inevitably lead to the total obliteration of the object being represented. Instead, they demonstrate previously unchallenged perceptions by violating them or by toying with their basic conditions.

Now let us just suppose that the vocalizations of extreme music are in fact monstrous. Under which of the aforesaid categories would they fall? If we, for the moment, put aside the lyrical content of thousands of metal songs, of which one can safely say that they deal with various manifestations of moral monstrosity, and if we thus focus our attention on the materiality of the voice, we eventually arrive in the area of the bodily monster—but not without taking a detour first.

Over the past decades, the voice has attracted great interest from various schools of linguistics, semiotics, and cultural studies, especially with regard to aspects of performativity, which is to say the connection between the voice and the sociopolitically entangled body from which it emanates (e.g., Barthes 1977; Pittam 1994; Zumthor 1994; Krämer 2003; Waldenfels

2003). And despite the concurrent debates about otherness and alternative body concepts, there has been paid startlingly little attention to the nature of monstrous voices. The few scholars who address the topic typically offer a simple, if not simplistic, way of understanding by advancing the thesis that monsterizations of the voice occur first and foremost by means of techno-logical manipulation. In an article on electroacoustic voice processing for contemporary opera, Jelena Novak muses that "[t]he concept of monstrosity enters the vocal sphere through technology that emphasizes the audibility of the cessation between the human and the inhuman manifested through the voice produced simultaneously by the body and a machine" (2010, 106). Similarly, Vito Pinto (2012, 58–60) puts much effort into stressing the per-ceptual inescapability of the severely processed voice. Although he acknowledges that already the emergence of unfamiliar ways of speaking can cause a sensation of monstrosity, it is for him the bizarreness of techni-cally distorted voices which outbids any other form of vocal transgression.

Viewed from this angle, the shortest (and probably most used) route to the acoustic construction of monsters would be the modification of a speak-er's voice with the help of widespread studio effects like pitch shifters, har-monizers, vocoders, ring modulators, audio choppers, and phase processors. We just have to cast a cursory glance over the history of film sound and game audio to get a sense of the vast availability of such procedures. Whether it is the massively overdriven howl of *The Thing from Another World* (Christian Nyby, 1951), the chains of psychedelic tape delay put atop the victims' agonized screams in *Night of the Living Dead* (George A. Romero, 1968), or the biphonic screeching of *The Evil Dead* (Sam Raimi, 1981), to name but one example for the long-standing Hollywood tradition of unnatural shifts in vocal timbre with the demonically possessed. All these different types of electroacoustically altered voices, as they are being kept alive thanks to a colorful assortment of digitally rendered extraterrestrials, orcs, witches, and ghosts, serve to furnish certain characters and situations with a touch of otherworldliness. Consequently, they are deeply engraved in our auditory memory, and although some of them may have silent forerun-ners—for instance in the Biblical account of demonic multivocality (see Thacker 2010, 197–200)— it is plausible to think that our ideas about vocal monstrosity are informed, above all else, by today's omnipresence of audio-narrative and audiovisual media.

Interestingly enough, excessive treatments of vocal sounds as the ones just referenced are scarcely of any importance when it comes to extreme metal. Of course we can be sure that no single metal voice enters into the audio mix without there being some sort of post-processing. But as is com-mon in the production of popular music in general, the procedures that are applied essentially involve the maximization of loudness through signal compression as well as the stereophonic positioning and spatialization of the pre-recorded material through panning, reverberation, and delay. Hence, the original timbre of the voice basically remains untouched or, at least, is not altered beyond recognition.[9] Likewise, the multitrack approach to vocals, which Natalie Purcell (2003, 58) regards as a specialty of Deicide, is certainly no achievement of metal. Here—and this holds true for both extreme metal and pop music—the vocalist employs different registers to yield homorhythmic lines which are then layered as a means of broadening the perceived vocal range. Other uses involve the composition of polyphonic vocal textures, as can be heard, for instance, toward the end of Pantera's *5 Minutes Alone* (1993) with Phil Anselmo accompanying himself in a counterpoint-like fashion. Kirill Gromada, singer in the two metal bands Pripjat and I, Nero and also a skilled sound engineer, explained to me the mixing of vocals and vocal layers as follows:

> It depends on the song, but if you want to obtain a certain effect, sure, then I place them [the vocals] differently across the panorama. Sometimes in such a way that they really shift from left to right or become more of a background, panned all the way to the right and left with one voice in the middle. This makes for a very wide field. But mainly I superimpose them head-on, that is to say in the center where the vocals should normally sit. [. . .] It's better to keep them together, because then you get this strengthening effect. It's simply that certain frequencies which are not covered by growling alone then become wrapped up by screaming. With that you get a huge spectrum, and when they are well coordinated, it's mega. [. . .] What's important is that I want to keep the voice as natural as possible. [. . .] The whole technology I put behind it aims at making it fit the mix, not at distorting something. [Plays back a song while switching back and forth between the final mix and the unprocessed vocal track] As you can see, the voice barely differs from that which you hear in the actual recording. It is of the utmost importance to me that one can hear each instrument, that one can hear it clearly and that one can hear it as being unaltered. (translated by the author[10])

This ideal of a voice that remains as unspoiled as possible, either onstage or in the studio, is something which I encountered in many conversations. About half of the interviewees from my ongoing field research (nineteen in total so far) in one way or another drew attention to the natural capacity of their vocal timbre. The topic was most frequently raised by people from technical death metal bands, which is to say by vocalists who place a high value on very controlled ways of growling and/or pig squealing. One could interpret this insistence on one's own vocal aptitude as further indication of metal's virtuosity, defined by Robert Walser as the "display of exceptional individual power" (1993, 76), against which the utilization of technological tools would probably have to be considered as cheating. This becomes particularly apparent in a statement by Chris Barnes, the former singer of Cannibal Corpse, whom quite a few of my interviewees referenced as an artistic role model:

> I've always got questions from people about my vocals. Like, "What effects do you use to get the vocals to sound like that?" I'd tell them it was natural and they wouldn't believe me. Even my sound guy at the time got sick of hearing it. I put it right on the record, so people who had the record knew what the story was. My vocals were always raw. We'd do effects on accents and intros, but never a broad spectrum of effects throughout. No flange or

reverb on a vocal throughout a song. I've been fighting that my whole career.
(Barnes 2008, reprinted in Mudrian 2009, 153)

Another thing I have learned from my interviews is that, irrespective of the
skepticism toward technological manipulation, a number of vocalists regard
the microphone to be an instrument in its own right. Generally speaking, a
voice that is closely miked brings about more weight on lower frequencies.
Apart from this proximity effect, which adds a considerable amount of vocal
boom (especially to growls), several extreme metal singers make use of so-
called cupping techniques with hand-held microphones, meaning that either
by placing one hand over the mic's head or by forming a basket with both
hands certain spectral components can be boosted systematically (see Figure
2). Since this might cause acoustic feedback onstage and in the rehearsal
space, some vocalists have "dropped the practice altogether" (Daniel
Schewior of Disposed to Mirth), while others insist on cupping as an indis-
pensable creative means and "simply tell the sound guy to lower the volume
on the stage monitors" (Martin Tubandt of Exsanguination / My Own Children's Drink).

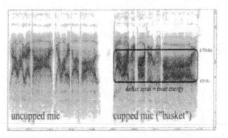

Figure 2: Spectrographic comparison of uncupped and cupped mid-range
growls, as performed by Thomas Appel of Inkarna. In this example, the
cupping of the microphone boosts the frequencies between 420 and 1.750
Hz, resulting in a more compacted sound.

But let us return to the question of a possible concurrence between the
vocalities of fictional horror and extreme metal. Metal's generic affiliation
with horror has been well established (e.g., Walser 1993, 160–65; Purcell
2003, 170–86; Barron and Inglis 2009; Clendinning and McAuley 2010;
Krautkrämer and Petri 2011; Phillipov 2012, 89–105). Considering the
countless analogies with regard to content, iconography, typography, and
musical sound, it hardly comes as a surprise that insiders and outsiders alike
should take the strangeness of the extreme metal voice for yet another sign
of this match made in hell. "When you hear a Death Metal vocalist", notes
the B movie producer and publicist Bill Zebub, "you should be under the
impression that you are hearing a demon" (qtd. in Purcell 2003, 11). Similarly, Jon Kristiansen's *Slayer*, one of the first fanzines dedicated to death
metal, grindcore, and black metal (all issues reprinted in Kristiansen 2011),
overflows with horror-related descriptions of vocals: Martin Walkyier, the

singer of Sabbat, is supposed to sound "like he is fuckin' possessed" (91), whereas the voice of Mayhem's former front man Maniac comes across as "total splattering chainsawcore" (112). Such remarks, categorical though they may seem, are rarely meant to suggest an actual demonic origin of the voice (this business is up to self-proclaimed exorcists like Bob Larson who makes clever in his "patients"[11]). Rather, they have to be read as a verbal play on genre conventions meant to express one's pleasure in figures of thought that exceed ordinary configurations of sense. Other than that, they surely help to solidify the impression of vocal monstrosity, as does the fact that in certain songs the vocals sound in conjunction with samples from horror movies.

By no means is it my intention to challenge the validity of these monstrous attributions.[12] However, data from my interviews suggests that the perceptions of audiences and musicians may differ significantly in this respect. Each time I seized the opportunity to ask a singer whether he or she saw a connection to the voices of horror cinema, I was either met with a shrug or with a critical stance on the subject. Five of the participants reported that their parents or other people in their social environment were genuinely shocked by their vocal endeavors because they associated with it a diabolical way of expressing oneself (one vocalist who was brought up a Catholic revealed to me that his grandmother, after hearing him practice, urged him to consult a priest). Still others, who have never been confronted with reactions that stark, were able to ironically distance themselves from the cliché. I vividly recall a get-together with several vocalists, in which we, among other things, discussed the motivation for singing in a metal band. At one point, Juan Gracia of Trailer Park Sex joked that he had learned his satanic voice from the cradle. To substantiate this claim he slipped into his mother's role and began to gently rock an invisible baby while growling out a lullaby.

A thing often mentioned to me was the importance of affective ideas as a driving force behind one's shaping of and command over the voice. Extreme vocalists strive to convey feelings of rage, brutality, intensity, aggression, or power. For that, they develop individual strategies. Daniel of Disposed to Mirth, for example, in preparation for studio sessions and live performances, got into the habit of looking at photos of real-life occurrences which, to use his words, really pissed him off. What is being pinpointed here is that the singers represent or express through their voice certain emotive states that may, but do not necessarily have to be associated with the affective meanings produced by horror. To clarify this still further we can again turn to Barnes, whom many, because of his signature growl and the gore-infused lyrics during his time with Cannibal Corpse, regard as a vocal monster par excellence. Yet it is remarkable how he, in hindsight, describes the genesis of his vocal style not so much in terms of monstrous mimicry, but as an emotional response to the stylistic traits of death metal at the beginning of the 1990s

For me, I was influenced by how I was feeling inside and how heavy and er-ratic the music was. The music was so groove-laden and technical. That's what inspired me—to push myself—to come up with the sounds I did. I liked Obituary, Death and Pestilence, but those bands didn't really inspire me vo-cally. I just wanted to destroy everything I thought was right. It was insanity put to music. A madman's brain on tape. (Barnes 2008, reprinted in Mudrian 2009, 148)

It is crucial to keep in mind that the majority of extreme metal and hardcore vocalists are self-taught (of my participants only one enjoyed a formal edu-cation as a jazz singer, but his studies at the conservatory notwithstanding, he told me that he had to unlearn many things for metal). Most of them start their autodidactic training by listening closely to their favorite singers and trying to imitate their vocals, which does seem to help with developing a basic feel for what is technically right and what should best be avoided. Based on that, people begin to further explore their vocal capabilities and eventually cultivate a personal style. Jonny Davy, the front man of the inter-nationally established band Job for a Cowboy, with whom I had the oppor-tunity of communicating via e-mail in June 2012, put it this way

It's even hard to pin-point any real role models in the metal vocalist world. I suppose Barney from Napalm Death and Travis from Cattle Decapitation are the first ones that pop into mind. My influences changed rapidly early on since the band was born, so I think that helped a lot. I never focused on try-ing to sound like anyone else, just focused on what I knew I could pull off and worked on building from there. In the end I was just a guy yelling in a microphone in our friend's parents' garage almost ten years ago. [. . .] At this point it's simply a reflex when I sing. With the range that I use I definitely have to put a lot more thought into it. I have to constantly change tongue movements, overtones, and at times it is exhausting. The only thing I force myself to remember is to simply sing from the diaphragm and to constantly have your floating ribs open for oxygen.

It can clearly be seen now that the passing down of extreme singing styles as well as their further development takes place, in essence, within the bounda-ries of the respective musical genres and is not erected upon the vocal per-formances of horror film actors or any technologically constructed monster voices. However, for the sake of completeness we must add that fantastic cinema does not inevitably rely on special audio effects, since "[a] good actor or impressionist, in fact anyone with enough practice, can become capable of changing his voice and giving it all kinds of inflections and di-mensions merely with the means nature has given him" (Chion 1999, 169). This results in the circumstance that every once in a while it is indeed possi-ble to determine at least phonatory analogies between the voices heard in extreme metal and other media. Beyond the frequently cited growl-like tim-bre of the Cookie Monster on *Sesame Street* (as portrayed by Frank Oz) one could think of many other memorable vocal dubbings of the sort, for in-stance Frank Welker's villainy voice for Dr. Claw on the animated series

Inspector Gadget or Andy Serkis's tremendous shifts in timbre in his role as Gollum. An even closer match can be established with regard to the noise announcing the presence of a vengeful spirit in the Japanese horror film *Ju-on* and its American remake *The Grudge*, as this sound is based on the same type of creaky voice that underlies certain inhale phonations found in grind-core and death metal. One can even encounter metal's pig squealing technique in places one would have least expected it, namely in the recent Universal Studios adaptation of the children's book series *Curious George*. All animal characters on the show are voiced by human actors, as is the occasionally appearing piggy Little Mike with its distinctive "bree" sound (e.g., in the episode *Ski Monkey*), demonstrating that what is cute and amusing in one context, can elsewhere appear heinous and demonic. Thus, if ever there was a domain of audio-related art in which the two spheres of the modal and the noise-like voice, as I outlined them above, were allowed to coexist in a mutually accepted manner, we would have to point at all the fantastic narratives of film, radio drama, and video game culture. Nevertheless, as constitutive as the extraordinary voice may be for the said genres, as accidental is its relation to the vocalities of extreme metal.[13] So even if our everyday perception suggests a causal relationship, we can assert that there is a correlation at best.

A more direct connection with the aforementioned category of the bodily monster becomes obvious in the vocalists' references to animal sounds. Although expressions like "growling" and the more current designations "pig squeal" and "frog noise" betray an affinity for zoomorphic thought, the significance of this aspect has not yet been fully realized outside the scene (except for Heesch 2011). The reproduction of animal calls in music is of course no novelty. But unlike the esthetically idealized appropriation of, say, birdsong in Western art music, the growls, squeals, and croaks of extreme metal, stylized though they still may be, aim at a far more direct incorporation of animalistic sound. Martin of Exsanguination brought to my attention a Youtube clip named "Crazy Koala Fight," which enjoys certain popularity among metalheads, for the rhythmic growls of one of the koalas bear a striking similarity to analogous vocal passages in deathgrind songs.[14] Another vocalist, who asked me to guard her identity because of the private nature of the following statement, told me this charming anecdote:

> I remember playing Princess Lillifee with my little nieces and a couple of their friends from the neighborhood. Eventually, one of the kiddos [. . .] thought that it would be a great idea to turn me into a piglet. The only thing I could come up with in this situation was to start doing my usual inhale stuff. The girls must have found it so cool that they wouldn't stop bewitching me. You know, like, "Wow, she's a real pig now!" [. . .] Now every time I come to stay we have to replay the whole thing. They are quite obsessed with it. [...] So much for evil music [laughs]. But what the heck? Making weird voices is supposed to be fun, one way or another. (translated by the author[15])

Academia and the Extreme Metal Voice

What struck me most while preparing for my field studies was the relative light heartedness with which scholars continue to write about the phenomenon at hand. More often than not, the tone becomes quite colloquial, and it is hard to tell in each case whether the sweeping generalizations of the voice can be ascribed to a lack of interest or a lack of knowledge concerning the vocal practices of extreme metal. Most of the definitions now on offer appear to rely on highly subjective accounts of auditory impressions. As a consequence, one can observe to a certain degree the seeping of journalistic jargon into scholarly works. When, for example, Deena Weinstein notes that "[v]ocalists growl as if gargling with razor blades and acid" (2011, 41), the meaningfulness of this description is essentially the same as in Ian Christe's dictum that "creatures like Glen Benton of Deicide tore out their larynxes to summon images of decaying corpses and giant catastrophic horrors" (2004, 239). Notwithstanding the tongue-in-cheek character of such remarks, one can little deny a subliminal tendency to pathologize the vocals under discussion here. This tendency manifests itself more severely in an article by the art historian Jörg Scheller, in which he analyzes the DVD lessons of the American-based vocal coach Melissa Cross

> "Screaming is an art", preaches Cross to her clients. They crouch in front of their mentor in a relaxed posture and with a concentrated look, while making noises in which asphyxia, oscillating sander and battle cries overlap. Cross explains how to add to the voice the right amount of "pebbles" or "sandpaper", how to "corrupt" the vocal cords and still keep a clear enunciation. After a few sessions they have grasped it at last: the throat artists do no longer scream just loudly and aggressively, but in a controlled and technically gifted fashion; for more safety in the workplace, so to speak. This has educational value not only for front-men with a bleeding pharynx [. . .]. (Scheller 2011, 287; translated by the author[16])

Jason Forster, a scholar of religious studies, uses aspects of phonation and vocal timbre as a means of updating persistent genre stereotypes

> [I]n place of the beast-like vocal spectrum found in Death Metal, in Black Metal we encounter a more hellish spectrum of sounds, dominated by what can only adequately be described as rasped and screeched attempts to sound as 'demonic' as possible [. . .]. Consequently, the effect Black Metal's vocal spectrum serves to generate is not so much primal as it is malignant – making it the perfect vehicle for the subgenre's unholy fervor. (Forster 2008, 9)

Now even if we shift our focus from such pejorative disquisitions to more neutral ones, it becomes evident that specific lines of reasoning prove to be quite durable. In an otherwise instructive essay on the role of violence in extreme metal, Ronald Bogue places the genre's vocal sonorities in a semantic field of quasi-satanic expression, unnaturalness, deformation and machinization (2004, 106–15). Bogue's retreat to academically ennobled

philosophical concepts—namely the Deleuze-Guattarian model of deterrito-
rialization—cannot obscure the fact that the vocals in question are being
neglected as musical practice, but instead defined according to criteria largely external to it. This particular point of view is not dissimilar to Novak's
and Pinto's reduction of vocal "monstrosity" to the sole aspect of technological manipulation, which, if we broaden our perspective, already at the advent of electroacoustic music around 1950 had severely negative consequences for its reception, when critics began to regard the newfound
possibility of decomposing and recomposing the human voice as an act of
denaturization (see Erbe 2009, 188–191).

To insist on ascriptions such as these can lead to paradoxical situations.
It is indisputably to Michelle Phillipov's credit to have outlined in her monograph *Death Metal and Music Criticism* (2012) some important character-
istics and esthetic differences in the vocal styles of Carcass (113–18) and
Cannibal Corpse (126–32). However, in following the categories erected by
Bogue she limits the vocals of death metal to a few selected aspects—
inflexibility, percussiveness, lack of expression, indecipherability—on the
basis of which she speculates about their disruptive effect on music (74–81).
Here again, the extreme metal voice is mainly defined for what it is not.
What has already been said and what we can be sure of is that its unfamiliar
sound sets it apart from culturally predominant vocal practices. And it appears as if this peculiar sonic trait overshadows all the obvious similarities
between noisy and tuneful singing. To begin with, the instances of growling
referred to by Phillipov are no more and no less percussive than is scat singing or Little Richard's vocal performance on his 1955 hit record *Tutti-Frutti*.
Second, if we allow for further examples from the death metal repertoire, in
which the function of the voice is not to punctuate or imitate instrumental
rhythms, it becomes perfectly clear that the durations and the rhythmic successions of the vowels being sung do not differ in the least from those which
can be found in traditional vocal melodies. For reasons of space, I cannot
provide an in-depth analysis to support this claim. But in simply picking up
the lyrics to some genre defining songs such as Death's *Regurgitated Guts*
(1987), Entombed's *Morbid Devourment* (1990), Obituary's *Body Bag*
(1990), Morbid Angel's *Sworn to the Black* (1993), or Deicide's *Christ Denied* (1995) and in trying to follow the respective vocal lines, one may find
it not too hard to imagine the words being sung melodically. Third, although
the majority of extreme metal lyrics can indeed barely be figured out by ear,
the degree to which this is the case varies significantly from one vocalist to
the next. As part of my field research I have recorded many audio samples
of the participants' individual voices. Through an auditory comparison of
different approaches to growling, screaming, and shouting, I have found that
intelligibility depends as much on phonation as it does on articulation. Especially in growling, some singers used their vocal tract to form certain vowels
against the linguistic norm to obtain different tones. In one particular instance, the realization of the growled vowel [o] in "glow" sounded more like
in "word" or even "bird." When later I asked the singer about this, he explained that he often would retract the tongue, its tip almost touching the

roof of the mouth, because this forced him to lower the larynx and produce a fuller sound. In other instances, vocalists chose to enunciate their lyrics more clearly (or less brutal, as one of them called it), hence improving comprehensibility in spite of the underlying noisy voice production.[17]

Scanning (Maybe not so) Monstrous Voices

To allow for a better understanding of the phonatory processes and biological mechanisms behind the extreme metal voice, I initiated a research project in cooperation with speech scientist and phonetician Sven Grawunder of the Max Planck Institute for Evolutionary Anthropology in Leipzig and ear, nose, and throat specialist Michael Fuchs of the Leipzig University School of Medicine. As part of our program, the full scope of which will be addressed as future work, we carried out a clinical study in late August 2012 with six vocalists. The fact that all participants were able to produce a wide variety of harsh vocal sounds enabled us to observe laryngeal movements with respect to different singing techniques and also compare individual results within each category. This resulted in a large quantity of data which is still being evaluated. Given the overall complexity of the material I can do little more than present temporary findings. With this outline, though highly incomplete, I hope to shed light on some of the things that have been discussed earlier in the chapter.

In conventional singing and speaking, tones are produced when compressed air from the lungs passes the vocal folds in the larynx and stimulates them to oscillate periodically. This regular vibration results in a primary harmonic spectrum, the timbral qualities of which are further shaped by adjusting the vocal tract (for a complete description see Sundberg 1987, 6–24). From our observations, vocal fold vibration either plays a less important role or is suppressed altogether when it comes to extreme metal singing. Instead, supplementary organic structures in the throat begin to function as oscillators, enabling the singers to initiate and prolong different types of vocal noise. To give a point of reference, I will first elaborate on a growl executed by Sebastian Urschel of Bitterness Exhumed (see Figure 3). His ability to sing even under a rigid viewing instrument, that is, with his tongue being fixed, turned out to be a great help at the outset of our experiment, for it allowed us to film the entire phonatory apparatus. Although a part of the sound is indeed generated by the vocal folds (a), the structures immediately above them, called the vestibular folds (b), are activated as well. During this combined oscillation, the epiglottis (c) is drawn toward the rear of the larynx, thus amplifying the sound to a considerable degree because of the increase in space above and behind the larynx.

Figure 3   **Figure 4**

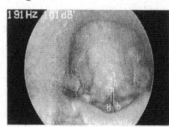   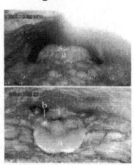

Now the important thing is that this particular mode of growl production cannot be generalized. Sebastian, who comes from a hardcore punk background and whose current band plays a mix of modern hardcore and sludge, is used to putting a tremendous amount of raw vocal power behind both his screams and growls. This perfectly matches the fact that his vocal folds are partially involved in sound production, as the vibrations on the level of the glottis add a tonal component to the otherwise rough sound (which makes it possible for Sebastian to even yield melodic lines on the basis of his growl-like voice). With other vocalists we noticed the vocal folds becoming very rigid instead. The transnasal laryngoscopies in Figure 4 depict two variants of an extremely low and noisy growl, as performed by Matthias Jähnichen and Andreas Langer from the brutal death metal band Endemicy. In Andreas's case, the epiglottis (a)—one function of which is to protect the windpipe during the ingestion of food—moves into a horizontal position and starts to flap. Behind it, the entrance to the esophagus (gullet) is pulled to the front. At the same time, the larynx becomes constricted significantly whereby the flexible part of the epiglottis makes contact with the arytenoid cartilages. Interestingly enough, this tapping motion goes hand in hand with the distinctive rattling quality of this particular growl. In the case of Matthias, however, the epiglottis (a) is pushed in the opposite direction and the primary vibration occurs on one of his aryepiglottic folds (b), resulting in a slightly different, more or less continuous sound.

As I can only briefly touch upon here, the funnel-like shape of the larynx in Matthias's growl is characteristic of the inhale pig squealing technique as well. This laryngeal configuration could also be observed during certain demonstrations of both voiced and unvoiced screaming techniques. Furthermore, Michael Fuchs, our team's physician, was astounded to see that part of the desired sound in extreme metal singing seems to come from the co-oscillation of mucus. At this point in our investigation there is good reason to believe that the fluttering of mucus and saliva in various locations of the throat not only contributes to the roughness of tone, but in addition helps protect the voice.[18]

Ironically, the loud and supposedly monstrous growls and screams of extreme music have a quiet cousin called whispering, in the sense that each of these vocalizations lacks pitch due to the tenseness of the vocal folds. Because it is mainly pitch that lets us identify a voice as being young or old, male or female, noise-like phonations provide our auditory system with hardly any reliable information about age and sex. One may choose to understand this ambiguity as monstrous. But in so doing, one must also recognize monstrosity's potential of going beyond stipulated cultural norms (see Barootes 2007). With this in mind, I would like to conclude the chapter with a persuasive argument put forth by Britta Görtz, front - woman in the thrash metal band Cripper: "The phrase 'you sound like a man' actually only reveals that no one knows what a growling woman sounds like . . . Since there are more men who do it . . . [women] sound like men and not the other way around. One could also say 'growling men sound like women.' It is interchangeable" (qtd. in Hecker 2012, 156).

Notes

1. On the concept of the sonic icon (or "sicon") and the role it plays in identifying particular genres, see Whittington 2007.

2. The episode in question was broadcasted June 19, 2012 on Frecuencia Latina. Several recordings of Ochoa's performance can be watched on the Internet, including http://youtu.be/n-VYl0cgnfs (accessed November 18, 2012).

3. Channel M6, November 20, 2012; see also http://youtu.be/V7EGCaANPNI (accessed January 14, 2013).

4. It is no secret that the entry requirements for suchlike competitions are very strict and the contestants carefully selected. Depending on the type of show, applicants must submit either a video or an audio recording to the production company (Rachel Aspe, for instance, sent in a filmed solo interpretation of a song by the metalcore band August Burns Red, which she made available through her Facebook profile). Once an applicant is deemed worthy of appearing on TV, a good deal of interaction between her, various staff members, and third - party representatives has already taken place prior to the actual air date (music selection and licensing, dress rehearsals, etc.). The trick then is to mask this kind of inside knowledge and pass off everything as a genuine surprise.

5. Comment by user chora on January 13, 2013, http://youtu.be/V7EGCaANPNI (accessed January 14, 2013).

6. A well-assorted list of female extreme vocalists from across the globe can be found under http://womenofextrememusic.tumblr.com (accessed January 14, 2013).

7. To name but a few artists and composers who made, or continue to make, outstanding contributions to exploring the possibilities of the human voice: Luciano Berio, Jaap Blonk, Henri Chopin, Bob Cobbing, Diamanda Galás, Vinko Globokar, Mauricio Kagel, David Moss, Natascha Nikeprelevic, Ute Wassermann, Gil Joseph Wolman.

8. See, for example, the brilliant collection by Niall Scott, ed., *Monsters and the Monstrous: Myths and Metaphors of Enduring Evil* (Amsterdam: Editions Rodopi, 2007).

9. Some goregrind bands that actually apply a pitch shifter for further lowering their growls (e.g., Rottrevore) are the exception that proves the rule. Other extreme metal recordings, on which the vocals have been processed quite noticeably, include the final track on Entombed's debut album *Left Hand Path* and the 1993 Morbid Angel song *God of Emptiness*.

10. Original wording: "Es kommt auf den Song an, aber wenn du einen besonderen Effekt erzielen möchtest, klar, dann lege ich sie [die Vocals] auch verschieden im Panorama. Manchmal so, dass sie sogar von links nach rechts wandern oder eher hintergründig sind, wirklich hart rechts und hart links, mit einer Stimme in der Mitte. Das ergibt ein sehr weites Feld. Aber hauptsächlich ist es so, dass ich sie direkt und frontal übereinander lege, also in der Mitte, wo der Gesang auch hingehört. [. . .] Es ist besser, sie zusammenzuhalten, weil du dann diesen Verstärkungseffekt bekommst. Es ist einfach so, dass gewisse Frequenzen, die vom Growlen nicht abgedeckt werden, dann vom Screamen abgedeckt sind. Das heißt du hast ein sehr großes Frequenzspektrum, und wenn die gut aufeinander abgestimmt sind, ist das mega. [. . .] Das Wichtige ist, ich möchte die Stimme so natürlich wie möglich belassen. [. . .] Die ganze Technik, die ich da drunter packe, hat nur zum Ziel, dass es im Gesamtmix zusammenpasst, aber nicht, etwas zu verfremden. [Gibt ein Stück wieder und schaltet gelegentlich zur unbearbeiteten Vokalspur] Wie du merkst, unterscheidet sich die Stimme nicht viel von dem, was du in der eigentlichen Aufnahme hörst. Ich lege sehr viel Wert darauf, dass man jedes Instrument hört, dass man es klar hört, und dass man es unverändert hört."

11. Larson's curse-lifting abilities are presently being marketed on several websites(www.youtube.com/user/boblarsonexorcism;www.boblarson.org; www. demontest.com). Although it is difficult to assess whether the individuals in his videos genuinely believe in being possessed, or whether they act as accomplices to Larson's entrepreneurial spirit, the presumed demonic presence perpetually reveals itself in a person's disguised voice. The adopted phonation types, often harsh and noisy in nature, bear a striking resemblance to the Hollywood version of the possessed voice. A few possibilities of comparison: the famous "redrum" monologue in *The Shining* (Stanley Kubrick, 1980); the opening scene of *Constantine* (Francis Lawrence, 2005); Jennifer Carpenter's vocal delivery for *The Exorcism of Emily Rose* (Scott Derrickson, 2005).

12. One has to be mindful, though, that even if interpretations of the sort mostly have no dire consequences, they can be used under certain conditions or in certain societies to justify persecution and political oppression (see Hecker 2012, 79–128; Winegarner 2013).

13. A notable exception, in which a singer drew upon his outstanding vocal capabilities to breathe life into a fictional demonic character, concerns Mike Patton's voice acting for the video game franchise *The Darkness*.

14. http://youtu.be/x8oLu7znwQ0 (accessed January 22, 2013). The sounds in question can be heard from 0:50 onwards. A more popular example for the imitation of animal voices in metal would be the trademark monkey scream of David Draiman from Disturbed.

15. Original wording: "Mir fällt gerade ein, wie ich einmal mit meinen kleinen Nichten und Mädels aus ihrer Nachbarschaft Prinzessin Lillifee spielen musste. Irgendwann hatte eines von den Kids [. . .] die grandiose Idee, mich in ein Ferkelchen zu verwandeln. Das einzige, was mir in dem Moment einfiel, war, mein übliches Inhale-Zeugs zu machen. Die Mädels müssen das so geil gefunden haben, dass sie gar nicht mehr aufhören wollten, mich zu verhexen. So nach dem Motto: 'Boah, die ist jetzt ein echtes Schwein!' [. . .] Immer wenn ich jetzt zu Besuch bin, müssen wir das ständig nachspielen. Die sind davon total besessen. [. . .] So viel zum

Thema böse Musik [lacht]. Aber was soll's? Abgefahrene Stimmen zu machen, ob so oder so, soll ja auch Spaß bringen."

16. "'Schreien ist eine Kunst,' predigt Cross ihren Klienten. Diese hocken in gelockerter Sitzhaltung vor ihrer Mentorin und blicken konzentriert drein, wenn sie Laute von sich geben, in denen sich Erstickungstod, Schwingschleifer und Schlachtgebrüll überlagern. Cross erläutert, wie der Stimme dabei die richtige Menge an 'Kieselstein' oder 'Sandpapier' hinzuzufügen ist, wie man die Stimmbänder 'korrumpiert' und dennoch eine klare Aussprache bewahrt. Nach ein paar Sitzungen haben sie es gelernt: Die Kehlenkünstler schreien nicht mehr nur laut und aggressiv, sondern kontrolliert und technisch versiert. Für mehr Sicherheit am Arbeitsplatz, gewissermaßen. Das hat nicht nur für Frontmänner mit blutendem Rachen einen Bildungswert [. . .]" (Scheller 2011, 287).

17. Some prominent vocalists who put this into practice are Angela Gossow (Arch Enemy), Vincent Bennett (The Acacia Strain), Phil Bozeman (Whitechapel), Randy Blythe (Lamb of God), Robert Meadows (A Life Once Lost) and Hernan Hermida (All Shall Perish).

18. None of the singers involved could be diagnosed with signs of voice disorder. Taking into account the findings from a previous clinical study on death metal growling (Eckers et al. 2009) it seems very unlikely that the vocal practices of extreme metal, contrary to popular belief, are more harmful than is any other form of singing. Besides, previous research indicates that the phonatory mechanisms in question, though scarcely found in classical and pop music, are quite common in some Asian and African singing traditions (see Grawunder 1999; Sakakibara et al. 2004; Auhagen et al. 2010).

ACKNOWLEDGMENTS

I would like to express my deepest gratitude to all the vocalists who so patiently endured my curiosity, right down to the poking about in their throats. Without the generous cooperation and trust of devoted musicians this kind of research would never be possible.

Chapter 5
Heavy Metal Music in the Caribbean Setting: Politics and Language at the Periphery
Nelson Varas-Díaz & Eliut Rivera-Segarra

Scholarly attention to heavy metal music has increased steadily in the past decade. Along with several conferences on the topic, and numerous books and journal articles, we seem to be witnessing a systematic interest on this musical genre, its participants, and culture.[1] This burgeoning interest and academic endeavor has been labeled as heavy metal studies (or metal studies) by engaged scholars. This endeavor, in general, represents good news for all interested in the subject of heavy metal. Still, just as with any emerging field of inquiry, initial steps need to be taken with precaution in order to avoid the pitfall of conceptualizing this emerging interest and academic work as a uniform field of inquiry, or even more problematic, addressing the multiple expressions of heavy metal music throughout different countries or regions as a continuum. Our chapter in this collection aims to shed some light on the particularities of a metal scene or community in the Caribbean setting as a contribution to the diversification of heavy metal studies and its areas of action/research.

Wallach, Berger & Greene, in their edited volume entitled *Metal Rules the Globe*, make an excellent argument for addressing the manifestations[i] of Heavy Metal music across the world through the lens of plurality, and not focusing exclusively on the commonalities of its manifestations throughout the globe.[2] Metal music, even when anchored in common definitions, is experienced differently in varied settings. Therefore, the authors suggest that there is a need to expand research on metal scenes outside Anglo-American contexts, in order to explore the nuances fostered by sociocultural forces in these different settings. That suggestion perfectly reflects the main objective of our study, which aims to document the sociocultural and political challenges faced by an emergent metal scene in the Caribbean island of Puerto Rico. But before we can reflect on metal in Puerto Rico, we need to elaborate on the island's social context.

The Context of Puerto Rico: A Breeding Ground for Metal Music?

Puerto Rico is one of the Greater Antilles located in the Caribbean. It is 114 miles long and 42 miles wide with an estimated population of almost 4 million. The social scenario in Puerto Rico is dire, to say the least. Almost 60 percent of families live in poverty and unemployment has surpassed 16 percent. This situation worsened in 2010 when approximately 30,000 government jobs were lost in just one year. Nearly 40 percent of the population receives aid from the United States' Nutritional Assistance Program and 64 percent receives aid for medical care. To make matters worse 15 percent of the population is illiterate. Poverty is pandemic, although heavily buffered by illegal economies.[3] This fosters an epidemic of violence with more than 1,000 violent deaths per year.[4;ii]

Puerto Rico's political scenario is also problematic. The island has never been politically independent. From 1493 to 1898 it lived under Spanish rule, which explains why its traditions are predominantly Hispanic and its everyday language is Spanish. In 1898 the island became a nonincorporated territory of the United States at the end of the Spanish-American War.[5] U.S. Congress, even today, withholds total control over areas such as the applicability of federal law and jurisdiction of federal courts, citizenship, commerce, currency, migration, patent laws, communications, mail, customs, air and sea transportation, military service, international relations, and treaty development.[5] There have been massive efforts to forcefully incorporate Puerto Ricans into the American ethnic "melting pot." Methods used for this purpose include: the imposition of English as the official language of the education system for over forty years, systematic political persecution of nationalist and pro-independence advocates, biological experimentation without consent, and compulsory participation in U.S. military conflicts. The colonial nature of the U.S.-Puerto Rico relation has been widely researched and documented in social sciences literature and reflects a country with distinctive Hispanic influences, confronted with its vague integration into the United States. Puerto Rico is deeply embedded in what academics have labeled the "colonial dilemma."[6] It is a Caribbean community existing as a nonincorporated territory of a larger and culturally different nation.[iii]

Considering the proposition made by Wallach and his colleagues that "metal music answers the question of how ethics fit into a disenchanted universe by offering a promise of community,"[2] Puerto Rico's problematic social scenario would seem like a perfect breeding ground for this music. And yet the metal community in Puerto Rico, although present since the early 1980s, is very much an underground phenomenon to which the general population does not pay attention.[9; iv] In fact, the small metal community that does exist is constantly challenged by multiple factors including lack of access to economic resources for music related activities (e.g., limited establishment of sustained metal concerts from non-local bands), a shortage of physical spaces for communal actions (e.g., shortage of metal specific clubs or venues), and lack of participation in locally developed events (e.g. events that are more costly to organize than what is generated through ticket sales), among others. And yet, even while facing these challenges the local metal community is ever present, even in small numbers.

A Metal Community in this Small Caribbean Island

As social scientists we are always intrigued by the use of the concept of "community" to describe a group of individuals. Although the concept is frequently used to describe groups of people, it can vary widely depending on the field of study that uses it. For example, psychology is usually concerned with the cognitive connection of the communal experience and addresses "sense of community" as a variable of interest.[10] Computer scientists have been more concerned with the pragmatic aspects of the communal, specifically its practical and common practices.[10;11] Sociology, based on the work of Benedict Anderson focusing on nations as communities, has paid more attention to the "imagined" qualities of the communal.[12] A community is "imagined" because although its entire population will never actually meet each other face-to-face, a sense of connectedness exists between them, fostering camaraderie even in light of the potential differences that exist between its members, and hence the emergence of the communal. Heavy metal studies has gravitated more toward the sociological approach, focusing on the way participants in metal scenes around the world share commonalities in identity discourses and imagine their local scenes and international interconnectedness.[13;14] Social scientists such as Sam Dunn and Deena Weinstein have stated outright that such a community exists at both the global and the local levels.[15;16] Still, research needs to systematically address how local sociocultural and political factors shape, or at least influence, the emergent local communities in varied places in the world. This is particularly important in settings that are peripheral, both geographically and culturally, to long-established metal scenes throughout the world. Such is the case of Puerto Rico, which is perceived by many as a tropical paradise deeply entrenched in its Hispanic roots and traditional music, such as bomba, plena, and salsa.[17;18] Although few would associate Puerto Rico with heavy metal music, it is ever-present in an underground community. It is our aim to document the sociocultural and political factors that exert influence over the emergent metal scene in the Caribbean island of Puerto Rico through systematic social research.

Method

In order to achieve the aim of our study, we implemented an ethnographic research design with both observational and in-depth qualitative interview techniques.[19] We selected this design in order to become better acquainted with a sector of the population in Puerto Rico that manifests itself as an underground movement, almost completely out of the public eye. Furthermore, these qualitative techniques allowed us to become participatory agents within the community as part of our data - gathering procedures.[20]

Our ethnographic outings were carried out from January to July of 2012 in venues at which the metal community usually meets in Puerto Rico throughout the year. These included mostly small clubs that are used as concert halls or meeting places for communal interaction (e.g., multiple concert events, a flea market specializing in metal merchandise, among other spaces). Our team totaled 104 hours of field observation through this period. All ethnographic outings were summarized through extensive notes, which were then shared and discussed among members of our team. Our discussions addressed commonalities in these observed experiences, while also exploring different interpretations of events in which team members expressed disagreement.

As part of the ethnographic component of our study, we also invited members of the community to engage in individual in-depth interviews. If they were interested in participating, their contact information was exchanged in order to establish a time and place for the interview that was to their liking. We provided participants with our phone numbers in case they had doubts about the study. Consent was acquired orally upon initiating the interview.

Each interview lasted approximately one hour. A total of thirty individuals participated in our in-depth qualitative interviews. Their socio-demographic data can be seen in Table 1. With this gathered data we engaged in our analysis.

Table 1
Socio-demographic distribution among participants

	Variable	Percentage
Gender		
	Male	64.3
	Female	35.7
Age		
	21–25	35.7
	26–30	42.9
	31–35	7.1
	36–40	14.2
Marital Status		
	Single	50.0

Married	14.3
Living with a Partner	21.4
Other	14.3
Sexual Orientation	
Heterosexual	85.7
Homosexual	7.1
Bisexual	7.1
Employment	
Employed	78.6
Unemployed	21.4
Religious	
Yes	28.6
No	71.4

In order to ensure the quality of our analysis, we started with a supervised transcription process to ensure fidelity. Team members were trained by the investigators on the appropriate way to transcribe an audio interview. After transcriptions were carried out, the team read the transcriptions while listening to the audiotapes in order to identify inconsistencies between them. The team met and corrected all errors in the transcriptions. Once this process was completed for each audiotape, the data analysis procedures began.

The research team met on a weekly basis to identify themes or patterns that emerged from our transcriptions. The team developed a list of these themes to keep as a master list for the analysis. These themes continued to be modified throughout the reading of all the transcriptions. Once those general themes were identified for all the interviews, the team searched for texts that evidenced them in the transcriptions. All selected texts for each theme were discussed in weekly meetings to ensure that they were appropriately selected by all members of the team. This consensus-based dispute-resolution procedure will generate an inter-rater reliability of 100 percent for the analysis. This step was carried out in order to ensure that the analysts agreed on the final interpretation of the coded passages and to avoid the inclusion of verbalizations that are unclear in their phrasing or overall meaning. The text selection and coding process was carried out with the use of qualitative analysis computer software HyperResearch (V.3.). Throughout the process several steps were taken in order to ensure the trustworthiness of the data.[21,22] These included: (a) supervising the overall transcription process of the audiotaped interviews and focus groups, (b) meeting with members of the research team to discuss the quality of these transcriptions, and (c) establishing group discussions throughout the data collection and analysis process so that team members could discuss concerns and findings throughout the data analysis process. The results from this process are presented in the following section.

Results

For the purpose of this book chapter we will concentrate on two particular issues that became present throughout our ethnographic observations and qualitative interviews, and that reflect the role of the island's social and cultural context in the process of building a metal scene. The first is the role of the island's political relation to the United States, and the second is related to the challenges of language and identity in this context.

Social Dynamics, Politics, and Puerto Rico's Colonial Dilemma

Our initial ventures into the underground metal scene in Puerto Rico yielded what could be interpreted as conflicting, and yet coexisting, interpretations with regards to the very existence of a metal community. While some participants described the existence of a communal perspective and a local metal scene, others seemed to focus on the dilemmas and tensions within it. It was clear from our ethnographic observations that communal practices were present. Some of these included collective events (e.g., concerts), shared histories (e.g., related to bands and previous events), and group specific venues of communication (e.g., through locally generated metal-related Facebook pages). And yet, the existence of this metal scene was sometimes described as tense with regards to its social dynamics, and suffering from lack of support from its own members.

This perceived lack of support manifested itself in several ways. First, there are manifested concerns over the lack of participation in local events. In fact, our ethnographic outings revealed that shows from local bands could have as few as twenty five audience members, and even when international bands participated in the underground scene,[v] at no time did we witness more than two hundred audience members. Second, community members voiced their frustration over the presence of small sectarian groups within the scene, which used loyalties to specific promoters to boycott other communal activities. Third, and probably most concerning, was that social interaction during concerts was described as potentially problematic at any given moment. Initially, lack of solidarity seemed to be a pervasive theme. For example, a local fan with long-standing ties to the metal scene described his participation in the Wacken festival in Germany. He stated the following:

> I was at Wacken and there were five people around me. One was Norwegian, one Polish, an Italian, one person from France . . . it was the like the UN! You looked at them, they looked at you, and they would raise their arms as if to say "look at us brother, we are here!" You do that in Puerto Rico and they would say, "What the fuck are you looking at?"

This perceived lack of solidarity and support for a local metal scene or a community was also evidenced in interviews with musicians and recording artists. The few Puerto Rican bands that record their music can face challenges in accessing the resources to develop quality products to disseminate among their fans. These challenges seem to take a toll on a potential sense of community, as lack of support seems to drown out feelings of interconnectedness to a local scene. A local musician echoed these feelings and experiences, when he told us the following:

> As a fan, I feel part of a larger international community. As a musician, I feel trapped in this Island where there are few spaces to take our music to. That has changed with the Internet . . . but I have yet to see that impact here.

The problem of sharing local metal music throughout the island was also addressed by an independent label owner when he stated that Puerto Ricans had a hard time consuming locally produced music. There seemed to be a feeling of a constant devaluation of the local scene and its output.

> Puerto Ricans here . . . I know people, and I can point them out to you, that won't buy a CD from a Puerto Rican band. Sometimes this place is like a bucket of crabs . . . when one tries to get out, another pulls him back in.

In light of these descriptions of lack of support and vague feelings of connectedness without specific communal actions,[vi] we decided to ask participants for their explanations for this phenomenon. Participants described the legacy of colonialism, specifically the island's political status, and its negative outlook on what is considered "local" as a potential explanation. They established direct links between the current state of the metal community and the political dimensions of colonialism. Participants described how local efforts made by metal bands were not supported, as they were not perceived to "measure up" to the musical quality of output in other settings. Although, this might be empirically true due to lack of funds or musical experience, among many other potential variables, it seems revealing that informants would be so keen to address the Island's colonial status as an explanation for their perceived lack of support and rejection of output by local bands. Their verbalizations echo research literature on the way the "colonial dilemma" influences how identity discourses and practices are negotiated in the Island.[6]

Based on the works of Frantz Fanon[23] and Albert Memmi,[24] scholars have pointed to how the colonial situation fosters the devalorization of the history and culture of local people. This leads to negative self-perception and self-portrayal. The colonial process promotes a sense of inferiority among the colonized. Everything associated with them is deprived of worth and a negative perception of the individual, group, and society as a whole is constructed. Although the colonial debate in Puerto Rico might seem unrelated to heavy metal studies, the

members of the local scene that participated in our interviews drew links between them. Although manifested in our interviews, participants were quick to
point out that most bands avoided talking about the political situation of the island through their music. One of them stated that "talking about nationalism in
Puerto Rico is like talking about Satanism (. . .) When you talk about the political in Puerto Rico you might as well be crucified." A political analysis of the
Island's current relation to the United States seems to be an ever-present discussion among members of the metal community, but few bands integrate it to their
musical or lyrical output.

One might argue that the island's political status is an unimportant subject
when trying to describe the local metal scene in Puerto Rico. We wish to stress
the opposite side of that argument, and highlight how the island's social and
political context shaped how community members describe and explain the challenges they face, how they interpret their situation, and provide meaning to the
difficulties they confront as a group. Therefore, the colonial dilemma needs to
be taken into consideration as an existing cultural and political explanation within the community as to why there is lack of solidarity among its members. Still,
this described lack of solidarity in no way should be interpreted as a manifestation of the nonexistence of a metal community. In fact, active participants in the
community stressed that their actions (i.e., manifested through self-funded radio
and Internet programs) aimed to foster and strengthen that existing community.
For example, for the past year the community has actively engaged in a weekly
web based live broadcast under the name of "RockSpot." It is hosted by four
local fans[vii] who discuss general metal news in Puerto Rico and the world. Our
research team had the opportunity to visit one of the live broadcasts of the show
and sit in as the "unofficial audience" for the night as part of our ethnographic
observations. At first glance, the show seems to be purely done for the fun of it,
enjoying music and company. And yet, in-depth interviews with the hosts revealed a more specific agenda behind their effort. One of them explained: "That
is why we are doing the show, to stop stereotypes and help people see that we
contribute to society, and maybe more than they think. We have never been a
threat to anyone. We just like a particular style of music." What seemed to be a
fun-based effort quickly turned into a more serious agenda, in order to reduce
stereotypes and strengthen the metal community in the Island. It is evident that
even while challenges exist, local metal fans continually work in the development of their community.
Participants frequently discussed the island's colonial dilemma and the subsequent devaluation of the local. Nevertheless, it should be stressed that the negative interpretations of insular identities do not go unchallenged. Although the
discussion on the colonial seems to be muted in the local bands' output, there
are other instances in which Puerto Rican national identities seem to be manifested as a source of pride within the community. For example, in several of our
ethnographic outings we have been able to watch a local metal band called

Death Arrangement (DA) perform as part of the programmed shows. DA is a band that emerged in Puerto Rico in 2008 and combined multiple genres of metal (e.g., death, thrash, and progressive) into a coherent sound that is quite distinctive in the local scene. They have made a name for themselves through a highly professional ethos, which is manifested through the use of quality backdrops in their concerts[viii] and having released two videos through web-based outputs. In fact, DA is probably one of the very few bands in Puerto Rico to have ever filmed a professional video for their songs.

What is interesting about DA for the purposes of our analysis is the manner in which they start each and every concert. Before beginning, the bass guitarist plays the first thirteen notes from the "Borinqueña". The "Borinqueña" is Puerto Rico's national anthem and is widely held by the vast majority of Puerto Ricans as an important song representative of a local national identity. We understand that this practice is an important piece of analysis for the local metal scene with regards to two dimensions. First, it serves as a mechanism to anchor the foreign (e.g., metal music) to a local national identity, as a way of expressing that Puerto Ricans can also engage in the creation of quality heavy metal music even when their surrounding culture seems to foster the contrary. Second, the "Borinqueña" has two coexisting versions that are politically used by locals as a reflection of their positioning on the colonial dilemma. The official version has lyrics describing the beauty of the island, while the revolutionary version mentions the need to extract oneself from colonial rule (from Spain at that particular moment in time) and engage in armed revolt. The second, of course, is widely used by political movements that highlight Puerto Rican national identities and separation from the colonial relation to the United States. We had the opportunity to interview DA as part of our study and learned that the use of the "Borinqueña" emerged quite naturally as part of their band practices, and was initially brought forth as an idea by their bass player who politically self-identifies as a pro-independence, and therefore anticolonial, individual.

Although participants described Puerto Rico's political status and colonial relation to the United States as a problematic situation that influences the local scene, it became readily apparent in our ethnographic outings that bands such as DA challenged such notions, even if for only a few moments in their sets. Although the band members are the first to make it clear that they do not wish to be political activists through their music, they also recognize the influence of Latin American artists in their musical upbringing.[ix] Still, it should be mentioned that challenges to the colonial discourse have been present in the last two decades in the local metal scene. For example, Puya is a native band that was born in 1992 out of the remnants of a trio of local virtuoso players entitled Whisker Biscuit. With the addition of a singer, Puya became the most salient Puerto Rican metal band of the decade. Based in Florida, they made extensive contributions to highlighting the potential sounds that a Puerto Rican metal band can achieve when integrating traditional metal with local instrumentation and national-related themes. Puya came to be known as one of the few metal bands to integrate a discussion on Puerto Rican national identity issues throughout their music. This was achieved sonically through the use of local instrumentation (i.e., percussion and string instruments such as the Cuatro[x]) and lyrical themes related to identity issues faced by Puerto Ricans embedded in the colonial dilemma. Puya sounds like a metal band on Latino-infused steroids. We can't think of a better way to describe it. Their initial album shows the Island of Puerto Rico behind chains, which could be interpreted as a manifestation of oppression over the nation. And yet, upon closer inspection it can be seen that joined hands, in a potential reflection of local solidarity, form the chain. Even their early artwork reflected the tension between the impact of the colonial and the emergence of a solidarity community. The lyrics to the song "Oasis" from their 1999 album *Fundamental* continue to evidence a strong concern for interpreting the local in a positive light.[25]

> I have been doing time all this time throughout the dry lands, looking for a path that was already written in my hand.
> Because what goes around must come back around to the first place it was found.
> Borinquén my friend is where it's at, and my beat will always tell you that.

After Puya's hiatus, its lead guitarist Ramón Ortiz went on to create Ankla[25] which continued the Latin-infused metal direction. Still, it is his most recent solo album entitled *Ortiz* in which his fusion of Puerto Rican traditional instruments and songs are seamlessly intertwined with metal music. In summary, through Puya, Ankla, and now his solo career, Ramón Ortiz has managed to bridge the gap between local culture, national identity, and metal music. One listen to his musical output and it almost seems to point towards a new direction to follow, one now full of pride, for a local metal community that is concerned over how the colonial process influences their development and survival. This concern over the political, and its manifestation through metal music, was described by one participant as a catalyst for a critical examination of Puerto Rico's relation to the United States. He stated:

> One thing that is important for me is that metal open the doors to have access to particular knowledge and specific political positions in my life. I have to say it was due to my listening of metal music (. . .). I believe in the Independence of Puerto Rico, and I believe in Socialism. How did metal lead me to that? Well if you listen to a Megadeth song, it is clear that the context of Puerto Rico is different, but you start to question that discourse which has been passed on to you that Americans are good. It is Americans criticizing their own system! They are supposed to live in a much better situation than us! Then you start to think.

As it can be seen through the verbalization of our participants, observations from ethnographic outings, and lyrics from influential bands in Puerto Rico, the colonial dilemma seems to be ever present for the metal community in the island

and it is not farfetched to position it as an important theme for analysis when explaining their challenges and aspirations. Although sometimes used as an explanation for the devaluation of the local and national, the colonial has also been systematically challenged through metal music. It is in this dichotomy that the colonial dilemma influences metal fans' interpretations of their context, while sometimes fostering cultural resistance.

The Challenges Posed by Language

As we stated earlier, communal practices have an imaginary dimension to them as these are not always geographical in nature, and all their members rarely know each other face-to-face. Still, these imaginary practices can also become materialized in communal actions. Throughout our study it became readily apparent that some local metal fans had historically shown interest in surpassing the symbolic nature of communal life, and engaged in concrete actions in order to materialize the heavy metal experience. Still, these experiences are also embedded in the local social, cultural, and political context of the Island. Therefore, they are also influenced by debates regarding politics and national identities. The metal community is therefore not imagined in a vacuum, and it therefore reflects its context. This was particularly evident in discussions related to language issues within the metal community. The debate seems quite simple enough and is manifested through a tension between the use of Spanish and/or English in metal related practices. Upon further examination is reveals itself as a more complex phenomenon in which national identities seem to be at play. Let us examine one particular example.

The Puerto Rico Metal Alliance (PRMA) is a group of local musicians, fans, and promoters who have established a joint web-based effort via Facebook and Myspace to "provide services that contribute to the development of a community of persons interested in metal music in Puerto Rico." Their vision mentions the need to establish "channels of communication" between its members. The Alliance even has a set of core values which include: "honesty, commitment, respect, and service." The PRMA's Facebook page has become a frequently sought-after space to find out about upcoming concerts from local and visiting international bands. Probably more important, it has become a space of group socialization in which older metal fans inform younger ones of Puerto Rican metal bands that are currently disbanded.

One would think that the creation of such a communal venue would be unproblematic, and yet the sociocultural and political realities of the island's context manifest themselves in the process. For example, one of the main debates regarding the creation of the PRMA was its name. While it is currently used in English, some founding members seemed to resent that Spanish was not used to correctly name the "Alianza Metalera de Puerto Rico" (Spanish for PRMA). One organizer explained:

> The political issue (i.e., the island's political status as a U.S. colony) always gets in the way . . . the fact that it's called the "Puerto Rico Metal Alliance" was an incredible debate topic. "It has to be in Spanish!" "It has to be in English!" people would argue. You could see the political clash. (. . .) That is something that maybe makes us different from the rest of the world metal community (i.e., language and political status). We are talking about a market, and English sells more that Spanish, like it or not. We had to take it to a vote, and finally English won out.

English truly won out, but not without members of the group feeling like it was a battle for a piece of national identity (manifested through language issues), rather than the name of the Alliance. In fact, a look at the PRMA's logo shows an indigenous symbol of the "coquí," which is a small frog endemic to the island, and is named after the sound they make at night.[xi] This symbol is commonly used by sectors of the population who are proud of the island's cultural heritage, including those that promote political separation from the United States. Therefore, in the PRMA's logo we can see the tension between the need for internationalization and fostering the local, with its implications for the value placed in language and local identities. Although they coexist on their Facebook page, our research evidences the ideological tension based on the colonial dilemma and its manifestation, in this case through language.

Still, the debate over language and its meaning for the metal community in Puerto Rico seems to be ever-present. A singer for a local metal band described how he preferred to sing in English, and perceived the push for integrating Spanish into local bands was a consequence of the emergence of the "Rock en Español" (Rock in Spanish) movement characteristic of the 1990s throughout Latin America. While describing this process within his band he mentioned the following:

> We always sang in English. At that time we didn't think about it. In the late, 90s we discussed singing in Spanish. That was when the boom of "Rock in Spanish" was in. Everyone here started playing in Spanish. I am not sure if it was because a nationalistic movement was brewing . . . . If you didn't sing in Spanish you were a sell-out. Some members wanted to do so . . . . and I said no. I won't sing in Spanish. It's not that I have anything against it . . . . I speak Spanish. I just can't see heavy metal in Spanish. That's like singing salsa in English.

This sentiment was not shared by all participants. A host for a local web-based metal-related show linked this type of position to language issues that emanate from the colonial experience. He stated:

I have had a friend of ours say, "Metal can't be sung in any other language other than English." "Therefore, metal in Spanish is an aberration." That is the position of the colonized!! They are colonized!!! Latin American has great bands . . . . Argentina has great bands . . . . Many of their bands criticized dictatorships. They used metal with feeling . . . as musical protest. Island life . . .[xii]

Of course, as with so many other cultural debates, answers are not simple or straight-forward. From these initial verbalizations it would seem that a crude equation was being implemented in which Spanish was a symbol of national pride, and English a manifestation of cultural subjugation to the colonial power. Although this might be true for some individuals, a look at the experiences of established bands seem to point toward the use of both languages as a reflection of being embedded in hybrid spaces. For example, Puya used both Spanish and English in their albums even while fostering an almost nationalistic perspective in their music. This in itself is a reflection of the strong migration history of Puerto Ricans toward the United States. Another example, the case of the band Dantesco, requires further examination.

Dantesco is an Epic/Doom metal band that emanated from Puerto Rico in 2003 and is still active on the local scene. From our perspective, and based on our ethnographic research, this is perceived by local fans to be the most important current band on the Island. They have achieved ambitions to which other local bands can only aspire. They have released five CDs and toured Latin America, several states in the United States, and countries in Europe. Their case is interesting for the debate regarding language issues as they have released albums in both Spanish and English. Their first full-length release, entitled *De la Mano de la Muerte* (Holding Death's Hand) was historic in the local metal scene both due to its professional musicianship and the use of Spanish as its main language in a metal release.[26]

The band's singer, who goes by the artistic name of Erico Dantesco, is a key component to the band's sound having cultivated his tenor-style voice throughout tours with opera companies in Europe. He holds a master's degree in philosophy from the University of Puerto Rico, which serves to make the band's lyrics complex, thoughtful, and saturated with historical references, far exceeding other local bands in beauty and depth. When interviewed about their use of Spanish for their first CD, he stated the following:

I started to write the first songs in Spanish because I had a vision of doing something really poetic. May Shakespeare and Dostoyevsky forgive me, but there is nothing like Spanish to write with passion. The strength it has, and the passion, allows you to write in an intense manner. That helped us. When people heard that they said wow! If we had done it in English, we would have been just another band.

Subsequent records have included songs in both English and Spanish. When asked if they were concerned that this might be interpreted by fans as unusual, he explained that language was not a barrier for them. He stated the following:

> The logic is that we do things like we want to. The next album (entitled *We Don't Fear your God*) will be in English. But afterwards we will continue to sing in Spanish as we have already given fans the satisfaction (of having a CD in English). But singing in English is not done for exposure. Our first CD was in Spanish and it was the one to take us to Europe, and had people listening to us in Japan and Russia.

The importance of Dantesco's reflection on the use of Spanish and English is dual. On the one hand, it stresses the importance placed on Spanish as a beautiful and poetic language (and therefore valid) that can be used by a local metal band. On the other, it systematically uses English as a way of expanding a fan base and communication with non-Spanish speakers. Still, the interchange between both languages does not seem to be anchored to the political, and the perceived loss of a national identity is not at play. Although this might seem contradictory to the verbalizations presented before, it evidences how the debate over language among the metal community in Puerto Rico is quite complex and interpreted from different perspectives, just like one would expect from other cultural phenomena. It can be both politically sensitive at times, and a manifestation of acceptable hybrid practices at others.

Aggressive Music at the Periphery

For an outsider, heavy metal music can be an intimidating entity to deal with. Its volume, speed, and sheer emotionality allow it to be systematically criminalized as a catalytic agent for aggressive practices. In this process, the concept of "aggression" in itself is ascribed a negative connotation as a potential challenge to social order. After all, most of us aspire to live and coexist in peaceful societies. Still, as the emerging literature on aggressive music suggests, it is the role of academic research to examine the underlying meanings and practices of this genre of music in order to describe the significances ascribed to it, and the message that those who create and enjoy it wish to transmit through it. This is no simple task, as social convention would suggest that we simply label it as violent and unneeded behavior.

This critical examination needs to take into consideration that the social meanings of heavy metal music will vary depending on the social setting in which it is created and manifested. Heavy metal studies, as an emerging field of inquiry, needs to avoid the pitfalls of engaging in academic imperialism, and neglecting to examine how metal scenes, that are not part of "traditional" metal scenes (i.e., particular cities in the United States and Europe), have existed in the past decades or are currently emerging.

The Caribbean setting, characterized by experiences of hybridity in terms of language, race, religiosity, and nationality due to its historical/geographical positioning, needs to be included in this research venture. Puerto Rico in particular, being the only traditional colony still left in the Caribbean, needs to be part of the emerging research ventures that academics are addressing as part of the study of heavy metal and other forms of aggressive music. Its particular context, as we have aimed to show in this chapter, brings forth the challenges created by its political relation to the United States and the multiple meanings ascribed to language selection for creating metal music. As we have shown, individuals in the local metal scene use this political situation as an explanatory starting point for some of the particular challenges faced by the community and the manner in which metal is produced and consumed. The complexities of building a metal scene at the periphery of traditional epicenters of aggressive music should not be ignored, in order to have a truly encompassing understanding of the role of heavy metal throughout the world. In the case of the underground metal scene in Puerto Rico, debates over nationality and culture in light of the colonial situation shape how the community imagines itself, and therefore how it interprets and produces its practices related to heavy metal music.

Notes

1. Karl Spracklen, Andy R. Brown, and Keith Kahn-Harris. "Metal Studies? Cultural Research in the Heavy Metal Scene." *Journal for Cultural Research* 15, no. 3 (2011): 209–12.

2. Jeremy Wallach, Harris M. Berger, and Paul D. Greene. *Metal Rules the Globe:Heavy Metal Music around the World*. Durham, NC: Duke University Press, 2012.

3. Nelson Varas-Diaz, and Irma Serrano-Garcia. "The Challenge of a Positive Self-Image in a Colonial Context: A Psychology of Liberation for the Puerto Rican Experience." [In eng]. *Am J Community Psychol* 31, no. 1–2 (Mar 2003): 103–15.

4. José Ortiz Rivera. "Cifra Récord De 1,135 Asesinatos En El 2011." *El Nuevo Día*, December 31, 2011.

5. Ronald Fernández. *The Disenchanted Island: Puerto Rico and the United States in the Twentieth Century* Florida, USA: Praeger, 1996.

6. Edwin Meléndez and Edgardo Meléndez. *Colonial Dilemma: Critical Perspectives on Comtemporary Puerto Rico*. USA: South End Press, 1999.

7. F. Tirado. "Lamb of God: "No Somos Satánicos"." *El Nuevo Día*, October 7, 2010.

8. Maritza Montero. "Community Action and Research as Citizenship Construction." [In eng]. *American journal of community psychology* 43, no. 1–2 (Mar 2009): 149–61.

9. Etienne Wenger. *Communities of Practice: Learning, Meaning, and*

88   Chapter 5

Identity. Cambridge, England: Cambridge University Press, 1998.
    10. Etienne Wenger, Richard A. McDermott, William Snyder, and
NetLibrary Inc. *Cultivating Communities of Practice: A Guide to Managing Knowledge*.
Boston, Mass.: Harvard Business School Press, 2002. http://www.columbia.edu/cgi-bin/cul/resolve?clio4241520.
    11. Benedict Anderson. *Imagined Communities: Reflections on the
Origin and Spread of Nationalism*. New York: Verso, 2006.
    12. Dave Snell and Darrin Hodgetts. "Heavy Metal, Identity and the
Social Negotiation of a Community of Practice." *Journal of Community & Applied Social Psychology* 17, no. 6 (2007): 430–45.
    13. Caroline Lucas, Mark Deeks, and Karl Spracklen. "Grim up North:
Northern England, Northern Europe and Black Metal." *Journal for Cultural Research* 15, no. 3 (2011): 279–95.
    14. Sam Dunn, and Scot McFadyen. "Global Metal." USA: Warner
Home Video, 2009.
    15. Deena Weinstein. *Heavy Metal: A Cultural Sociology*. New York:
Lexington Books, 1991.
    16. Frances Aparicio. *Listening to Salsa: Gender, Latin Popular Music,
and Puerto Rican Cultures*. Music/Culture. Hanover, NH: Wesleyan University Press/University Press of New England, 1998.
    17. César Miguel Rondón, Frances R. Aparicio, and Jackie White. *The
Book of Salsa : A Chronicle of Urban Music from the Caribbean to New York City*. Latin America in Translation/En Traducción/Em Tradução. Chapel Hill: University of North Carolina Press, 2008.
    18. Paul Atkinson. *Handbook of Ethnography*. London ; Thousand
Oaks, Calif.: SAGE, 2001.
    19. Alice McIntyre. *Participatory Action Research*. Qualitative
Research Methods Series. Los Angeles: Sage Publications, 2008.
    20. Thomas Schwandt. *Dictionary of Qualitative Inquiry*. Thousand
Oaks, CA: Sage, 2001.
    21. Yvonna Lincoln, and Egon Guba. *Naturalistic Inquiry* Beverly
Hills, CA: SAGE, 1985.
    22. Frantz Fanon. *The Wretched of the Earth*. New York,: Grove Press,
1965.
    23. Albert Memmi. *The Colonizer and the Colonized*. 1st American ed.
New York,: Orion Press, 1965.
    24. Puya. *Fundamental*. Universal International, 1999.
    25. Ankla. *Steep Trails*. Bieler Bros Records, 2006.
    26. Dantesco. *De La Mano De La Muerte*. TDNE, 2005.

ⁱ We use the concept of "manifestations" in its most ample sense in order to describe all the practices, individual and collective, that are part of the metal experience. These can be as varied as listening to metal music, participating in concerts, building a local scene, and/or describing the emergence of a particular subgenre, among other activities.
ⁱⁱ Although the social situation of the Island is unavoidably negative, Puerto Ricans have been found to be among the happiest countries in the world on several surveys carried out

by recognized international organizations. This has been attributed to the importance placed on family and social support in Puerto Rican culture.

iii Just as with any politically controversial topic, arguments can be made about the Island's benefits of its colonial dilemma. For example, Puerto Rico receives federal aid for housing, nutrition, and education that make it different from other Caribbean islands by increasing quality of life and access to goods. Still, for the purposes of our analysis, we will focus on the cultural implications of the US/Puerto Rico relation and how members of the local metal scene interpret it.

iv The exception to this rule might be when international bands visit the Islands and rile up the religious right in moral panic. This was the case of Lamb of God as recently as 2010.

v Three examples of such events include visits from Alcest (France), the Absence (US), and Havok (US) during 2012.

vi Although descriptions of the communal in our interviews seemed to focus on the challenges faced, we should stress that upon observation an evident sense of community was present as manifested through engagement in local events, Internet forums, and verbalizations of concern over the future of the scene.

vii These individuals are fans, some of which at some point have been involved in the development of local concerts as promoters and have ties to local television outlets. They are: Rafa Bracero, Elliot Diez, Lechón Atómico (stage persona for Juan Solá Sloan), and Hugh Lynch.

viii Although this might seem like a normal process for established bands, this is one of the very few groups to have such graphics in the entire Island. In a setting with very little resources, such a "minor" detail is interpreted by local members of the scene as an important step in having a professional band.

ix DA also developed a metal version of Celia Cruz's song entitled Bravo (DA covered the adaptation made by Enrique Bunbury and Nacho Vegas of the original song). Celia Cruz is a famous Cuban-American singer who was known world-wide as the "Queen of Salsa" or "La Guarachera de Cuba." In referencing her music, DA show their links to Caribbean inspired music, even when their audience may be unaware of it. In our interviews, they also listed Silvio Rodríguez (Cuban folk singer) and La Lupe (Cuban-American salsa singer) as influences, both controversial figures in Latin American music for their political opinions (Silvio) and performance style (La Lupe).

x The "Cuatro" Puerto Rico's national instrument. Shaped like a small guitar, it has ten strings separated in five courses. It is commonly used to play Puerto Rico's traditional music, which is closely linked to life in the countryside or inner part of the island.

xi This symbol has been used by bands like Puya and Nonpoint, to reflect their strong Puerto Rican roots even when residing within the continental United States.

xii This last sentence was mentioned with disdain. It should be noted that the participant linked this issue to "island life." This is a very insightful comment as the same debate is being carried out by the metal community in the Island of Cuba. This was the subject of a web-based poll during June 2012 at the metal site http://www.cuba-metal.com. The options for the survey were Spanish, English, and Spanglish.

Chapter 6
No Fun: Noise Music, Avant-garde Aggression, and Sonic Punishment
Ross Hagen

When I attended the Four-day No Fun Festival in Brooklyn in 2007, the noise duo Deathroes performed a set with a pair of massive strobe lights pointed directly at the audience. The strobe lights were not synced together and began to slowly become more and more frenetic over the course of the half-hour set until they peaked with a blast of white light. It was impossible to look directly at the stage. Audience members either looked away or shut their eyes, in which case the blinding strobe lights caused fractal patterns as the light filtered through the blood vessels in their eyelids. The sound itself was a mass of slowly evolving drones and feedback performed at a crushing volume, to the point of physically resonating within the body. Several audience members draped themselves over the bass cabinets of the venue's speaker system to more fully feel the sound. Looking back at the audience, it was a strikingly serene tableau compared to the aural and visual oppression coming from the stage. The sensory overload caused by the visual and sonic stimuli rendered movement and even complex thought almost impossible. At the end of the thirty-minute set, it was almost like awakening from a dream, with only a vague memory of what just transpired.

When scholars discuss aggression in musical styles and scenes, it is often described as a purgative, Artaudian catharsis in which the music symbolically depicts aggression and provides a release for it. However, rather than symbolically enact violence and aggression through confrontational lyrics or displays of musical power and virtuosity, noise music attempts to visit physical and psychological violence upon the audience through sheer volume and sonic density. The tactics used by noise musicians mimic many of those employed by military and police forces in standoffs and interrogations, and audiences at noise concerts often approach the experience as a physical and psychological trial and transformation. Noise concerts provide the experience of domination and being dominated, but within a controlled environment. In addition to enacting physical and psychological aggression, noise music is an extension of the twentieth-century avant-garde's attempts to undermine traditional artistic and capitalistic values. Noise performance particularly questions notions of artistic skill, competence, and success in favor of a "de-skilled" and egalitarian approach. The noise musician becomes more of a facilitator of the experience as opposed to a performer who possesses skills the audience does not.

Much of this chapter is the result of my own personal engagement with the Colorado noise scene as a performer and concert attendee from 2002 to 2010 and interviews conducted for my doctoral dissertation in 2010.[1] Although the coterie of noise musicians who lived in Denver in the 2000s certainly has a distinctive character, many of its qualities are likely shared by other local noise scenes and by the larger global network of noise aficionados. In particular, the demographics of the noise scene on both global and local scales seem to skew overwhelmingly toward young white men, and perhaps as a result much of the discourse around noise music is implicitly masculinist. When describing the effects of noise music for audience members, the listeners can be understood to be largely male. The participants in the Denver noise scene that I interviewed also had backgrounds working in electronics, audiovisual technical work, or computer programming, and several hold degrees in art or music. I would not be surprised to find intersections of interests and education among participants in noise music scenes in other regions, but I do not have supporting data.

Defining Noise and the Noise Scene

Defining "noise" as a theoretical entity requires a multifaceted approach. Torben Sangild's 2002 essay "Aesthetics of Noise" identifies three different ways that noise has been defined in scholarship: subjective definitions that define noise as sound that is unpleasant or unwanted, a communicative interpretations that define noise as something that disrupts a signal or a message, and a purely acoustic definition that defines noise by its use of irregular frequencies, as opposed to the strict mathematical ratios that underpin much Western music.[2] Sangild also interprets the use of noise within or as music along four lines. Noise is used as an expression of the abject, a means to reach the sublime, an expression of multiplicity, or as a transgressive and subversive element. Within these threads, a common ideal is that noise is simultaneously an excess of sound and frequency and a pre-existing "ur-sound" from which music, language, and meaning arise.[3] This ideal is encapsulated in white noise, which refers to sound in which all frequencies across a given spectrum are equivalent—it contains no clear referent pitch or collection of pitches because it contains all possible pitches. From a symbolic standpoint, noise can then simultaneously represent both a lack of meaning and an excess of meaning.

When performing noise music, maximum volume often seems to be the primary concern, matching the symbolic excess with an excess of decibels. Musicologist Joanna Demers posits that this emphasis on extreme volume is one of the aspects that sometimes renders noise "meaningless," because it acts directly on the body, bypassing semiosis and symbolic meaning.[4] The extreme volume literally makes the sound tactile as it resonates within the body, sometimes to the extent that air being pushed by the speakers presses the clothing against one's body. Indeed, the discourse of noise often privileges the physicality of the sound involved. Sections of maximum volume and sonic density are referred to as "walls," implying both physical size, solidness, and an impenetrable character.[5] Robert Walser noted a similar effect in heavy metal where the extreme volume causes the music to "conflate inner and outer realities for the audience," with the result that the music is "felt within as much as without."[6] As a result, timbral shifts in the performance are felt physically by the audience. Listening to noise in some ways forces one to focus on these minute details in succession because the totality of the sound is often so immense and all-encompassing that it defies attempts at holistic comprehension.[7] As with other forms of "extreme" music, notably death metal and grindcore, the fractured nature of the musical pieces and the absence of recognizeable song forms invite a new experience of musical time and pleasure.[8]

Sangild also proposes a useful framework for dealing with sustained "walls" of noise. Deathroes and similar harsh noise performers do not necessarily use noise as an expressionist gesture of pain, anger, chaos, or Dionysian ecstasy. Indeed, there is little in the way of climax, tension, or release to give their noise any sense of traditional expressivity. The sound is maximal, but the overall form and flow is essentially minimal, creating a hypnotic experience that Sangild refers to as a "screaming mantra."[9] In this mode, the noise "wall" creates a sense of detachment rather than ecstatic release or inner reverie. The listener is then also suspended in the moment, as the sound generally provides no indication of progress from beginning to end; it is, as noise musician Todd Novosad, of the Denver noise acts Novasak and Zoologist, notes, "all middle."[10]

History and Genre

For noise musicians, many aspects of their scene are geared toward maintaining this spirit of aggression and artistic transgression, even as noise has become increasingly normalized within the world of underground music. As Paul Hegarty notes, even as noise opposes itself to music, it almost invariably becomes accepted into musical practice, a transformation that is accelerated by its existence as a definable genre.[11] However, noise music traces a history through the artistic avant-garde, particularly among artists and movements that took a more hostile stance toward traditional artistic attitudes and norms. In some ways, its sonic aggression could be considered to be wielded against these aesthetic values as well as against its audiences.

Although noise music is generally a late twentieth-century phenomenon, the first major document within the history of noise is the Italian futurist Luigi

Russolo's 1913 treatise, *Art of Noises*. Within it, Russolo advocates the elevation of mechanical, industrial, and military noise as the new music of the modern era, and proposes a number of categories by which man might harness noise in the service of art.[12] The media theorist Friedrich Kittler likewise looks to the conceptualization of sound as frequency and the invention of sound recording in the late nineteenth century as the point of a fundamental shift in our understanding of noise and its relationship to music.[13] Sound recording technology at its heart does not make a distinction between "music" and "noise," unlike our sense of hearing, which our brain filters in order to focus on the most relevant sounds, or the European tradition of notation, which focuses entirely on discrete pitches. Taken together, these developments threatened to deny music the place of privilege it had enjoyed over the centuries as all sounds became equal. The invention of tape recording during World War II and its subsequent availability to consumers in the 1960s also provided new ways to manipulate and deconstruct sound, detached from strictly linear time.

As far as noise's emergence as a distinct genre, David Novak locates the separation of noise from other styles of avant-garde music in 1970s Japan, particularly at experimental listening parties in Kyoto where noise eventually coalesced into a form of improvised and untutored artistic performance.[14] These performances and recordings were then exported to the United States and Europe, where artists and audiences accepted noise as a full-fledged musical genre.[15] One can also point to the influence of Lou Reed's 1975 album *Metal Machine Music*, a work, possibly intended as a joke, which consists entirely of modulated guitar feedback mixed together at different speeds. Even if noise would seem to challenge and undermine notions of fixed genre, it is accepted as a full-fledged style by its fans.[16]

The artistic avant-garde has also bequeathed its aesthetic agenda to noise music, particularly those aspects that purposefully undermine traditional conceptions of music and art in the West. Hegarty contends that true avant-garde movements question accepted ideas of "finished pieces, competence of performers, composition, [and] means of production (of sounds, of pieces)."[17] In visual art, this impulse can be clearly observed in works such as Marcel Duchamp's "ready-made" pieces like *Bicycle Wheel* and the famous urinal, *Fountain*, and in Robert Rauschenberg's *Erased de Kooning*, in which Rauschenberg erased a drawing by fellow artist Willem de Kooning. The works and philosophies of John Cage have also been particularly influential to noise musicians because many of his pieces collapse the differences between art and everyday life, or music and everyday noises, proposing a world in which all activities and interpretations are equally valid.[18] The anti-commercialism of the Dadaist Fluxus movement in the 1960s, combined with its utopian agenda to abolish the idea of art, is continued in many practices of the noise scene.[19] Scholar Catherine O'Meara also makes an astute comparison between the visual overload of large minimalist sculptures and the auditory "overload" effect of noise music, noting the prevalence of architectural metaphors in critical writings about noise music.[20]

Noise music's history also traces a trajectory alongside garage rock and punk rock music in the 1970s and early 1980s.[21] These genres of rock music generally value energy and passion over talent and embrace a "do-it-yourself" ethos that often disdains the capitalist model of music production, distribution, and promotion. As Dick Hebdige noted in *Subculture: The Meaning of Style*, one punk fanzine encouraged aspiring musicians by printing chord charts for three basic guitar chords with the caption, "Here's one chord, here's two more, now start a band."[22] Once electronic instruments and tape recorders became readily available to the general consumer, noise music's avant-garde lineage became aligned with this do-it-yourself aesthetic. The networks of noise scenes around the world are also similar to punk scenes' independent distribution and production networks, allowing bands to release their records without concern for widespread commercial appeal beyond their own niche.[23]

An additional aspect of noise music is that its musical and sonic qualities provide few stylistic markers related to its place of origin.[24] Noise music seems to be simultaneously from everywhere and from nowhere, a quality it shares with other forms of electronic music such as techno and house music.[25] With the exceptions of pioneering noise artists from Japan and British artists like Throbbing Gristle, there are comparatively few aesthetic values associated with actual geographic place in the noise scene. Even for famous artists the associations with locality are arguably more dependent on knowing that these noise musicians are from a particular place rather than identifying shared sonic characteristics among geographically related artists. For example, the genre appellation "Japanoise" has been troublesome for some Japanese artists because it creates a "scene" out of a number of diverse artists who may have little in common and also hints at a certain exoticization.[26]

Noise in Performance

Within the performance of sonically aggressive noise music, improvisation and unpredictability are paramount. Many noise musicians employ arrays of electronic equipment, often miswired in order to produce uncontrollable and chaotic results. An audio mixer wired so that it sends its output back through its input is one of the most common methods for creating chaos via a feedback loop, resulting in thick tones, high-pitched screeches, and rhythmic pulses. This kind of miswiring could be considered an act of aggression against the equipment itself, as it may ultimately ruin it. In some cases noise musicians use pieces of equipment that are literally broken, reveling in the sounds of damaged electronics. In addition to "instruments" like a mixer, a typical noise "rig" might include a number of guitar effects pedals, synthesizers, contact microphones, and any number of other electronic devices all connected together. Some performers prefer to use a computer, sometimes with custom-made software. Still others take a more primitivist approach, employing a variety of power tools including metal grinders, drills, mig welders, and occasionally even small explosives. The Japanese group Hantarash became notorious in the 1980s for a number of legendary concerts in which the band members wrought havoc with heavy machinery including bulldozers and backhoes, in some cases injuring themselves in the process.[27] One American group, Rosemary Malign and the Eugenics Council, became notorious for setting off smoke bombs and M-80s during their performances, sometimes sending audiences scattering for cover.

A small cottage industry exists to provide noise musicians with customized or hand-built instruments, including small companies like Trogotronic and online stores like NoiseFX.com. The information page for Trogotronic states that their instruments are "primitive and noisy," noting that "some of the vintage models are probably a fire hazard and others have very dangerous high voltage within,"[28] promising the noise musician a uniquely pugnacious piece of equipment. Another example, the Weevil, a small electronic instrument created by the BugBrand company, features a "power-starvation" button that chokes off the power supply to its sound-generating oscillators, causing the sound to sputter.[29] Instrument builders also often "circuit-bend" battery-powered toys like Speak-and-Spells or Furbys, wiring new connections within the circuitry that allow them to distort and change the device's sounds, a practice that has been the inspiration for several conferences and how-to books.[30] Noise events often resemble electronics expositions as much as a concerts, as enthusiasts and performers talk shop and compare their setups and procedures. The novelty of the setup is part of the inherent value of the show, and some noise fans have come to disdain mixer feedback and guitar-based noise simply because of the ubiquity of such techniques. The central idea is that each noise musician creates his or her own unique process, using a myriad of customized instruments, effects units, and homemade components.

These types of intentionally chaotic performances and processes are replicated in computerized methods for performing noise. Noise musicians who perform using laptop computers often use software that allows for parameters within their performances to be autonomous or self-perpetuating. Like the miswired arrays of audio electronics, misused computer technology has the potential to produce uncontrolled sounds ranging from small clicks and pops to walls of distortion.[31]

Regardless of their individual systems for creating noise, noise musicians use technology to decenter or even sever the traditional relationship between a performer's intent and the resulting sound. Paul Théberge notes that the relationship to physical gesture and sound production becomes arbitrary in electronically produced music in general.[32] Noise performance often extends this capriciousness beyond gesture and makes turmoil an end in itself, devising situations in which the final sounds are only marginally controlled by the performer. The process may even become self-perpetuating and literally render the noise musician a spectator to his or her own performance.[33] This aspect of noise performance especially runs counter to traditional notions of performance and skill that inform most concert experiences. The chaos and loss of control within a noise performance is often experienced not only by the audience but also by the performer, who in this situation may be more accurately considered a facilitator of the electronic equipment's exploits. As with other physical, psychological, and psychedelic ordeals like sweat lodges or fasts, the leader of the group experiences the event along with the other participants as opposed to doing things to the participants.

The misuse and abuse of electronic equipment in performance also creates a very real risk of malfunction. Consequently, equipment failures are not uncommon in noise, and seasoned noise fans and performers often accept meltdowns as valid outcomes. These chaotic and unpredictable aspects of noise likewise require the performer to engage in a type of radical acceptance in which all results are equally valid, up to and including catastrophic equipment failure. In an interview, Todd Novosad described artistic failure as possible only if the performer is visibly unhappy with the results and poisons the atmosphere with his or her attitude.[34] Indeed, actual equipment failure may be greeted as a triumph by the audience and as proof that the performer's activities entailed genuine risk and even potential damage.

By tolerating, and even celebrating failure, noise becomes permissive and inclusive of all comers and all outcomes. Indeed, noise music's acceptance of failure is perhaps its most radical turn from the traditional discourse of music and art, which celebrates victory, achievement, and success, along with the accompanying sense of exclusivity.[35] If displays of musical virtuosity, such as the archetypal electric guitar "shred" solo, are symbols of aggression, or at least a sense of individual power,[36] noise departs from this model. The aggression of noise is directed then, not entirely at a physical audience, listener, or other figure or institution, but also at normative concepts of skill and artistic value. It is aggressively egalitarian, even as its sonic and artistic qualities cultivate a certain elite esotericism.

The focus on live performance in this chapter would seem to diminish the recorded output of noise musicians, which is noteworthy in and of itself. In particular, noise artists are notoriously prolific, with many of them producing dozens if not hundreds of recordings over the course of their careers. Some recordings may simply be documentations of live performances with or without audiences, although noise artists may also approach recording as a more intentional exercise in composition. In most cases, the individual recordings are produced in vanishingly small quantities, often fewer than fifty copies. Paul Hegarty proposes that, at least in the case of the Japanese artist Merzbow, this hyper-fecundity is a way to deconstruct the impulse for collecting among music fans by rendering it nearly impossible to amass a complete collection of an artist's releases.[37] On the other hand, the situation also invites the fetishization of rare releases as expressions of subcultural capital, with some rare releases fetching hundreds of dollars.[38] However, many of the psychological and physical effects of noise music are dependent on the live experience of noise with the proper amount of sound amplification. Recordings of noise are unable to re-create these effects under most circumstances. Headphones are in some ways able to approximate the all-enveloping experience and, as Jodi Berland notes, "earbud" style headphones are able to seemingly bring sounds directly within the body.[39] However, the experience of recorded noise music almost necessarily lacks the fully embodied physicality of sound sought in live performance. The aspect of the noise experience that revolves around recordings is more of a collector culture focused on noise recordings as art objects, although these objects possess a certain subcultural cachet and reflect antipathy toward the consumerism of the music industry.

Social Control, Dominance, and Submission

The aggression of noise as a sonic entity is not limited to its "musical" setting, and the treatment of noise in other situations informs the experience of the noise music performance. For most people, exposure to sustained, meaningless noise is highly objectionable, and noise is often limited and eliminated if possible. Theorist Jacques Attali argues that the attempted regulation of background noise, a continuous and unavoidable phenomenon, is one of the more basic hallmarks of civilization.[40] For Attali, the creation of musical order out of chaotic noises assists in maintaining and legitimizing the social order. In American society, noise is often actively policed through laws that ban, for example, the use of engine brakes on semi-trucks or loud music during evening hours. In the latter case, music becomes noise solely by being undesirable in a particular time and place.[41] Many social spaces, such as restaurants and libraries, are defined through their suppression of noise, although some eating establishments deliberately maintain a higher sound level to encourage faster turnover.

The disruptive and psychologically draining aspects of noise have more recently been adapted as a means of crowd control and psychological warfare. The "meaningless" aspect of noise can trace a heritage within military propaganda and communication, especially after tape recording provided a means for editing, rearranging, and disguising coded messages in the 1940s and 1950s.[42] More recently, American Technology Corporation has developed a crowd control and hailing device called the Long Range Acoustic Device (LRAD) which produces a directed high-pitched sound beam beyond or near the threshold of pain with a maximum effective range of five hundred yards.[43] Police forces have used LRAD devices to disperse protesters, and commercial sea vessels have used them against pirates.[44] Police and military forces also frequently use loud noise and objectionable music to psychologically wear down subjects in standoff situations such as at the Branch Davidian compound in Waco, Texas.[45] Steve Goodman notes that sound can also be used more generally against a population in order to harass, intimidate, and create a climate of fear, citing in particular the Israeli military's use of sonic booms from low-flying military aircraft against civilian populations in the Gaza Strip. Goodman further theorizes that much of the potential for social control and violence through sound resides in realms in frequency he terms "unsound," consisting of subsonic and ultrasonic frequencies that cannot be "heard" but which physically act upon the body and mind.[46] In these cases, social or criminal disruption (itself a type of social "noise") is dispersed or intimidated by sound that has been sanctioned by the state and wielded by military forces. On an individual level, sustained exposure to loud music and noise has also been used as a psychological torture technique in detention camps such as Abu Ghraib.[47]

Noise performance presents similarly unwanted or weaponized sounds in a space where they can be experienced voluntarily as an exercise in aggression, domination, and submission. From the audience's perspective, a noise performance is in some ways an enactment of these scenarios of social control, involving a temporary surrender to a highly disorienting experience within a safe space. Audiences at noise performances often approach the experience much in the same way that one might take part in a sweat lodge, marathon, or other psychologically or physically demanding event. Indeed, there is a distinctly masculinist tone to the discourse, privileging endurance and fortitude in the face of sonic violence and punishment. One is reminded of a legend about the early twentieth-century composer Charles Ives supposedly shouting down a disgruntled concertgoer by telling him, "Stop being such a God-damned sissy! Why can't you stand up before fine strong music like this and use your ears like a man?" As a result, disorienting and even distressing qualities are highly prized by the audience at a noise show. The disorienting, and sometimes literally nauseating, effects are part of the "fun." Noise performer Rasmussen related to me that he enjoys placing slightly detuned frequencies at opposite ends of the stereo spectrum precisely because of the disorienting effect. What he describes are "binaural beats," which have been claimed to enhance meditation, assist in pain and addiction, or to produce psychedelic effects, the latter of which inspired a brief run of alarmist news stories in 2010.[48] The psychedelic and transcendent aspects of the noise experience are often the ultimate goals of audience members, as the overwhelming sound of noise music does invite a certain sublime bliss once one is indoctrinated into its world.

Some performers of noise music also thrive on physically interacting with, confronting, and occasionally even assaulting members of the audience. The physicality of the sound is then accompanied by a literal physical assault, which may or may not be playful. For example, the band C.O.C.K. E.S.P.'s members attack one another while wearing silly costumes, creating a fracas which sometimes spills out into the audience as a sort of absurd mosh pit. Returning to the No Fun Fest in 2007, the American performer Slogun (John Balistreri) attempted during his set to engage and dominate the audience in a more serious manner by berating them, throwing beer on them, and employing a small entourage of fellow performers who rained blows and kicks from the stage. This was not received particularly well by the audience, although at the end of the set one audience member did oblige Balistreri by pulling him off the stage and starting a fight. This situation suggests that audiences at noise music performances seek out symbolic violence and the enactment of domination, but balk once the threat of violence and physical pain becomes actualized. In this particular case, Slogun and fellow performer Sickness (Chris Goudreau) had poisoned the audience against them by drunkenly punching members of the crowd during the headlining set by Japanese artist Painjerk the previous night, but the line in the sand seems to remain.

Performances such as these perhaps demonstrate that the aggressiveness of noise has a limit, even as it seems to propose a field of complete sonic excess. Once the symbolic sonic violence became literally physical and harmful, many participants found their pleasure and personal transcendence disrupted. Yet physical interaction and even violence may not always be a transgression for noise performers and audiences. Indeed, it can be an accepted and desired part of the experience of musical aggression, as many mosh pit veterans can attest. For many participants, the result of the sonic and physical aggressiveness of a noise performance is the sense of hypnotism, disembodiment, and trance as described in reference to Deathroes' set. But this state seems to be contingent on the audiences' willing submission to the experience. The actions of Slogun could be considered an attempt to reassert the aggression and confrontation that noise embodies, and to throw it in the faces of those who simply want to have an "extreme" experience without any personal risk.

The experience of domination also comes to the fore in noise performance, as the performer wields a measure of psychological control over the audience as a facilitator of the experience. Domination plays a role even in more traditional musical experiences, in that listening to music often engenders submission to the will of the composer, as posited by theorist Edward T. Cone.[49] Fred Maus extended this notion into the realm of sadomasochism, noting that many aspects of musical experience and discourse mirror the active/passive relationship of S&M, particularly the uniquely strict environment of the classical concert hall.[50] However, while the classical concert attempts to control the listener's experience through social strictures requiring silence and stillness, noise concerts attempt to overwhelm the listener with sound and eliminate the option of ignoring it. The extreme volume and density of a minimalist "wall" noise performance even becomes akin to a sort of sensory deprivation, a sort of aural equivalent to a blindfold. Julian Henrique theorizes that loud and tactile sonic environments of this nature create this sense of immersion because they suppress and displace other senses, especially vision, in favor of hearing.[51] The lack of development in noise music likewise sharpens the listener's perception of subtle shifts in timbre or pitch.[52] It is worth noting, however that the individual listener submits to the physical domination of the experience while simultaneously exerting some control over his or her individual experience of being voluntarily dominated.[53] A final key difference between the domination of noise music and that enacted by other musical traditions is the fact that noise music's aesthetic ultimately allows almost any interested participant to become the facilitator of the experience.

The fascination with dominance and submission extends beyond the sonic experience of noise concerts into the visual component of noise releases and performances. A number of noise recordings feature graphic cover artwork depicting violence, bondage, torture, or fascistic imagery. In many of these explicit images, the victims are female, raising the specter of whether or not the dominance enacted through noise is an explicitly masculinist dominance. As noted, the demographics of noise scenes are skewed heavily toward young men, a quality it shares with many other underground "extreme" music scenes. However, the intent behind these images is often ambiguous and unclear, as the noise music in the recording rarely contains any hint as to whether the imagery is meant to affirm and promote these themes or whether it is meant to indict them and expose their horror. In some cases this visual element may simply be included for shock value, as extreme imagery to accompany extreme music. The British industrial act Throbbing Gristle used video projections of violence, warfare, and pornography ostensibly as a means to break taboos and expose the omnipresent violence of Western society.[54] The audience members are in a sense made complicit with such content as well, a particularly challenging and uncomfortable notion for proponents of tolerance and artistic open-mindedness who are suddenly faced with material that is openly hostile to liberalist worldviews. Additionally, there is no guarantee that any critical or satirical element in the performance will be recognized as such, as Jason Hanley notes in his study of the industrial groups Ministry and Laibach.[55] Within the noise scene, such imagery may also not be seen as particularly transgressive, and participants in extreme music often deliberately ignore many of the more troubling political aspects of such material in order to reorient the content as humorous or light-hearted, a tactic Kahn-Harris terms "reflexive anti-reflexivity."[56] One might ultimately posit that the use of such shocking and apparently transgressive imagery alongside noise music is simply an extension of the audience's experience of domination and disorientation.

The Endgame of Total Aggression?

Noise as an artistic entity has always contained this component of aggression and a fetishization of "extremeness." Yet, for all of the deliberate unpredictability and chaos that noise cultivates, as a genre it often displays a remarkable consistency, perhaps akin to the flat lining of atonal music in the absence of a need to resolve musical dissonance. The musical and sonic characteristics are sometimes so consistent that few identifying characteristics distinguish one noise artist from another, a situation compounded by the diverse range of sounds often explored by individual artists. Ultimately, the chaos of noise becomes normative, expected, and perhaps even obvious and boring. Returning to Sangild's "screaming mantra," we might question if such a thing could even be considered "aggressive," at least within the world of noise music, where its effects are regarded as transcendent rather than transgressive. In effect, after a period of time it becomes almost a form of loud silence.

Noise music also is clearly no longer as aggressively counter cultural as it once was. It faces many of the same dilemmas as the punk movement and other music scenes that define themselves, at least partly, by their antagonism toward mainstream culture. The emergence of noise as a defined and marketable genre leads some critics to consider that the transgression and rebellion of noise is something of a mirage, that (in true Adornian fashion) it gives the listeners an illusion of transgression and difference while still adhering to many conventions of the popular music industry. It is perhaps no surprise that some critical theorists have seen the ultimate triumph of the culture industry in noise's marketing as yet another self-consciously cool and adrenaline-fueled "extreme music." After all, if the "death of music" is ultimately just another commercial product, is there anything that cannot be commoditized? At the 2007 No-Fun festival in New York City, the seemingly anarchic and anti-commercial ethos of the performances was offset by the extensive tables of merchandise, reinforcing theorist Nick Smith's concern that noise concerts are often essentially commercial events populated by "young white men buying expensive tickets, t-shirts, recordings, videos, and drinking alcohol."[57] For as much as the discourse of noise music and noise fans attempts to place the scene beyond commercialism, sometimes simply by virtue of its imposing sonic profile, its sonic aggression is perhaps ultimately eclipsed by the aggressiveness of Western capitalism and DIY entrepreneurship.

The existence of a noise "scene" in and of itself may even constrain the anarchic, aggressive, and artistically democratic spirit that noise attempts to embody. As Elizabeth Grosz and others have noted, the communal egalitarianism of utopias comes with significant controls and constraints, often resulting in an essentially totalitarian state.[58] Hakim Bey likewise theorizes that anarchic performance traditions are imperiled by any attempt at permanence, because permanence creates a need for structure, which ultimately constrains creativity and may invite surveillance by authoritarian figures.[59] Within some noise music circles, loud, dense, harsh-sounding noise has become an orthodoxy, albeit a somewhat informal one. The idea that noise may have a correct sound seems antithetical to its aesthetic goals, but this consistency likely enables noise to persist as a defined genre and has allowed it access to larger, official venues.

The migration of noise performances to these larger, licensed venues may also ultimately inhibit some types of performances, even if one disregards problems regarding explosives or other dangerous equipment. The layout of the venues themselves can encourage or discourage particular modes of performance. In particular, a venue with a stage implies a certain contract with the audience, creating the expectation that the performance is separate from the audience, who amass as witnesses. For example, the confrontational nature of Slogun's set at the 2007 No Fun Fest might have been better received in a venue where he was not separated from the audience by a stage. Although some, if not most, audience members would still have drawn the line at being literally assaulted rather than enacting assault through sound, the crossing of that line would not have seemed so out of place.

The experience of noise music raises a number of questions about musical aggression and the ways in which audiences and performers experience it. For example, even if many seem to approach noise music as a test of fortitude, audience members may also experience bodily pleasure and manipulation through the physicality of noise music. For example, Denver noise musician John Gross reported to me that in several cases women at noise performances told him they become sexually aroused by the intense low-frequency sounds.[60] This statement raises the possibility of gendered appreciations of noise music that the scene's masculinist discourse may ignore. Indeed, Tara Rogers notes that electronic music in general has been rife with militaristic terminology, misogynist album art, and a history of overlooking the contributions of women composers.[61] Although noise music and the avant-garde potentially destabilize the discourses of power, virtuosity, and individual achievement that permeate most Western music, they replaced one discourse of power with another, retaining notions of conquest and techno-scientific innovation while casting "tradition" as the victim. Even the aesthetic of failure in noise music has potentially gendered qualities, as a male producer's fetishized "glitch" may easily become coded as a "mistake" in the hands of a female producer.[62] One might wonder whether the experience of oppression and domination could just as easily be one of awe and wonder at exploring nuanced and novel sonic palettes. Even as some theorists and fans worry over noise music's increasing visibility among underground music fans and arbiters of coolness, these new audiences may bring different modes of appreciation to the scene.

NOTES

1. Ross Hagen, "Fandom: Participatory Music Behavior in the Age of Postmodern Media," (PhD diss., CU-Boulder, 2010).
2. Torben Sangild, "Aesthetics of Noise" (Copenhagen: Datanom, 2002) http://www.ubu.com/papers/noise.html (accessed May 20, 2012).
3. Michel Serres, *Genesis*, trans. Geneviève James and James Nielson (Ann Arbor: University of Michigan Press, 1995), 7–14; Michel Serres, *The Parasite*, trans. Lawrence R. Schehr (Baltimore and London: The Johns Hopkins University Press, 1982), 121–28.
4. Joanna Demers, *Listening Through the Noise: The Aesthetics of Experimental Electronic Music* (New York: Oxford, 2010), 15.
5. Catherine O'Meara, "New York Noise: Music in the Post-industrial City, 1978–1985" (PhD diss., UCLA, 2006), 93–94.
6. Robert Walser, *Running with the Devil: Power, Gender, and Madness in Heavy Metal Music* (Middletown, CT: Wesleyan University Press, 1993), 45.
7. O'Meara, "New York Noise," 93.

8. Michelle Phillipov, *Death Metal and Music Criticism: Analysis at the Limits* (New York: Lexington Books, 2012), 73–88.

9. Torben Sangild, "NOISE—THREE MUSICAL GESTURES: Expressionist, Introvert and Minimal Noise," *Journal of Music and Meaning* 2 (Spring 2004), http://www.musicandmeaning.net/issues/showArticle.php?artID=2.4 (accessed May 20, 2012).

10. Todd Novosad, quoted in Hagen, "Fandom," 107.

11. Paul Hegarty, *Noise/Music:A History* (New York: Continuum Books, 2007), ix.

12. Luigi Russolo, *Art Of Noises*, trans. Barclay Brown (New York: Pendragon Press, 1986).

13. Friederich Kittler, *Gramophone, Film, Typewriter*, trans. Geoffrey Winthrop-Young and Michael Wutz (Stanford, CA: Stanford University Press, 1999); Melle Jan Kromhout, "'Over the Ruined Factory There's a Funny Noise': Throbbing Gristle and the Mediatized Roots of Noise in/as Music," *Popular Music and Society* 34, no. 1 (February 2011): 23–34.

14. David Novak, "2.5x6 Metres of Space: Japanese Music Coffeehouses and Experimental Practices of Listening," *Popular Music* 27, no. 1 (2003): 15–34.

15. Novak, "2.5x6 Metres of Space," 28.

16. Chris Atton, "Fan Discourse and the Construction of Noise as a Genre," *Journal of Popular Music Studies* 23, issue 3 (2011): 324–342.

17. Hegarty, *Noise/Music*, 11.

18. John Cage, "Composition as Process," in *Silence: Lectures and Writings by John Cage* (Middletown, CT: Wesleyan University Press, 1973), 39.

19. Paul Hegarty, *Noise/Music*, 27–29; Michel Oren, "Anti-Art as the End of Cultural History," *Performing Arts Journal* 15, no. 2 (May, 1993): 2.

20. Catherine O'Meara, "New York Noise," 94.

21. Hegarty, *Noise/Music*, 89–101.

22. Dick Hebdige, *Subculture: The Meaning of Style* (New York and London: Methuen and Co., 1979), 112.

23. Tim Gosling, "'Not For Sale': The Underground Network of Anarcho-Punk," in *Music Scenes: Local, Translocal, and Virtual*, eds. Andy Bennett and Richard A. Peterson (Nashville, TN: Vanderbilt University Press, 2004), 168–86; David Hesmondhalgh, "Post-Punk's Attempt to Democratise the Music Industry: The Success and Failure of Rough Trade," *Popular Music* 16, no. 3 (1997): 255–74.

24. Novak, "2.5x6 Metres of Space," 28.

25. Susana Asesino, "The Nortec Edge: Border Traditions and 'Electronica' in Tijuana," in *Rockin' Las Americas*, ed. Deborah Pacini Hernandez, Héctor Fernández L'Hoeste, and Eric Zolov (Pittsburgh: University of Pittsburgh Press, 2004), 312.

26. Mikawa Toshiharu,"Noise in Japan (Part 2)," http://japanoise.net /j/ incapa 15.htm (accessed July 28, 2012).

27. GinSatoh, "Hanatarashi Hanatarashi part 2" http://www5a.biglobe.ne.jp/ ~gin/ rock/ japan/hanatarasi/ hanatarashi 2/hanatarashi2.html (accessed July 28, 2012).

28. Trogotronic, "Trogotronic Information," http://trogotronic.com (accessed February 5, 2010).

29. Tom Bugs, "Weevils: BugBrand, Audio Electronics," Bugbrand.co.uk, http://www.bugbrand.co.uk/index.php?main_page=index&cPath=1_4&zenid =2e33e55d3d6f95cfe8487f883c27f8e9. (accessed February 6, 2010).

30. Reed Ghazala, *Circuit Bending: Build Your Own Alien Instruments* (Indianapolis: Wiley Publishing, 2005).

31. Kim Cascone, "The Aesthetics of Failure: 'Post-Digital' Tendencies in Contemporary Computer Music," *Computer Music Journal* 24, no. 4 (Winter 2002): 12–18.

32. Paul Théberge, *Any Sound You Can Imagine* (Hanover, NH: University Press of New England, 1997), 199.

33. Pulse Emitter, interview by Adam Cornelius, *People Who Do Noise*, DVD, directed by Adam Cornelius (Portland OR: Cold Hands Video, 2007).

34. Hagen, "Fandom," 109.

35. Sara Jane Bailes, *Performance Theatre and the Politics of Failure: Forced Entertainment, Goat Island, Elevator Repair Service* (New York: Routledge, 2011), 1–5.

36. Walser, *Running With the Devil*, 76–78.

37. Hegarty, *Noise/Music*, 156–57.

38. Nick Smith, "The Splinter in Your Ear: Noise as the Semblance of Critique," *Culture, Theory and Critique* 46/1 (2005): 43–59.

39. Jody Berland, "Postmusics," in *Sonic Synergies: Music, Technology and Community, Identity*, eds. Gerry Bloustien, Margaret Peters, and Susan Luckman (Burlington, VT: Ashgate, 2008), 34.

40. Jacques Attali, *Noise: The Political Economy of Music* (Minneapolis, MN: University of Minnesota Press, 1985), 122–24.

41. Bruce Johnson and Martin Cloonan, "Policy," in *Dark Side of the Tune: Popular Music and Violence* (Burlington, VT and Aldershot, Hampshire: Ashgate, 2008), 161–194.

42. Melle Jan Kromhout, "'Over the Ruined Factory There's a Funny Noise.'"

43. American Technology Corporation, "LRAD / Product Overview," http://www.atcsd.com/site/content/view/15/110/ (accessed September 13, 2009).

44. Bruce V. Bigelow, "Device Helped Thwart Pirates," *San Diego Union-Tribune*, November 9, 2005, http://legacy.signonsandiego.com/uniontrib /20051109/ new s_1b9cruise.html (accessed February 5, 2010).

45. Catherine Wessinger, "Deaths in the Fire at the Branch Davidians' Mount Carmel: Who Bears Responsibility?," *Nova Religio: The Journal of Alternative and Emergent Religions* 13, no. 2 (2009): 25–60; House Committee on the Judiciary, *Events Surrounding the Branch Davidian Cult Standoff in Waco, Texas*, 103rd Cong. 1st sess., 1993,http://www.archive.org/stream/eventssurroundin00unit/eventssurroundin00unit_ djv u. txt (accessed Jan 10, 2010).

46. Steve Goodman, *Sonic Warfare: Sound, Affect, and the Ecology of Fear* (Cambridge, Mass. And London: MIT Press, 2010), xiii–xiv, 9–11, 183–88.

47. Suzanne Cusick, "'You are in a place that is out of the world...': Music in the Detention Camps of the Global War on Terror," *Journal of the Society for American Music* 2 (2008): 1–26; Bruce Johnson and Martin Cloonan, "Music as Violence," in *Dark Side of the Tune: Popular Music and Violence* (Burlington, VT, and Aldershot, Hampshire: Ashgate, 2008), 147–160. Musicologist Jonathan Pieslak writes in his study of the use of music by American soldiers in Iraq that painting these interrogation techniques as torture may not always be appropriate. The military's current procedure requires the interrogator to be in the room while the music or noise is being played, to guard against damaging the subject's hearing. Pieslak's interviewees state that the primary goal in playing such music is to create an unsettling mood. Jonathan Pieslak, *Sound Targets: American Soldiers and Music in the Iraq War* (Bloomington and Indianapolis: Indiana University Press, 2009), 78–99.

48. Ryan Singel, "Report: Teens Using Digital Drugs to Get High," *Wired*, July 14, 2010, http://www.wired.com/threatlevel/2010/07/digital-drugs/ (accessed August 2, 2012).

49. Edward T. Cone, *The Composer's Voice* (Berkeley: University of California Press, 1974), 157.

50. Fred Maus, "The Disciplined Subject of Musical Analysis," in *Beyond Structural Listening?: Postmodern Modes of Hearing* (Berkeley: University of California Press, 2004), 35–43.

51. Julian Henrique, "Sonic Dominance and the Reggae Sound System Session," in *The Auditory Culture Reader*. Eds. Michael Bull and Les Back (Oxford: Berg 2003,) 451–480.

52. Demers, *Listening Through the Noise*, 93.

53. O'Meara, "New York Noise," 92–93.

54. Hegarty, *Noise/Music*, 108–111.

55. Hegarty, *Noise/Music*, 109; Jason J. Hanley, "'The Land of Rape and Honey': The Use of World War II Propaganda in the Music Videos of Ministry and Laibach," *American Music* 22/1 (Spring 2004): 158–74.

56. Keith Kahn-Harris, *Extreme Metal* (New York: Berg, 2007), 145.

57. Smith, "The Splinter in Your Ear," 55.

58. Elizabeth Grosz, "Embodied Utopias: The Time of Architecture," in *Architecture from the Outside: Essays on Virtual and Real Space* (Cambridge, Mass: The MIT Press, 2001), 132.

59. Hakim Bey. *T. A. Z. The Temporary Autonomous Zone, Ontological Anarchy, Poetic Terrorism* (Brooklyn: Autonomedia, 1985).

60. Hagen, "Fandom," 224.

61. Tara Rodgers, *Pink Noises: Women on Electronic Music and Sound* (Durham: NC: Duke University Press, 2010), 6–10.

62. Le Tigre, quoted in Rodgers, *Pink Noises*, 7.

Chapter 7
The Last Report: Throbbing Gristle and Audio Extremes
Brian Cogan

Introduction: Throbbing Gristle, The Most Important Band You've Never Heard of.

One of the most fascinating categories of music, extreme music, continues to baffle and confuse those used to pedestrian concerns such as "rhythm" and melody" in their chosen genre of music. While some forms of extreme music *do* sometimes have rhythm and melody, most extreme music is difficult (but perhaps rewarding) to listen to because it challenges the patience and sometimes sanity of a listener. While the category is not necessarily a recent one (Debussy, Stravinsky, and Gershwin could all have been lumped into this category in the past, not even to mention Stockhausen, etc.), in recent history one of the most important pioneers of extreme music (and lifestyle) were the Mancunian band Throbbing Gristle.

Throbbing Gristle was one of the most uncompromisingly brutally abrasive bands in musical history. Everything from their name (Throbbing Gristle is "Yorkshire slang for an erection"[1]) to their abrasively militaristic image, their use of casual references to fascist and other taboo imagery, and their relentless cacophony of musical experimentation, marks them as one of the key pioneers in modern extreme music. As media critic Douglas Rushkoff noted, Throbbing Gristle is considered by most critics to be "the father of all industrial bands."[2] Not only is Throbbing Gristle the father of all industrial bands, they may also be, in the words of Federico Nessi "the most important band of the last century."[3]

But then why are they so influential, but yet almost unknown to most listeners? Based on sales alone, it seems that most people, even those with a fairly intricate grasp of "alternative music," have no idea who Throbbing Gristle were, and even if they had heard them, the obvious temptation would be to rush for the off button on the stereo or radio.

Throbbing Gristle were among the most abrasive bands of all time, but they did not start out that way. Throbbing Gristle was formed after the demise of

COUM Transmissions, a notorious British performance art group that included members Genesis P-Orridge (formerly Neil Megsun) his then girlfriend Cosey Fanni Tutti (Christine Newby) and later, Hipgnosis designer Peter "Sleazy" Christopherson. In 1975 with the addition of technician and keyboard-ist/programmer Chris Carter, they morphed COUM into a full-time musical pro-ject, Throbbing Gristle that lasted until 1981, and reformed for several years after 2000 until the untimely death of Christopheson in 2010. Throbbing Gristle reimagined the relationship of the performer and the audience and used their music as a way of sometimes literally attacking people, making their audience feel uncomfortable and challenging their expectations of music and perfor-mance. Their music was loud, brutal, and designed not just to offend the ears, but the brain as well. As Drew Daniel noted, "The sounds of early Throbbing Gristle were unearthly, entirely unexpected, whirling comets of strangeness."[4] And, as I have noted, "Throbbing Gristle virtually single-handedly created a new genre, Industrial Noise, using extreme behaviors to create extremely pro-vocative and disturbing forms of art."[5] They directly influenced contemporaries such as Clock DVA, Whitehouse and Nurse with Wound and influenced a gen-eration of other bands from the underground (Coil, Neubaten, etc.) but also, along with their music, their dabbling with fascist imagery certainly influenced later, more mainstream artists such as Nine Inch Nails and Marilyn Manson, and may have been an influence on the death metal and black metal scenes

But the strangest thing about Throbbing Gristle may not have been the mu-sic they created, but *why* they created their particular blend of the fascinating and the grotesque. They were "inspired by the sixties tradition of performance art and happenings,"[6] and two members of TG, Genesis P-Orridge and Cosey Fanni Tutti, were members of the now belatedly recognized important pioneer-ing British performance art troupe COUM Transmissions, which, as mentioned earlier later morphed into Throbbing Gristle. COUM came from a performance art background and much of the work that pioneering performance artists are acclaimed for even today can be directly linked back to the foundational works performed by COUM. COUM was admittedly influenced by the darkness of 1960s bands such as the Velvet Underground and artist/performers such as John Cage, and performance artist Marina Abramovic's early works such as *Rhythm 0*, (where she lay naked on a table for six hours, surrounded by seventy two dif-ferent objects such as a rose, honey, a knife, guns, etc., leaving the artist exposed and in possible danger). This approach to performance influenced and later mir-rored the performance art of COUM, where the transgressive was made into art for the masses via increasingly bizarre and dangerous performative acts.

But Throbbing Gristle was also formed during a period when punk rock was becoming an exciting and much reviled new genre in Britain. Unlike the United States, where punk was on the fringes of the commercial mainstream, England's relatively small size allowed for a great acceptance of punk, as least as far as the charts were concerned. In punk, Throbbing Gristle saw a similar spirit and by the time COUM had transformed into Throbbing Gristle, they had already start-ed to appropriate some of their ideas in translating their vision into music. But, with a crucial difference as, "Most punk bands felt that working within the system was a necessary compromise to get the message of punk out to the masses,"[7] however, "Throbbing Gristle ignored formal ideology and worked towards redefining issues such as freedom, the body and the extremes to which music and performance could be taken."[8]

Throbbing Gristle made extreme music their mission, and they were not afraid to use the media as a tool to gain further exposure. The band, and particularly Genesis, were "captivated by the Warholian notion of using fame, hype and controversy themselves as an artistic medium."[9] As Genesis himself was to note to punk historian Jon Savage later, "We hadn't thought of becoming part of the music business. We were a comment on culture, and hypocrisy and double values."[10] Throbbing Gristle had a distinct (if oblique) philosophy and in many ways, Throbbing Gristle was "an attempt to popularize academic concepts and blend them into what people *thought* was a popular culture medium."[11] Although this may sound a little disingenuous in retrospect, to the members of Throbbing Gristle, it was equally important that people understand what their art; despite every effort they made (including hiding from the audience) to confuse and overwhelm their fans. Throbbing Gristle was the epitome of a mélange of low culture and postmodernism. The only musical question was if the fans were willing (and able) to follow them on their mission, no matter how musically adventurous they became.

Yet, this extreme mixture of calculated aggression and challenging music made Throbbing Gristle an enigma to many in the seventies. This is also why so few serious examinations of TG have been published since their original demise and eventual comeback over the last decade. Drew Daniel, author of the *20 Jazz Funk Greats* book from the $33^{1/3}$ series notes, "In some ways, Throbbing Gristle . . . are difficult to write about because of their oblique, even hostile relationship to music qua music."[12] They are not easy to put in a genre because they despised the idea of genre solidity and ideology. As Daniel notes further, "TG's calling card is a constitutive hostility to belonging: to a genre, to a gender, to a lifestyle, to a music scene, to a society."[13] Because they are so unexplainable in many ways, so incredibly challenging both during their initial existence and in recorded form afterwards, they remain confusing to many who are not ardent fans or professional musicologists. In the following sections, I will elaborate on how Throbbing Gristle grew from a performance art group who used extreme performance to become the founders of modern industrial music and culture. Unknown or not, I intend to illustrate that they are in-disputably important. Media theorist Douglas Rushkoff in particular credits P-Orridge for "daringly and almost single-handedly bringing body piercing, tribalism, and the harsh styled 'industrial' sound to Western culture."[14] Although the band eventually broke up due to massive internal contradictions (some will be detailed later), their influence goes beyond music and into the modern worlds of body modification and extreme outsider culture. In some ways, Throbbing Gristle were not just the precursors of modern extreme music and culture, they were its creators.

Throbbing Gristle as Performance Art

While Throbbing Gristle is a guiding force behind both industrial and the more extreme aspects of punk culture and music, in many ways they also directly connect back to the most positive aspects of the 1960s counterculture, most importantly, the urge to reinvent and toss aside the shackles of contemporary society. Throbbing Gristle may have helped invent a new, dark way of looking at the world, but from the early days of COUM Transmissions, they were also expanding on a sort of experimental theatre/performance art piece that had been lurking in the margins of the 1960s counterculture. Instead of taking their cue from the hippies, loose collection of left-wing ideologies (it can be argued that Genesis and Cosey had been hippies for at least some of their career), COUM took their inspiration from the fringes of the 1960s counterculture, specifically from art movements such as Fluxus (and its ancestors such as Dada, surrealism and Cabaret Voltaire) as well as the dark experimental music of the Velvet Underground, and performance art of pioneers such as Herman Nitsch, Joseph Beuys, Alan Kaprow (who coined the term "happenings to describe his work) as well as Andy Warhol's work with the Exploding Plastic Inevitable. COUM started out in 1969 as a loose commune of artists that lived communally and even shared clothes. The already established group was eventually joined by Genesis P-Orridge and then by Cosey Fanni Tutti, before the rest of the members eventually left and in 1971, the two continued on under the groups' name. As COUM, the two of them took the original group's mission in a darker more experimental style as "together, the two dedicated themselves to performance art that involved body modification, ritual scarring, immersion in various bodily fluids, sodomy and other forms of ritualistic pain and pleasure designed to test their bodies to the limit and test the audiences capacity for disgust."[15] They were dedicated to pushing the limits of the human body and performance art, even if for some performances even Genesis had no idea what it meant. In one performance in a park in London, which featured, "P-Orridge with his face half covered in make-up wearing a black rubber suit, whipping a chained 'dog' in SS leather overcoat in the middle of a public park in London with a child's pram nearby filled with maggots and hens heads and limbs.[16] COUM Transmissions started getting more outrageous starting in 1972 at an event called "The Alien Brain" which demonstrated their debt to Fluxus. Some performances included "various combinations of soiled tampons, maggots, black eggs, feathers, and syringes full of blood, milk or urine might figure as props" along with the usual blood and milk enemas and mutual penetration with a double dildo. What is perhaps even more shocking is how many of these performances were supported by British Arts Council grants.[17]

Genesis and Cosey were determined to expand the parameters of what could be considered art. As Genesis later remembered, "In COUM Transmissions I started to do cuts, scrape my body with sharp nails not razor blades, to me that didn't feel ritualistic enough; it had to be a dagger or nail or implement—not something clean and neat, but something which was dramatic and difficult and somewhat intimidating to *me*."[18] The nebulous theory of COUM Transmissions was "if you're opened up and you're aware of all possibilities and don't try to shut off anything, or repress anything, then things are transmitted through you just like they are with shamans or anything else."[19] To Genesis, this was not just experimenting; this was how he wanted to live his life. As he noted in an interview, "I think I was influenced by reading Kerouac's books about the Beat Generation, and books about Dada and surrealism. The thing that I was always interested in was the actual *lifestyle*—not so much the work that they produced but the way they lived and the fact that they did live out their lives like an art work"[20] But how extreme could COUM go in search of art? At one performance, after drinking half a bottle of whiskey (he didn't drink at the time) Genesis started cutting himself, as he put it:

> "I started cutting a swastika shape into my chest about nine inches square with a rusty nail; then I turned it into a Union Jack (the British flag), and then just scratched and cut all over the place. I'd also been eating these twigs I'd found outside in the mud in a building site and it turned out that they were poisonous. The combination of everything, the rusty nail that I'd found, the whiskey and the dehydration and the branches made me very ill and I started to vomit and dehydrate. I was rushed to the University hospital and by the time I got there they couldn't find a pulse. I had astral projections."[21]

By 1974, Throbbing Gristle were internationally recognized by critics as artistic innovators, but even by then Genesis was looking for new ways to open up the group's repertoire. They began to incorporate more nonmusical instruments such as bicycle wheels in order to make audio a more prominent part of their programs. In March 1974, they met Peter "Sleazy" Christopherson at a show and Sleazy, so nicknamed because he was fascinated by the sexual aspects of COUM's performance, joined the group in March 1975. As they incorporated Sleazy into the performance pieces, they incorporated more and more of what could almost be called "music" into their performances. This shift was because, as Genesis said, "we wanted to go into popular culture away from the art gallery context and to show that the same techniques that had been made to operate in that context could work. We wanted to test it out on the real world."[22] Soon, they moved away from the bodily fluids and more toward music. As Ford wrote, "What made COUM's music stand out . . . was the "do-it-yourself" attitude, with its unconventional instruments operated by non-professionals playing to an unconventional score."[23] When they recruited an actual musician and electronics expert, self-admitted rabid ABBA and Pink Floyd fan Chris Carter, into COUM, it was clear that the art world was no longer the best avenue to showcase their ideas, as they were moving toward becoming an admittedly unconventional band.

Throbbing Gristle got its official start at COUM's last show in October 1976 at an exhibit called "Prostitution" which featured forty nude photos of Cosey from pornographic magazines, as well as a plethora of used tampons. The so-called "shock" over this show led to Tory politician Nicholas Fairbairn denouncing the use of public money to fund such an exhibition, angrily proclaiming, "these people are wreckers of civilization."[24] Throbbing Gristle could not have been more pleased with the first "review" of their new direction. They would do their best over the next half decade to try and fulfill the role that Fairbairn had given them. As Simon Ford noted, Throbbing Gristle "transformed art into popular culture."[25] But what kind of popular culture was prepared for the darkness of Throbbing Gristle?

The Second Report

By the time of their first full-length record, *The Second Annual Report*, TG had created something new, even when lumped into the burgeoning punk scene in which they were not really participants. Unlike most early punk records, Throbbing Gristle's first recorded musical compositions were not reworking of traditional blues-based music as many of their punk contemporaries were attempting. Instead Throbbing Gristle tried to make sure that their music went along with their artistic DIY based agenda, that in the spirit of punk, it was resolutely primitive and lo-fi. Presumably, to most listeners who bought the record thinking it would be akin to most of the punk rock prevalent at the time, they soon discovered, sometimes to their horror, that "this was not a punk rock record, this was not a rock record, and this was not even music."[26] Instead, what baffled listeners discovered was that *The Second Annual Report* was "a bleak abstract landscape of synthetic dirges and continuing ideas from the days of COUM."[27] While they had become a "band" and started to make "music" they were still taking COUM's impulse to make people question the limits of their understanding to a larger audience. It was clear that Gristle's "quest was to create a total body experience, immersive and assaultive. They jettisoned songs, melody and groove in favor of the overwhelming *force* of sound itself."[28] Even while recorded under less than optimal conditions, *The Second Annual Report* is still a startling record. *The Second Annual Report* "consisted of spontaneously improvised noise jams recorded in a lo-fi manner and frequently featured random snippets of found media rather than through-composed material, it sounded crude, impassive, too raw to count as 'real music.'"[29] The record also rewarded those who paid close attention to the lyrics (mostly by Genesis), which further elaborated on the aims of Throbbing Gristle. As Drew Daniel also noted, the lyrics were "bristling with references to abnormal psychology, avant-garde literature and the margins of performance art, TG were low on form but high on content; each record was a virus of subcultural info animating a musical host."[30] It seems clear in retrospect that for most young punks, fond of the abrasive and the transgressive, this was hard to understand. As Daniel put it, "The clammy, weedy, thin unpleasant sounds of Throbbing Gristle's needle high end and the dull ache inspired by their relentless low-end throb weren't the sound of petty gripes about 'no fun' they literally *were* no fun."[31]

To Genesis and the rest of Throbbing Gristle, this was very intentional. They wanted to make the listener uncomfortable, but to them the music was only part of the message; the unsettling lyrics, taped voices, and found sounds were an equally important part of the Gristle experience. In an interview with a Japanese fan, to answer, "Why are you doing music," Genesis replied that,

> Well one reason, it's a platform for propaganda. And it's also a way for us to apply our ideas to show that without any musical training or background, through applying our philosophy to music, we made the music work as well; therefore, we're not just talking bullshit. The philosophy must have something in it or the record wouldn't have worked or we wouldn't have had an influence worldwide.[32]

Genesis also explained the peculiar logic behind the title of several Throbbing Gristle records. "And we called the records *reports*, which is to say that they were like home movies of *sound*. They were reports; they weren't like necessarily complete musical gems."[33] Gristle took the punk aesthetic with its convenient allusions to anarchy (most of which were released by major labels in the UK) and announced quite openly that what they were doing was nothing less than a William S. Burroughs attempt to wake the audience up to the manipulation of the power elites by any means necessary. As Roni Saarig noted "Industrial musicians wanted to focus on issues of the modern age where propaganda and the access and the control of information were becoming the primary tools of power."[34] To become a fan of Throbbing Gristle was almost like joining a cult. They were not there to be accessible and fun, they were there to attack anyone who had the guts to listen. As Simon Reynolds wrote, "TG's gigs were sadistic assaults on their audiences, not just barrages of songs, but of lighting too (convulsive strobes, high powered halogen lamps aimed in people's faces)."[35] This is also because Throbbing Gristle did not rely on conventional musical instruments. Even though they did use some instruments such as bass and cornet in many of their songs, they also used innovative and ahead-of-their time- innovations in tape loops and primitive sampling to create their soundscapes. Chris Carter created a "gristle-izer" or primitive sampler for Sleazy to play. "Its one octave keyboard triggered an array of cassette machines, each loaded with found sounds ranging from TV and movie dialogue to everyday conversations surreptitiously recorded by a roving Sleazy."[36]

This meant that the creepy voices, ("found sounds") sometimes of children and sometimes of criminals that were incorporated into the music were as important as the found sounds and lo-fi rumbles. Throbbing Gristle took their role as artists seriously and as Roni Saarig noted, Throbbing Gristle were "not so much a band as a group of art terrorists who chose sound—noise, tape effects,

documentary material, and songs as well—as the best medium for their attack."[37] The songs were not meant to be enjoyed, but to alert the listener to the
reality of the world they lived in. To Throbbing Gristle, that world was a malev-
olent one indeed. "They investigated a post-industrial nightmare that included
fascism and its related atrocities, the dehumanization of factory labor, and social
deviance in all forms."[38]

Throbbing Gristle also worked on making their appearance onstage as intimidating and unsettling as their music. They freely used imagery and ideas that
led to many complaining of "Gristle's ambiguous relationship with fascism."[39]
Among their visual outrages were their use of a photo of Auschwitz as logo for
their independent record company, Factory Records. An early single was titled
"Zyklon B Zombie," "named in deliberate bad taste after Nazi nerve gas."[40]

As Simon Reynolds noted, "P-Orridge saw his lyrics as a continuation of
the way the Velvet Underground had expanded rock's songwriting to take on
taboo areas such as sadomachicism and heroin."[41] Their new emphasis on fascism and the military led to one of their most famous singles, "Discipline"
where the front cover photo was of the band standing in uniform in front of "the
building that had once served as the third Reich's ministry of propaganda."[42]
They even called the large factory-esque building that they lived and worked in
the "Death Factory." The Death Factory was originally next to London Fields in
Hackney, a traditional gravesite for plague victims, hence the nickname for the
bunker. But Genesis also went on to note that "but we always saw the Death
Factory as a metaphor for industrial society as well."[43] A new type of music also
need a new genre and Genesis's friendship with performance artist Monte
Cazzaza led to them using Cazzaza's phrase "industrial music" to describe their
sound and to begin wearing camouflage outfits and then "embarked on an experiment in totalitarian psychology that got a bit out of hand."[44]

When Genesis was irked by a band of itinerant travelling people[45] who had
set up camp in a field behind the Death Factory, he decided that the band would
fully explore the implications of their music. They decided to torture the camp
through use of ultralow frequencies. For a few years, Throbbing Gristle had
been trying to "research into harnessing, "groups of infra and ultra sound
equipment such as pizo horns and signal generators."[46] They were attempting to
"research into harnessing of sound to provoke controlled physical and psychological reactions in the listener."[47] They began to bombard the traveling people's
camp late at night with their signal generators, and much to the band's pleasure,
it seemed to work. Their pizo horns and signal generators led to "sensations
forming in the ears, of broken sleep, nightmares, headaches, bad feelings."[48]
Eventually, and after many sleepless and unpleasant nights, the traveling people
left the area "thinking it was haunted or cursed."[49]

This cruel manipulation confirmed for Genesis his worst fears of the power
that propaganda held. To Genesis, Throbbing Gristle is "disturbing because it
illustrates the power of suggestion and manipulation. The power in the hands of
those who write the captions under the photograph, the voice over to the TV
news. Art, newspapers, radio, the camera—all can be made to lie, even if they're

telling the truth: by omission, deception, misinformation. That interests us and we tend to play on that as a group."[50] They had realized the power of their ideas, but perhaps their most disturbing album was one that looked, and in some ways sounded, almost pleasurable.

20 Jazz Funk Greats

By 1979 Throbbing Gristle had mastered their nontraditional approach to music and had established to critics that abrasive, brutal noise was a legitimate form of musical expression. They were quickly followed by other bands either inspired by them or who had recognized a kindred spirit in the first three TG albums. However, Throbbing Gristle did not want fans to follow their lead; even the bands they supported such as DVA Clock and Nurse With Wound were different from Throbbing Gristle in many important ways. Throbbing Gristle also realized that extreme music for its own sake was a musical cul-de-sac. They had pushed the boundaries of noise to something brutally beautiful, now they could make a lateral move. Their next record was a deceptively titled affair called 20 Jazz Funk Greats, with a front cover depicting the band dressed in their best hip clothes on the top of a cliff. Of course, the cliff itself was notorious for the many suicides committed there every year. But that was for the astute listener to discover for themselves. The record (there is a little jazz and funk on it, but mostly experimental pieces that are almost recognizable as songs) was confounding to Throbbing Gristle fans and made them listen even more closely to the lyrics than before.

As usual, the main topics of the record were power and manipulation. Genesis's musical efforts "took the cut and past methods of colleague William S. Burroughs and applied them to music on a conscious effort to expose the hidden language of power and manipulate it to countercultural ends."[51] The record 20 Jazz Funk Greats "brought Throbbing Gristle's love affair with misinformation to a climax."[52] Genesis had not only studied the effects of abrasive music on the mind and body, he was also interested in the more subtle way that background music affected the listener. He was particularly interested in studying "the science of the effects of sound of the body and developed music to alter consciousness, evoke fear, or even stimulate orgasm. He called this music 'anti-muzak' and it is meant to have an effect on the mind and body antithetical to Muzak Corporation's soundtracks. Instead of putting listeners to sleep, Genesis wants to wake them up."[53]

While the songs on 20 Jazz Funk Greats may have been overtly "listenable" the content and messages were taking things in even more extreme directions. The voice recorded on "Persuasion" may have been of a friend of Sleazy who was a pedophile,[54] the sounds on the tape the pedophile provided of a boy giggling (the band claims that the recordings, while made by an admitted pedophile- were completely devoid of sexual content), was a result of Sleazy's desire to make associations that made the listener uncomfortable, where the affect is "sinister in that context" and that "I was very interested in how people's perceptions change out of context."[55] Many other extreme bands hearing this, decided to up the ante, (Nurse with Wound as an example) and tried to incorporate even more shock for shock's sake.

This was just what Throbbing Gristle found so frustrating in their musical peers. Throbbing Gristle had attempted to be subversive and question the relationship of people to their greatest fears, serial killers, etc., but the inherent shock value they had used for art's sake was that it "had worked all too well, cementing the association of industrial music with gruesome tales of serial killing, rape, child molestation and child murder."[56] This lead to a situation where "it ultimately proved stifling and tedious to the members of the band who had to watch as their anti-humanist gestures were photocopied and distorted endlessly by arrivistes, who brought plenty of iron-stomached bloodlust, but forgot to pack the critical savor faire."[57] By the time of their next release, the live *Heathen Earth*, it seemed that the only logical step was to break up. After a particularly brutal romantic breakup in which Cosey left Genesis for Chris Carter, the band was splintering anyway and eventually the band split into two camps. One with Carter and Fan Tutti staring a new industrial-based dance band called Chris and Cosey, and Genesis and Sleazy forming the long-running Psychic Television, which Genesis continued in various permutations for the next three decades. While Throbbing Gristle was done for the moment, their influence was felt not just in the new abrasive form of music that they had pioneered, but also in their extreme choice of lifestyles.

Genesis and Tribal Culture

In 2005 Genesis P-Orridge put his money where his mouth was. In an experimental piece of elaborate dental hygiene, Genesis had all of his remaining teeth replaced with gold. But this was only the continuation of a lifestyle based on art and experimentation that had first flowered with COUM. To Genesis, choosing to live his life as an experiment meant that he would accept any challenge and take his body to the ultimate limits of pain and sensation. Along with his wife the artist Lady Jaye Breyer, Genesis also embarked on a mission to make the two of them into one pandrogynous being. In this experiment, Genesis, who had already heavily inked and tattooed his body, anticipating "tribal culture" by at least a few decades, changed his body with hormone injection and mutual breast implants for himself and Lady Jaye. Genesis also changed his name to Genesis Breyer P-Orridge, a name he has kept since the unexpected death of Breyer in 2007.

The reinvention of body as art was not just done for art's sake. For several decades part of the worldview of Genesis has revolved around art, ritual transmission of information, and secret societies. To Genesis, the world is run by a vast conspiracy with a small group of people keeping control of the world who "have maintained a monopoly over sexual, magical and mystical traditions in order to keep the masses at bay."[58] As Douglas Rushkoff noted, his worldview is that "the uninitiated are not allowed to be aware of or participate in this, or it will dilute, or ultimately destroy the mystical source of power."[59] Genesis elaborated that the only way to understand the world was to understand the secretive nature of the power elite. As Genesis said, "we live in a world where everything is magic and metaphor. Language is used to manipulate things in accordance with a small minority's idea of their destiny: the inherited, implicit and inviolable right to maintain power."[60] As Genesis revealed to V. Vale, the publisher of *RE/Search*, the first journal to report on industrial and tribal culture, "Basically, everything that we do is just aimed at trying at trying to find out how people's minds are manipulated...and then short-circuit that."[61]

To this extent, Genesis not only remade his body, but also throughout his solo career, made sure that he continued in opposing the dominant secret power elites and challenging people to attack and resist the secret world around them. He founded the half-cult/half band Psychic Television and worked with Brion Gysin and Burroughs to develop a "cut and paste style of subversion" under the term, "industrial culture."[62] "Throbbing Gristle was really more of an ongoing performance art piece in real time. Genesis hoped to reinstall culture with primitive magical techniques, while exposing people to the blatant manipulation foisted upon them by a top down media infrastructure."[63] In overcoming the limit of mind and body, Genesis P-Orridge and Throbbing Gristle showed not just how extreme music could be, but how extreme life could be as well.

The Final Report

When Throbbing Gristle broke up in 1981, it did not seem likely that they could ever reform. Not even counting the tension between Cosey and Genesis as ex-lovers, they had also done so much to confound expectations in their lifestyle, but also to make most bands that followed in their footsteps look tame and commercial in comparison. However, their legacy, in any band that uses extreme music, including bands that never heard of them but use industrial music, obviously influenced Neubaten, Nine Inch Nails, etc. Their influence extended to not only industrial bands but also any band that assembles their own instruments and participates in DIY culture. Most industrial music in the eighties and beyond has a debt to pay to Throbbing Gristle, even though most of them do not really understand that what Throbbing Gristle was doing was more of a project and way of life than a musical movement. Nonetheless, "just like the Velvet Underground (one of the only groups Throbbing Gristle acknowledged as an influence) it sometimes seemed that everybody who heard Throbbing Gristle started their own band"[64] However, unlike the Velvets, who only re-formed for a European tour in 1994, Gristle did re-form in 2002 and performed music again until

Genesis left the reunion in 2007 and Peter "Sleazy" Christopherson died of un-known causes in November 2010. This, along with the tragic death of Lady Jaye in 2007, made the chances of them ever re-forming again almost nonexistent. But still their legacy, particularly of Genesis's vision, persists. To his fans and critics, Genesis and his music have been confounding in terms of his caginess and brilliant at the same time. As media critics Douglas Rushkoff put it, Genesis "has made a career of reconstructing culture."[65] Throbbing Gristle in particular deconstructed music so thoroughly both in art and in practice that to this author, it is difficult to listen to traditional music in the same way after listening to them. As Simon Reynolds noted, "The remarkable thing about Throbbing Gristle's legacy is that they almost single-handedly created one of the most enduring and densely populated fields of post punk mucus, despite having a rather disdainful attitude towards music per se."[66] Genesis always maintained that Throbbing Gristle was about being "always be awake and ready to alter, to be aware that you're mortal and life is about formulas, and that expressions of life (art or music) shouldn't be about formulas either. To be aware and not lazy."[67] Throbbing Gristle, for all of their inherent contradictions, urged their listeners not to live lives of quiet passivity, but to recognize the methods of control and conformity that were inherent in the system, and not resist this control with all their might. For attentive fans, both becoming aware of the vagaries of one's environment and even listening to the abrasive music of Throbbing Gristle may not be a pleasant experience, both are worthwhile and both are vital.
The mission is terminated.

Notes

1. Ford, Simon *Wreckers of Civilization: The Story of COUM Transmissions and Throbbing Gristle* (England: Black Dog Publishing 1999) 5.16.

2. Rushkoff, Douglas. *Media Virus: Hidden Agendas in Popular Culture* New York: (Ballantine Books, 1994), 306.

3. Nessi, Federico "Throbbing Gristle" Artlurker.com http://www.artlurker.com /2008/09/throbbing-gristle-by-federico-nessi/.

4. Daniel, Drew. *33 1⁄3 20 Jazz Funk Greats* (New York: Continuum, 2008) 2.

5. Cogan, Brian. *The Punk Encyclopedia* (New York: Sterling, 2008) 86.

6. Cogan, Brian. "Do they owe us a living? Of Course they do!" Crass, Throbbing Gristle and Anarchy and Radicalism in Early English Punk rock" *The Journal for the Study of Radicalism,* vol 1, no. 2. 2007 pp.77–90, 84.

7. Cogan 2007, 78.

8. Cogan, 2007, 8.

9. Cogan 2007, 85.

10. Savage, Jon. *England's Dreaming: Anarchy, Sex Pistols, Punk and Beyond* (New York: St. Martin's Press, 1991). 423.

11. Ford, 5.17.

12. Daniel, 2.

13. Daniel, 160.

14. Rushkoff, 306.

15. Cogan 2008, 84.

16. Ford, 4.20–4.21.

17. Reynolds, 126.

18. Vale, V. "Genesis and Paula P-Orridge" *RE/Search Modern Primitives* (San Francisco: Re/Search Publications 1989), 167.

19. Vale, 1989, 72.

20. Reiko, "Throbbing Gristle Interview" in *RE/Search #4/5,* V. Vale ed. (San Francisco: Re/Search Publications, 2007), 80.

21. Vale, 1989, 168.

22. Ford, 5.18.

23. Ford, 4.6.

24. Reynolds, Simon. *Rip it Up and Start Again: Postpunk 1978-1984* (England: Penguin 2005), 128.

25. Ford, 5.18.

26. Daniel, 10.

27. Dyer, Simon. "Throbbing Gristle Biography" in *RE/Search #4/5,* V. Vale ed. (San Francisco: Re/Search Publications, 2007), 62.

28. Reynolds, 128.

29. Daniel, 130.

30. Daniel, 13.

31. Daniel, 12.

32. Reiko, 86.

33. Reiko, 89.

34. Saarig, Roni. *The Secret History of Rock: The Most Influential Bands You've Never Heard,* (New York: Billboard 1998), 182.

35. Reynolds, 131.

36. Reynolds, 127.

37. Saarig, 183.

38. Saarig, 183.

39. Reynolds, 130.

40. Saarig,185.

41. Reynolds, 131.

42. Reynolds, 134.

43. Savage, 422.

44. Reynolds, 133.

45. The term is a revision of the old appellation "tinkers" or a roving band of people of uncertain ethnicity, possibly connected to the Roma people.

46. Ford, 9.18.

47. Ford, 8.10.

48. Ford, 9.19.

49. Ford, 9.21.

50. Dyer, 63.

51. Rushkoff, 311.

52. Saarig, 185.

53. Rushkoff, 311.

54. Daniel, 113.

55. Daniel, 114.

56. Daniel, 130.

57. Daniel, 130.

58. Rushkoff, 307.

59. Rushkoff, 307.

60. Rushkoff, 308.

61. Vale, V. "Genesis P-Orridge Interview" in *RE/Search #4/5,* V. Vale ed. (San Francisco: Re/Search Publications, 2007), 67.

62. Rushkoff, 309.

63. Rushkoff, 309.

64. Reynolds, 138.

65. Rushkoff, 310.

66. Reynolds, 135.

67. Reynolds, 136.

Chapter 8
Black Metal Soul Music:
Stone Vengeance and the Aesthetics of
Race in Heavy Metal
Kevin Fellezs

*"Some people refer to us as a Christian metal band! Christian! You know, I told
the guy, that's not what we are. I can understand, they hear the Bible references
—but that's the blues! That's from the blues. I'm just carrying on [the black
musical] tradition in rock'n'roll. It's a code, you know, and a part of who I am.
"It's ignorance [by blacks to the fact] that black people [have always been involved in rock'n'roll]. Then on through the '60s, you don't see [black people] —
they're re-categorized. It's based on the ignorance of our own people – letting
something that they built, that they were at the foundation of — it wasn't just
them, you had other people involved but they definitely played a large part of
the invention of [rock music]."*
— Mike Coffey, leader of Stone Vengeance[1]

    Near the beginning of his incisive study of heavy metal, Robert Walser as-
serts, "A heavy metal genealogy ought to trace the music back to African-
American blues, but this is seldom done. Just as histories of North America
begin with the European invasion, the histories of musical genres such as rock
and heavy metal commonly begin at the point of white dominance. But to emphasize Black Sabbath's contribution of occult concerns to rock is to forget
Robert Johnson's struggles with the Devil and Howlin' Wolf's meditations on
the problem of evil" (1993, 8). African American guitarist and Stone Vengeance
founder Mike Coffey does not hesitate to trace rock music and by extension,
heavy metal, from the blues

    I listen to stuff from the '20s. Charley Patton, Blind Lemon Jefferson, Blind
    Blake, Robert Johnson from the '30s. Lonnie Johnson, who's just as good,
    probably a little better than Robert Johnson. Robert Johnson just got popular
    because Eric Clapton put his stamp [of approval] on him. But you ask BB King
    and all those guys, [they'll tell you that] Lonnie Johnson's bad as hell, man.

Skip James. That's what happens when you put the drums and the bass behind the guitar, it's rockin' now! *You can't get heavy metal — if you don't have that guitar, it'll be something else.* You can have a loud bass and drums but without that guitar, it's another music. *The guitar is primary because of the blues.*

While Walser allows the blues to shimmer behind the remainder of his book without further comment, I want to note the ways in which black (African American) heavy metal musicians confront the reality that, as Walser and other heavy metal scholars such as Deena Weinstein readily acknowledge, heavy metal is a genre with an audience that is "mostly young, white, male, and working class" (Walser 1993, 3).

Moreover, black heavy metal musicians must also confront the practices of a music industry that bases its decisions about marketing, artist development, and genre configuration on that reality. These assumptions cum practices inadvertently silence black rock musicians by reinforcing tautological links between genre and race that ensure audiences, critics and music industry personnel identify certain musical sounds and gestures with particular types of bodies. While the global reach of contemporary metal complicates Walser and Weinstein's assertions about the core constituency for heavy metal, the overarching racialization of rock as a "white" genre remains, particularly in the United States, black African metal bands notwithstanding.[2]

Stone Vengeance is a heavy metal band comprised of entirely African American musicians and, while enjoying a primarily white male audience, formed their aesthetic in recognition, even celebration, of their blackness. Initially formed in 1978, Stone Vengeance have remained a cult favorite for a small yet dedicated core audience who can be found "on every continent but Antarctica," as Coffey boasts. Their fans have named them the Lords of Heavy Metal Soul, a moniker, while clearly meant to praise, speaks to Stone Vengeance's racialized positioning outside the inner sanctum of "metaldom," pointing as it does to a long history of primitivist tropes concerning black Americans' "soul," a nonintellectual, body-oriented essence that opposes the figuration of thrash metal as a complex musical form. As John Sheinbaum warns rock scholars, while rock's increasingly canonical historical narrative presents white rock musicians as artists and black soul musicians as craftspeople, "race-based constructions of difference we may hear should not lead us, unthinkingly, to assert that [music produced by white or black musicians] somehow possesses different levels of value" (2002, 127). Sheinbaum's point — that an unspoken and therefore often unacknowledged idea lurking behind critical judgment holds that exemplary black musicians are unschooled "soulful performers" while ideal white musicians are highly trained "skillful artists" — reveals the predetermined ways in which black cultural production enters critical discourse in an already-subordinate position.

My interest in Stone Vengeance lies in this very predicament: the relationship between race and value as experienced by musicians who challenge conventional genre boundaries through an embodied difference to assumed genre expectations.[3] In fact, my initial interest was in studying the 1980s San Francisco thrash metal scene that had served as Metallica's formative ground. However, as I began researching, I became increasingly interested in Stone Vengeance because of their longevity — most of the other bands from the original scene have long since disappeared.[4] More important, as the sole representatives of African American musicians in the scene, Stone Vengeance provide a uniquely productive vehicle for reflecting on the relationships among processes of racialization, critical appraisals of aesthetic and historical value and music industry assessments of commercial interest precisely because Stone Vengeance makes visible the underlying tenets for recognition by other metal musicians, critics, fans, and music industry personnel — all of whom begin their appraisal of bands and musicians on presumptive notions of genre, including the bodies deemed appropriate for a particular genre. As Fabian Holt argues in his insightful study of popular music genre, a *"genre can be viewed as a culture* with the characteristics of a system or systemic functions [and] are identified not only with music, but also *with certain cultural values, rituals, practices, territories, traditions, and groups of people."*[5] It is reasonable to assume that the "cultural values, rituals, practices, territories, traditions, and groups of people" associated with thrash metal do not normally call to mind African American musicians or black musical traditions. Yet as Stone Vengeance effectively posits despite working within a genre discursively constructed as a space for the expression of white masculinity, thrash metal can be thought of as part of a black American musical tradition.

Before allowing Coffey's narrative to center my discussion, I want to be explicit about not taking his comments at face value. However, throughout all my work (and not exclusively for this chapter), I aim to highlight musicians' voices in order that we might gain knowledge from their perspective. Too often musicians' voices are muted or muffled by scholars, critics, and fans with a real loss in the ways in which historical narratives, aesthetic choices, and music industry practices are framed. By giving ample space to Coffey, I hope to serve as an interested interlocutor of Stone Vengeance's working aesthetic in heavy metal as an articulation of a black aesthetic. In this way, I mean to foreground Coffey's role as musician — both agentive and reactive, both expressive and constitutive — in negotiating musical discourse, audience desire and critical hermeneutics.

For example, at one point in a conversation with Coffey and drummer/vocalist Darren Tompkins, I referred to Jimi Hendrix and his role in shaping psychedelic hard rock and, consequently, heavy metal through his technical mastery of the blues combined with the sonic assault of hard rock and his creative use of distortion.[6] But the mention of Hendrix elicited a heated reply from Coffey. After quickly assuring me that he loves Hendrix's music, Coffey became decidedly less appreciative of the aims to which Hendrix's representation has been mobilized by rock critics and fans, particularly after his death. I quote Coffey's response at length

I always think about it. People act like they really love Hendrix. But, you know what? If that is the case, it wouldn't be so hard for black people to get *in* to [i.e., make it in] this music. So I feel like, well, Hendrix is gone and he's no longer an obstacle or a threat or something — so it's easy, [he's] safe to like. That's what I feel about Hendrix because people like me, and you . . . we're children of Hendrix through the discipline of rock'n'roll.

But there's no apparatus to help us *at all*. So, I think it's bullshit. I think it's a fake love affair with Hendrix. It's just he's gone, and money can be made off of him, you know what I mean?

Think about it. He didn't make it here in the States. We have to *look* at that. He was *struggling* in the States, just like us. Just like Living Colour wouldn't have made it if it wasn't for Mick Jagger, you know what I mean? So it's bullshit, dude.[7]

Noting how a fetishized Hendrixian presence allows white rock fans to proclaim their admiration for a dead black musician while disenfranchising living black rock musicians, Coffey insists that despite the adulation Hendrix receives within rock culture, the real status of black rock musicians is evident in the racialized conditions that remain within the music industry and within rock discourse writ large that keep black musicians from full participation within rock even, as Coffey points out, for an artist as revered as Hendrix.[8] Coffey's view that the figure of Hendrix has allowed an obscuring of the lack of apparatus lack of structure, of legitimization, of support, of authority — for other black rock musicians in the commercial music market provides the chance to briefly address the underlying issue of musicking, thrash metal or otherwise, as labor.

Something Else

Stone Vengeance was not successful in turning home court to their advantage in the burgeoning San Francisco Bay Area metal scene of the 1980s. Despite moderately large sales of a homemade cassette recording at the Record Vault, an important heavy metal music store in San Francisco at the time, Stone Vengeance remained a club band unable to secure a recording contract with heavy metal labels such as Megaforce, Roadrunner, or Combat or touring opportunities as an opening act for better - known bands.[9]

The musicians of Stone Vengeance provide a perspective that is important *precisely because of* their positions as working-class black musicians, whose professional music careers confront the intertwining pincers of race and class as articulated in musical discourse, including practices and norms within the music industry. Born and raised in the black working-class neighborhood of the Bayview–Hunter's Point area of San Francisco, California, Coffey, Tompkins and Starks see their creative efforts as both art and commerce.

Indeed, the fact that Stone Vengeance performances are self-conscious acts of labor formed a large part of our discussions. Coffey and Tompkins recognize that their musical labor is harnessed to racialized conceptions of professional musicking that are reinforced structurally through music business organization norms and practices (not to mention institutes of music education). Coffey points to racialist thinking as impacting his professional efforts: "[Record] labels are set up for white groups. I learned that a long time ago. I didn't go into this with my eyes closed. I knew we were black and I knew about racism. But I just didn't think it would be this hard. I really didn't. *I was willing to work hard and prove myself and put in the work.*"

In fact, Coffey is quick to note, "Black people like money just like anybody else. [Black musicians] didn't just walk away from rock'n'roll. We had no apparatus; the white folks owned the distribution, they owned the record labels, they owned the publishing. What the fuck did black people know? They just wanted to make some money. And, they [would have been interested in] whatever [type of music that was popular in the way that] rock'n'roll became. We would've been *in* it — *if we weren't pushed out.* But you know they were pushed out just by looking at what was going on with a Little Richard and then a Pat Boone." Coffey's point about the way in which Pat Boone's anodyne covers of Little Richard and others' more raucous rock'n'roll hits went on to greater sales among mainstream audiences also points to the ways in which the racialization of genre have left black musicians

Similar to Coffey's reminder about the way in which Robert Johnson was legitimated through Clapton's imprimatur, Maureen Mahon notes the troubled entry of another African American rock band, Living Colour, into the mainstream rock market: "Whether one reads Living Colour's alliance with [Mick] Jagger as the calling in of a debt, the ultimate sellout, or a savvy manipulation of resources, it exemplifies the race and power dynamics of the music industry. Most disturbing for Black Rock Coalition members was the fact that a white star had to validate a black band before it could gain recognition" (2004, 156). While race is not the only element in play, it is difficult to deny that racialized conceptions of musical genre form a significant part of the larger context in assessing a particular band's perceived mainstream marketability. Further, these assessments usually carry negative repercussions for black musicians engaged in genres not typically identified as "black music" genres (e.g., rhythm and blues, rap).

In defending his choice to pursue an interest in heavy metal, Coffey maintains that black American music has always dealt with the themes identified with heavy metal: individualism, antiauthoritarianism, antibourgeois sentiments connected to working-class alienation and a morbid fascination with death and apocalyptic imagery that is often drawn from anti- or, perhaps more accurately, pre- or non-Christian beliefs. Stone Vengeance treats these themes *as a fundamentally black aesthetic,* thereby presenting thrash metal as part of a larger black music tradition.[10]

Stone Vengeance articulates their heavy "metalness" in explicit dialogue
with ideas about, for instance, black masculinity. But their performances repudi-
ate popular culture stereotypes of blackness. Coffey describes the band's outlier
position in heavy metal by recalling a scene in the film, *Blade* in which the black
"half-vampire daywalker" played by Wesley Snipes is helped by a black woman, who asks him, "You're one of them [a vampire], aren't you?" Blade replies,
"No, I'm something else."[11]

Coffey continues, "That's what we are. We're not what the white guys are
[i.e., conventional rock groups]. We're not what the black guys are [i.e., conventional funk or hip hop groups]. So, to manage a band like us, you have to think
about that because we don't fit. Because there are no record labels looking for
black rock bands. You have some [black rock bands] that are out there [now] but
we were the first black *heavy metal* band. Stone Vengeance is notable for being
the first black *thrash heavy metal* band. More and more people now are starting
to see that."[12] The continued silence around Stone Vengeance in the increasing
catalog of heavy metal texts, however, belies Coffey's assertion.[13] What might
Stone Vengeance's invisibility reveal?

Black Thrash Roots

Coffey is adamant that rock is based on the blues. While he admires guitarists
such as Randy Rhoads, Ulrich Roth, Ritchie Blackmore, and Yngwie Malmsteen
for their efforts to combine elements of European art music with hard rock, he
insists, "If you don't like the blues, I guarantee you, your heroes like the blues
[he is specifically discussing Rhoads, et al.]. Black Sabbath, you know they
were called Earth at first, a blues band. Van Halen was into [Eric] Clapton.
AC/DC — they *crazy* about the blues. KISS — listen to Ace Frehley, that's the
blues. *All* of those guys who established heavy metal were into the blues."

Coffey points out that the relationship between the blues and rock extends
beyond the "merely musical," noting,

> You can't take the blues out of it. People ask, why do you sing about Satan?
> That's the same thing in the blues, it was the devil's music. It's the same shit
> today. We sing about god, the devil, sex — it's the same thing. You can't really
> get away from it. They can only pull that on people who don't know the history
> of the music.
>   But I studied the music. When I got into it, I would go to the library and
> read the history of [rock music]. So, I know where it came from – it came from
> what they called "race music" or "that nigger bop" music. It was [initially per-
> ceived as a] strictly black [music] and then it became rock'n'roll, which was [a]
> strictly white [music]. I remember some guy tried to come with some bullshit,
> trying to say that Elvis Presley had his rockabilly, his country style — trying to
> take away from the black influence. But that's not what [Sam Phillips] said. He
> said, "If I can find a white man that sings like a black man, I'll make a million

dollars." *He wasn't looking at Elvis's country roots, he was looking for Elvis to sound like a black man.*

This is no small point for Coffey. Phillips, whose Sun label had primarily recorded African American rhythm and blues musicians, was looking for a white singer who could sing with an authentic black feeling in order to leave the secondary race record market and move into the mainstream popular music market. While Elvis Presley might have given Phillips what he wanted, the singer's career with Sun Records was brief (1953–1956). By 1960 Elvis was charting with ballads such as "Are You Lonesome Tonight?" and "It's Now or Never" for RCA rather than reproducing the energetic rock'n'roll sound of his earlier Sun recordings "Hound Dog" or "Baby, Let's Play House." As Elvis's recordings indicated, the rapid transformation of rhythm and blues into rock and roll in the late 1950s eventually advanced rock to the center of American popular music culture in a process captured by Reebee Garofalo's apt description as a movement from "black roots to white fruits."[14]

However, Coffey's early music listening experiences pierced through rock's whitewashed veneer. His involvement with heavy metal was a natural outcome of being exposed to a wide variety of music despite growing up in a working-class African American neighborhood. Coffey: "I was exposed to a lot of music [through] the radio. And I remember hearing 'A Day in the Life' on the radio. That was one of the songs, the Beatles' 'A Day in the Life,' that *stuck* with me. I was like, there's something about that music — just *magical*." Coffey is unequivocal about the Beatles as source and inspiration for making music central in his life, displaying his continuing reverence for the band by the Beatles posters that hang in his band's rehearsal space and his frequent references to them in interviews.

In fact, *The Beatles at the Hollywood Bowl* (Capitol 1977), a live recording compiled primarily from two performances at the Hollywood Bowl in 1964 and 1965, was the first recording Coffey purchased. While his claims to having listened to the record over one thousand times may be hyperbolic, it indicates the central place the recording occupies in his musical development. He was initially disappointed as the sounds of a noisy, screaming audience first greeted him. However, his buyer's remorse soon turned to appreciation as his room filled with the sound of electric guitars. He recalls, "They start off with 'Twist and Shout.' And, dude, it was the *sound* of it. So, [the reason] I got into wanting to play music [was through a] fascination with the electronic side of it. The sound of *amplified* blues, man. *The sound of the equipment*. The *power* of just a few instruments on a stage being amplified and the *power* rolling off that stage." Like many rock fans, Coffey was attracted to two elements in rock that partially define its aesthetic: loud volume and complexity in the service of expressing power.

Coffey's attraction to rock's volume as an instantiation of power indicates the resistive, even rebellious, potential rock music holds out for him. Coffey's immersion in the forceful "sound of amplified blues" allows him to wield power through rock's volume and use of distortion against unspoken "genre rules," a term I borrow from Simon Frith to describe the formal and (mostly) informal set of evolving rules – prohibitions, restrictions, qualifications — that determine the ordering of sounds, and the bodies who produce them, into specific genres.[15]

Returning to Coffey's musical roots, he points to the influence of the free-form FM radio of the late 1960s and 1970s, whose DJs introduced him to classical music by Igor Stravinsky, jazz by Sun Ra and, most important, the metal of the New Wave of British Heavy Metal (NWOBHM). As noted, Coffey idealized the music of the Beatles but it was the wide spectrum of music that was played on San Francisco Bay Area stations during the 1970s that freed him from the music of his neighborhood. As he put it, "I felt so liberated" by the radio.[16]

Two isolated instances in 1977 constitute Coffey's entire formal instruction on guitar. He had learned "Day Tripper" by ear. However, he still hadn't learned how to tune a guitar in standard tuning and would "de-tune" guitars at music stores to sound like the one he had at home. One day, perhaps intrigued by his detuning, an employee at Angelo's House of Music asked Coffey to perform a song. After performing "Day Tripper" with a single finger, the employee informed him that he was playing incorrectly and taught him not only how to perform "Day Tripper" more easily but taught him standard tuning, as well. Around the same time, Joseph Smiel, a German American music teacher at Woodrow Wilson High School, gave Coffey a single lesson, which consisted of showing the beginning guitarist some basic skills such as proper hand positioning and giving him a ripped-out chord chart from a Mel Bay guitar instruction book.

Music stores also provided a way to learn about developments in hard rock and heavy metal. Coffey remembers, "I'd see a white guy [who] looked like he rocked and ask him, 'Which band do you like?' because I wanted to find out about new bands. Now, I knew about the big bands like Judas Priest and Iron Maiden." Tellingly, Coffey searched for "white guys" rather than black musicians for recommendations about rock bands. While Judas Priest and Iron Maiden formed the foundation for his music, Coffey also began taking cues from the punk scene:

> When I heard Iron Maiden, that band really made me feel pretty good about what we were doing because I liked their music so much that it let me know that we were on the right track. I mean, we were already playing hard shit then but bands like them inspired me further. We were just like Metallica and others. We were taking our influences from the New Wave of British Heavy Metal and the hardcore punk. *That's* what made thrash — it was a mixture of those two. The speed and aggression of the hardcore punk mixed with the NWOBHM. Man, we just made a hybrid of it.

Keeping in mind that Coffey was captivated by "A Day in the Life" because of its compositional intricacies, his attraction to thrash metal exemplifies Glenn

Pillsbury's assertion that thrash metal's musical complexity serves to promote masculinist values such as musical virtuosity that are deeply embedded within Eurocentric models and taste hierarchies. In accepting Pillsbury's contention that Metallica's "production of identity through complexity" (2006, 60) rests on ideas about whiteness and masculinity, however, I mean to point out that Stone Vengeance's articulation of musical complexity in thrash metal rests on *opposing* stereotypes about blackness and masculinity in which black masculinity is equated entirely with the body rather than the mind. Importantly, Stone Vengeance uses thrash metal's musical complexity to demonstrate their musical abilities *beyond* those normally equated with black musicians, namely rhythmic complexity and emotional expression, *without abandoning* them as anyone familiar with thrash's speed and visceral appeal can appreciate.

Coffey continues,

> Motorhead — you gotta give them credit, too. Songs like "Iron Fist" and some of that early stuff – that was an influence. Even Loudness from Japan — we listened to all that shit. Venom was one of my favorites, Iron Maiden. Judas Priest before all of them 'cause I was into the Priest, all their '70s stuff. The early stuff like "Sad Wings of Destiny" and "Sin After Sin" and "Stained Class," all of that. Great shit. That's where we got our scream from — Rob Halford was the man. Raven, John Gallagher. Those were the two guys, we started going [screams]. Also, a small part, Robert Plant.

Coffey and his band mates drew from the same pool of artists as their white counterparts despite their relative isolation in a working-class black neighborhood. In an ironic reversal of white teens who accessed black R&B and early rock and roll through radio broadcasts in the 1950s, the members of Stone Vengeance gained entrance into the hard rock world of the 1970s through the countercultural mediation provided by predominantly white DJs on independent FM radio stations. The ironies would not end there.

Black Thrash Routes

Similar to burgeoning teen-aged rock guitarists everywhere, Coffey decided to start a band, recalling, "It was a rock band from the beginning. I wanted to *rock*. Boston [and Ted] Nugent were already in my head." However, as a largely self-taught guitarist who was attending a predominantly African American high school, Coffey had little of the conventional connections to other heavy metal musicians that white suburban schools in the United States offered to most heavy metal fans. Instead, Coffey tried to meet likely band members through music stores. Coffey recalls, "[Bassist] Anthony [Starks] and I were hanging out at Guitar Center,[17] trying to get another guitar player. We'd meet different white guys because [by the mid-1970s], I [had given] up on meeting another brother

[African American] who wanted to [perform rock music]. So, I'd try to meet these white guys. They'd talk good but they wouldn't show up to rehearsal, they wouldn't even call back." Still, a white musician briefly held the drum chair in Stone Vengeance: "Arthur would hang with us at the house and at school. He was kind of a loner because there weren't that many white people at Woodrow Wilson [high school] at that time." But soon, Arthur quit, telling Coffey, "I just can't see a black rock band making it."[18] Eventually giving up on finding another guitarist, Coffey began to envision a guitar-based power trio.

Coffey initially named his band the Dreamers, but after about a year, he wanted a more appropriate name for a heavy metal group. He recalls it was in 1978 when

> It took me a couple of weeks to come up with [Stone Vengeance] because I knew a name meant everything. There was a spiritual base of what I wanted to say but not [as] a "religious" band. It's not that. I just know that people use religion to control people in certain ways so I'm not into following [any religion] under [those conditions].
>
> So, the "stone" is from the Bible. The stone that the builders rejected — that's us. That stone is a people, an ancient people. The builders are the 'civilized' nations of the world. Black people are rejected.
>
> That's what the stone represented to me — the despised, the rejected, the hated. The builders – those that build civilizations — scorned [us], looked down upon us. That has been our experience in this music.
>
> You see the star and all that in our [band logo] and [people] don't know what that means. But it's heavy symbolism. You have six points, each one is sixty degrees, 6 times 60 equals 360 degrees, that's a circle, a circle of knowledge with 6 points of light. You have the skull, which everyone knows represents death. So, it's a balance. Knowledge is power, knowledge is life — if you have knowledge, you can survive.

As Walser cogently argues, "Heavy metal's fascination with the dark side of life gives evidence of both dissatisfaction with dominant identities and institutions and an intense yearning for reconciliation with something more credible" (1993, xvi–xvii). Clearly, Coffey sees Stone Vengeance as part of a long history of enduring African American cultural resistance, embodying the "rejected" legacy and rhetorically prevailing over death. Stone Vengeance's preoccupation with heavy metal iconography and a shared ideological resonance with its dark themes are derived from a legacy of black American biblical "readings against the grain," echoes from the spirituals of black slaves as well as the secular and often sacrilegious concerns of the blues — musical anchors distinct from, for example, the Norse mythology ascribed by Norwegian black metal groups.

In addition to Pillsbury's description that thrash emerged from "reworkings of British metal groups such as Diamond Head, Iron Maiden and Motorhead," Coffey includes the blues as a means to recognize heavy metal as a black American musical practice (2006, 3). Moreover, Stone Vengeance's rebuffs by the music industry echo the marginalized position from which Coffey announces an African American thrash metal band named to invoke the long history of black repudiation of "the builders of civilization." Coffey is unambiguous on this point

> Stone Vengeance has existed and survived by my iron will. I would not give up. I knew Stone Vengeance was a square peg but I have enough pride as a black man that I wasn't going to force myself into a round hole. I was never going to do that. We're nice guys and people will tell you that we're one of the easiest bands to work with in the business. But we're not what you would call Uncle Toms. And that is part of the reason that freezes a lot of people, because in this country, the black man is made to look a certain way and if you can't be used or ridiculed — some people just don't like that. They feel more comfortable if you're in a position where you're not taken seriously. So you can be a joke, know what I mean?

Black Outlaws

Coffey identifies Stone Vengeance as a San Francisco thrash band that emerged from the same early 1980s scene in which Metallica and Exodus cut their teeth:

> Back then, when [the] heavy metal [scene] was starting [to form in San Francisco], the bands that were playing sounded like either [Judas] Priest, Iron Maiden or they were more commercial sounding. But there [weren't] that many bands. There was us, Metallica coming up [from Los Angeles], Slayer, Exodus. And from what I remember, honestly, we were probably the first to come out of San Francisco. Because Metallica was not from here. Slayer wasn't from here. Exodus was from the East Bay somewhere.

Yet, even in an underground metal scene in which they were literal "home boys," Stone Vengeance remained external to much of the social aspects of a scene through which musicians interact in competitive as well as collaborative ways. Coffey admits,

> We were already [blending NWOBHM and punk influences] and I didn't even know we had any peers. *Because I didn't really hang with rockers.* I found out about Metallica through the Record Vault [a well-known San Francisco metal music store in the 1980s]. They said, "You gotta check these guys out." This was when Dave Mustaine was still in the band. And Kirk [Hammett] was with Exodus. When I first saw those bands, I was like, "Oh! This is where *we* belong!" Because, to me, the only people that were doing what I was diggin' was Iron Maiden, Venom, Raven and all those [type of] bands.

Coffey disclosed that while Stone Vengeance never hung out with many other rock bands except when playing shows together, a number of them were fans:

You know, you talk to 'em, you meet 'em [backstage]. [Deceased Metallica bassist] Cliff Burton liked our music a lot. The guys in Laaz Rockit, they liked us. Suicidal Tendencies, they liked us. So many people. [Charged] GBH was *crazy* about us! All the guys in Metallica were cool with us, hanging out with us backstage at the Stone [a San Francisco rock club] when we were playing with Trouble and Slayer. This was when [Metallica] had just gotten signed with Elektra.

Yet despite well-intentioned music industry insiders who offered to manage the band, they all eventually came "up against forces that they didn't anticipate." When asked to describe those forces, Coffey was straightforward:

Well, just the racism. For instance, when we tried to book ourselves into certain clubs. People tell me that it's a shame that Stone Vengeance hasn't been in the Fillmore, hasn't been at the Warfield. There were just a few clubs [that would book us]. We never had a shot like [the other San Francisco] bands. I would see bands in a club like at Ruthie's Inn in '84, and they're getting signed a year later. And I'm hearing some of our influence on them. But we're just getting left in the underground. Exodus got signed, all of those bands were on major labels. Testament, Exodus, Heathen — all these bands benefited from a scene that we helped build. They came along later and we got the least out of it.

Additionally, when asked whether he endured any provocation from African American neighbors, Coffey admitted that he faced "all kind of insults. Yeah, I remember the insults, man. The pressure of that made me more determined." It is not only white audiences who, tacitly or explicitly, exclude black participation in rock music. Black audiences have been "taught" to uphold musical segregation, as well. Indeed, Coffey admits that while "there were always some black people in the 'hood that could dig [our music], but of course we didn't fit in, we were outcasts, man. Definitely Stone Vengeance is outlaws" (Joseffer 2010, 165).

It is more than a matter of increasing Stone Vengeance's audience, however. As Coffey states, it is a matter of personal connection to his own community

The same thing that Hendrix wanted, is what I would really want. [Our audience has] always been predominantly white. [But] I've really always wanted to get black people that like rock — and there's a lot of 'em out there — to come. We already have a good amount of Latinos. But more — I would just like to have everybody, you know, because I'm black. You know, that's still my people and Latinos, that's my people, so you want them to be able to be proud of you. And not to take anything away from the white audiences because a lot of those people have supported us but not as much as they've supported others. I'm aware of that. We [Stone Vengeance] have a few friends. I don't need a bunch of friends, I know who they are. I know who our friends are, I'm very careful about that. But I'm going to tell you, Kevin, all the pain, all the disappointment, I took it the hardest because this is my band. I don't think I've forgotten any of the disappointments, the frustrations.

Under those circumstances, Coffey went about setting up his own DIY (do it yourself) network, recalling,

You know how it was in those days. The network was the tape, the cassette tape. I would always take a cassette, put it in an envelope and send it to fans, whoever wanted it. All over the world, man. I was sending shit behind the Iron Curtain when it was still the Soviet Union. So we had fans there, then. So you can imagine what was happening when a person would get his hands [on it] because it was illegal. And I would get these letters from all over the world. Sometimes I would get money. It would've cost more [to change into U.S. currency] but I would send it to them anyway. And that's how I did it, man.

In 1985, Coffey used his contacts with the Record Vault to promote Stone Vengeance in a similar DIY fashion

I'd take a cassette tape — it wasn't even a demo! I took a boombox, set it in the studio, rehearsed with the guys. So I took it to the Record Vault, they listened to it and they asked me, "Can we sell this?" [Laughs] "Yeah, if you think so." And, apparently, man, they *knew* so. So they gave a copy to Ron Quintana and he played it on KUSF, which is good for us because that was exposure.[19]

Besides being a radio disc jockey, Quintana was an avid heavy metal collector who produced the fanzine *Metal Mania* and whose influence would be crucial in the development of the San Francisco metal scene. But Coffey's attempts to grow beyond contacts with individual fans or the market of a local, if influential, heavy metal retail store were disheartening and revealed the ways in which the world of independent-label thrash metal reproduced the larger music industry's racialized sensibilities. Steve Waksman's important study of the cross-genre impact of punk and heavy metal includes a chapter on the role of the independent, or indie, label in developing the heavy metal scene in the 1980s. Focusing on SST, Metal Blade, and Sub Pop, Waksman notes how each label "did not forsake genre as a tool to achieve their ends." Importantly, however, "Once these labels were established, they did not merely reproduce the already defined aesthetics of the genres with which they were associated [but] updated and redefined in line with changing local conditions and the importation of new sounds from afar" (2009, 255).

Yet Coffey, in describing his own interactions with indie labels, reveals the limits "updating and redefining already defined genre aesthetics" held in Stone Vengeance's particular case

I remember we would get record companies back in those early days that would be interested. So nobody can tell me, "No, it's not racism." OK, in the '80s —

this happened numerous times — I would get a letter from a record label and they would be interested in signing the band. A record company doesn't write you unless they're already familiar with your music and they're interested.

But they didn't know what we looked like. They would just hear the music — "Oh, I'm interested." [They knew we were an] American metal band. They'd ask me for a press kit, wanting to see what we looked like. Then I would send them a picture and they would just back up. Or, this is what they would say – and it's a trip because initially they would be totally enthusiastic — "we're totally interested, send us a bio, send us a picture." Then all of a sudden, they freeze: "You don't have the right look."

It happened so much that when I would get interest [later], I wouldn't send them shit. I'd go make a Xerox copy of [our photo] because I didn't want to waste the time or the postage sending them my music for nothing. I'd rather keep my music and give it to a fan instead of sending it to them when they aren't going to do anything with it. So, I started to just send them a picture and that would end that.

A final example: Stone Vengeance was remastering their first compact disc recording, *To Kill Evil*, and the mixing engineer, Jeff Risdon, knew a casting director who was looking for a heavy metal group for a movie that was being shot in the San Francisco Bay Area. But Coffey told Risdon, "Look, man, I appreciate what you're saying but when they say they're looking for heavy metal, they're not looking for us." But Risdon insisted and, as a favor to him, Coffey called the casting director, telling her that Stone Vengeance is an African American heavy metal band. After talking with the producers, the casting director informed Coffey that the producers felt that having a black metal group in the film would be "presenting a whole other type of statement."

Conclusion

Coffey notes,

> See, when I tell people this stuff, I'm talking from what white people said, not from what *I'm* saying. *We never intended to make a statement. We just wanted to rock.* But to white people, [Stone Vengeance is] "another statement." I don't know what kind of statement exactly — I can *guess* — but think about it, a black band trying to play [heavy metal]. We just happen to be black but we have to be making a statement now. *We can't just rock. So, it shows that we are perceived [through race].*

My central interest has been to trace the roots and routes Stone Vengeance mobilizes in order to tease out the band's claims for thrash metal authenticity and authority based on foundational black American blues traditions. But as the quote above suggests, while Coffey foregrounds Stone Vengeance's interpreting of rock as a black musical expression, he also desires to be known simply as a "thrash metal musician" rather than as a "black thrash metal musician." Yet Coffey's positionality — embedded in a narrative of aural trespassing and sonic acculturation that complicates the links between phenotype and audiotype by seeking to redefine the look and sound of embodied difference in thrash metal — is caught within the complications such desires entail. On one hand, regardless of how Stone Vengeance may simply "want to rock," Coffey is unable to dislodge the racialized terms of engagement set in motion by the band's performances and recordings.

On the other hand, Stone Vengeance makes a strong case for considering thrash metal as a black musical tradition by remembering the links between the blues and rock. The argument not only legitimizes the band's position within rock but also forces a reconsideration of commonplace notions of the links between musical genres and performing bodies. The band's professional experiences underscore the ubiquity of these ideas and highlight the difficulties black musicians face in their attempts to expand conceptions of heavy metal from a space of white working-class masculinity into a more inclusive genre.

Stone Vengeance may be finally receiving overdue recognition. Remarkably, after over thirty years, there is a renewed interest globally for Stone Vengeance's recordings and live performances. The access to worldwide audiences through new media outlets such as YouTube and Facebook has opened up fresh possibilities for the band. Continuing festival appearances and favorable critical reviews speak to Coffey's disciplined work ethic and steadfast determination to keep Stone Vengeance relevant. In fact, Stone Vengeance has been reinvited to the Metal Assault Festival in Würzburg, Germany, along with an offer to tour South America in 2011.

In a largely instrumental Black Sabbath–inspired song, "Wrath Cometh," Coffey sings a single line, "And in the end, we are justified by revenge." The stone, in other words, will someday prevail over the forces that reject and despise it. Indeed, Stone Vengeance's music persists as a vital testament to metal's core principle of individual empowerment rallied against larger structural and discursive forces while allowing the band to demonstrate that thrash metal's roots run deep within the enduring legacy of black American blues traditions.

Notes

1. Interview with author, 10 Dec 2009. All Coffey quotes are from author interview unless otherwise credited.

2. Indeed, the articles that deal with African metal carry titles such as "'White music' in the black continent?" (from http://newschoolthoughtsonafrica.wordpress.com /2010/10/05/white-music-in-the-black-continent/>). While many African heavy metal bands are composed of white Africans, the hypermasculinist orientation of heavy metal

remains wherever it has taken root as a quick investigation of the Myspace pages for black African heavy metal bands such as Crackdust or Wrust attest.

3. In fact, this chapter is part of a longer project in which I will investigate various non-white heavy metal bands including the Filipino American thrash band Death Angel and others.

4. For a view of the rise of a resurgent thrash metal scene in the San Francisco Bay Area, including a brief mention of Stone Vengeance, see Ben Richardson's "Headbanging History," *SF Bay Guardian* (Dec. 14, 2010). Available at: http://www. sfbg.com /2010/12/14/headbanging-history (accessed 2010/12/18). However, of the many bands that came out of the 1980s San Francisco Bay Area metal scene — Exodus, Heathen, Megadeth — it is only Metallica that enjoys a truly international audience, in terms of critical value, musical influence and commercial presence.

5. Holt, 23, 19, added emphasis.

6. See Weinstein, *Heavy Metal*, in which she traces the link between psychedelic rock and heavy metal, beginning with Hendrix; see, in particular, pages 16-18. See also Waksman, *This Ain't the Summer of Love*, for a broader look at the various ways in which heavy metal was influenced by psychedelic, or acid, rock.

7. In an expanded version of this article, I spend some time thinking about Coffey's comment that "people like me and you . . . we're children of Hendrix through the discipline of rock'n'roll." He is discussing people of color here ("people like me and you") and the notion of being a "child of Hendrix" evokes a shared sense of alterity to cultural norms. His ideas about the constituent elements for a "discipline of rock'n'roll" provide interesting avenues for thinking through his workingman's ethos dedicated to a regular schedule of individual practice sessions and band rehearsals.

8. See Kevin J. H. Dettmar, "Racism, Experienced: Listening to Jimi Hendrix — then and now" (*Chronicle of Higher Education*, 2 Apr 2010: B13–B14) for a lucid account of Dettmar's personal interaction with the discourse around Hendrix and the racial implications of that interaction. Coffey also notes that the critical reception for Band of Gypsys — Hendrix's band with drummer Buddy Miles and bassist Billy Cox — was cool at best, suggesting that race played a part in the ways the Hendrix Experience and Band of Gypsys were evaluated.

9. The importance of music stores in the development of the heavy metal scene of the 1980s is an understudied phenomenon. However, Steve Waksman mentions Johnny and Marsha Zazula's record store, Rock'N'Roll Heaven, as a major source of underground metal recordings as well as being "*the* place to hang out for specialist Heavy Metal music on the East Coast" (2009, 235, original emphasis) and emphasizes the role music stores played in shaping local heavy metal scenes throughout the US.

10. As detailed later in the text, Coffey renamed his rock band the Dreamers to Stone Vengeance in San Francisco in 1978. The Black Rock Coalition formed in New York City in 1985. Stone Vengeance was isolated for the most part from other black rock fans and musicians. Unaware of the Black Rock Coalition (BRC) until Living Colour's success gave BRC national exposure, Stone Vengeance has remained outside the BRC orbit to this day due in large part to Stone Vengeance's genesis prior to the formation of the BRC as well as the band's thrash metal orientation.

11. Coincidentally, a Stone Vengeance composition, "I Vampyre," almost made it onto the *Blade* soundtrack.

12. There were a handful of other African American heavy metal groups in the 1980s who formed in the wake of Stone Vengeance, most notably Znowhite, Black Death, Sound Barrier, and Death.

13. The lack of an African American presence in the following books (not meant to be exhaustive but merely indicative of a larger trend) illustrate my point about Stone Vengeance's literal silencing in an increasingly "official narrative" of heavy metal historiography and scholarship: Jeffrey Jensen Arnett, *Metalheads: Heavy Metal Music and Adolescent Alienation* (Boulder CO: Westview, 1996); Ian Christie, *Sound of the Beast: The Complete Headbanging History of Heavy Metal* (New York: It-Harper Collins, 2004); and Natalie J. Purcell, *Death Metal Music: The Passion and Politics of a Subculture* (Jefferson, NC: McFarland, 2003). To be fair to Coffey, he may be referring to the growing acknowledgment of Stone Vengeance in fan discourse.

14. Reebee Garofalo, "Crossing Over: From Black Rhythm and Blues to White Rock'n'Roll," in *Rhythm and Business: The Political Economy of Black Music*. Edited by Norman Kelley. (New York: Akashic, 2002). Additionally, similar to Coffey's complicated view of Hendrix, while he is clearly critical of some of the uses "Presley" has served within rock discourse, he was also frank about his admiration for Presley's music.

15. See the chapter "Genre Rules" from *Performing Rites: On the Value of Popular Music* (Cambridge, MA: Harvard University Press, 1996).

16. For more on the underground FM phenomenon of the 1970s, see Richard Neer, *FM: The Rise and Fall of Rock Radio* (NY: Random House, 2001).

17. A national United States retail music instrument chain store.

18. Coffey only recalls the drummer's first name, Arthur.

19. The "Wrath Cometh" Rehearsal Demo, as it was later titled, included the songs, "Stone Vengeance," "Time is at Hand," "The Great Controversy," and "The Persecution."

All lyrics used with permission courtesy of Michael Coffey.

Chapter 9
"The Time Is Right to Set Our Sight On Salvation:" The Strange Tale of How the Hare Krishnas Came to Play Hardcore Punk
Colin Helb

In the September 1991 issue of *Back to Godhead*, the "Magazine of the Hare Krishna Movement" first published by His Divine Grace A. C. Bhaktivedanta Swami Prabhupada in 1944,[1] the "From the Editor" notes that a "group of teenager kids have commandeered a full sixteen pages of this issue."[2] The editor notes that the publishers of *Back to Godhead* are not interested in hardcore music, they are only interested in the music because of its connection to the Krishna Consciousness movement. The article that follows, "Hardcore Hare Krsnas: The Straightedge Connection," penned by "Bhakta Vic Shelter" (a/k/a then-guitarist for Shelter Vic DiCara) conveys his personal journey to that brought him to the intersection of hardcore punk music and the Krishna Consciousness movement and the pages of *Back to Godhead*. With humor and introspection, DiCara not only relays his personal progression from relatively small bands, Beyond and Inside Out, to his appreciation of New York band Cro-Mags (who have long played with Krishna Conscious imagery and philosophies), to his early interactions with Youth of Today and Shelter vocalist Ray Cappo, to his publishing of a Krishna Conscious hardcore 'zine titled *The Enquirer*, to ultimately joining Cappo in Shelter. This article presents a concise, yet thorough introduction to the players who could be seen as the cornerstones for the marriage of otherwise seemingly at odds worlds of Hare Krishnas and punks. And, while the years immediately following 1991 could be seen as a time when this peculiar and specific scene was strongest, there is more to this story.

At Pennsbury High School[3] in Fairless Hills, Pennsylvania, it was not uncommon in the early 1990s to see a "hardcore kid" wearing a T-shirt featuring Hindu god Jagannath,[4] carrying a *Japa* bag full of prayer beads, and chanting the "Hare Krishna Mantra" between classes. At the time, Ray Cappo was living at an ISKCON (International Society for Krishna Consciousness) temple in the

Mount Airy neighborhood of nearby Philadelphia. He was working on his new
band, Shelter, and launching a new record label called Equal Vision Records
while living a chaste lifestyle as a monk. Cappo's band, at the time comprised of
other Hare Krishna devotees, played the area often—Philadelphia, Trenton, New
York City, and Reading. When not performing, the members of the band attended services, philosophical discussions, and shows. Seemingly always in possession of literature or simply ready to discuss Krishna Consciousness with kids at
shows, Ray Cappo and others involved with Shelter, Equal Vision Records, or
the Philly temple danced a line between cult-like recruitment and seemingly
altruistic proctor for philosophical, theological, ethical, and cosmological debate
and discussion with no hidden agenda.

As a child of a baby boomer, I was delivered a healthy dose of anti-cult caution inspired by a history of the 1960s counterculture's involvement with Scien-
tologists, Moonies, Hare Krishnas, and Jonestown; common corruption and in-
authenticity of gurus, sages, and alternative religions; and a general distrust of
organized religion. But these were rock stars . . . sort of. The better known associates of Equal Vision Records played in important bands, knew important
bands, and did important things (especially in the eyes of a fifteen- year- old
kid). They knew cool bands coming through town playing larger venues and, if
your timing was right, you could hang out with those cool bands too. They were
nice people.[5] On Wednesday evenings, the upstairs of a vegetarian restaurant
called Govinda's on Philadelphia's then-thriving South Street offered free vegetarian food and conversation. But, although the members of Shelter were active
members of the regional hardcore scene (a politically and culturally varied regional scene), they were also missionaries. The devotees, armed with books
written by ISKCON founder Srila Prabhupada, were well-practiced, philosophical queries, and a desire to keep *everything* Krishna-centric: meals, conversations, friendship, and hardcore punk rock music.

Beyond Shelter, entire bands pledged allegiances to ISKCON to become a
"Krishna Conscious band," bands were formed to be Krishna-focused, and
(more common) individual members of bands, many already straightedge and
living an abstinent lifestyle, explored Krishna Consciousness on varying levels
of devotion. At Pennsbury High, a straightedge hardcore band called Concerned
who were beginning to play shows with some of the regional scene's more re-
spected and successful bands like Mouthpiece, Lifetime, and Ressurection, began to make a spiritual shift toward a more Krishna-centric identity signaled by
a name change. The band, now known as Prema, would eventually sign to Shelter's Equal Vision Records and released 1994's *pebble* (while still in high
school) and 1996's *drivel* (a year and a half following graduation). The lead
singer of the group, Mike Corcoran, whether intentionally or not, led a small
Krishna Conscious movement in the halls of Pennsbury High School not unlike
Cappo's leadership in the larger encompassing scene.

As a kid growing up in the local hardcore scene, Krishna Consciousness
never seemed all too alien of a presence to me. There were skate punks, gutter
punks, old school hardcore kids, emo kids, mall punks, poseurs, straightedge

kids, skinheads, vegetarians, vegans, and Krishnas. There seemed to always be Krishnas, and there seemed to always *have been* Krishnas in hardcore.

I was already well aware of the presence of Krishna Consciousness in the local hardcore and punk scene when I first saw Shelter in concert on a cold January evening at Trenton, NJ's City Gardens.[6] Being a nascent music scholar, I had done my homework and knew of Shelter's impressive lineage featuring the former vocalist from Youth of Today and then guitarist from the short-lived California band Inside Out that also featured a young Zack de la Rocha of Rage Against the Machine fame. Beyond that, I knew Shelter was a Krishna band. They were a religious band, a pious band, if you will, of monks. But, among the vows taken by these monks, there certainly was no vow of silence.

Following the opening band—a young New Brunswick band called Bouncing Souls—Shelter took to the stage not from some off-limits "green room," but from the back of the house carrying drums, little cymbals, tambourines, and bells. They danced joyously dressed in flowing saffron robes. They carried upon their faces a looks of peace, intensity, happiness, and seriousness. They (the members of the band and several other devotees) chanted

> Hare Krishna[7], Hare Krishna, Krishna Krishna, Hare Hare
> Hare Rama, Hare Rama, Rama Rama, Hare Hare

This? This was "hardcore royalty?" This was punk? This was supposed to assist me in dealing with teenaged angst? Was my mom right? Maybe the Hare Krishnas were a cult of drug-addled hippies. What's going on here? Maybe . . . but, just as my tendency for teenage rejection seemed to be inspiring me to reject *this* alternative as well, the sounds of jangly bells and small finger cymbals was replaced with the searing feedback of DiCara's Jackson guitar through a Marshall amplifier, and the famed acrobatics of Cappo's kicks and crowd-surfing antics erupted from the peaceful bounce of a dozen devotees' trancelike voyage to the stage.

It became clear to me. I got it. At least, I think I got it.

Hare Krishna Hardcore Punk . . . Yeah, That's a Thing

In some ways, this chapter is an attempt to makes sense of, and answer questions I developed twenty years ago: How did Hare Krishna hardcore come into being? What, if any, is the connection to the Hare Krishnas of the 1960s counterculture? And, why is it that though I do not find this connection between Krishna Consciousness and punk rock music strange, do so many others I talk to ask me, "that's a thing?"

Granted, Krishna Conscious hardcore is a subculture of a subculture *of a subculture*. If we can imagine a subcultural set of Russian nesting dolls, Krishna

Conscious hardcore rests inside straightedge hardcore, which rests inside American hardcore punk, which rests inside "general punk," which rests inside popular music. This is a small and concentrated subculture and, while its popularity did spread beyond the consumption by other devotees of Krishna Consciousness, its niche audience is rather small.

In simplified terms, the story of Hare Krishna–related hardcore music in the 1990s is the story of two interconnected bands: Shelter and 108. Many of the players in this scene can trace a direct connection to or from one or both of these bands, Equal Vision Records, New York City straightedge hardcore, or other related entities. But, in order to better understand the cultural context of Krishna Consciousness' relationship with straightedge hardcore, punk music, and popular music in general, I believe it is important to trace the historic relationship between ISKCON and Western culture, specifically Western popular music. It is my intension that by tracing this relationship, that which may seem an odd and unusual pairing—aggressive and often perceptively violent punk with that of peaceful Eastern mysticism—-to the initiated can be understood, if not appreciated.

This chapter will, by way of historicizing the culture, explore a time line of Krishna Consciousness's influence upon Western subculture as a tool of escapism, spiritual and aesthetic influence, and cultural identity in order to attempt to "make sense" of the seemingly at-odds notions of aggressive punk music and the projected serenity of the inner peace sought by the Krishna Conscious philosophies. It is an attempt at an understanding of Krishna Conscious hardcore beyond an enigmatic "blip" in the history of straightedge hardcore, as it seems to often be dismissed as, by way of constructing a lineage for the subculture. That lineage will include brief explorations of the relationship between Krishna Consciousness and Western subculture; between Krishna Consciousness and popular music; between Krishna Consciousness and punk; and finally the rise of Krishna Conscious hardcore amid the straightedge movement of hardcore. It is my intension to aid in the understanding of both *how* the seemingly bizarre subculture of a subculture came into being and to begin to understand that, although seemingly bizarre when viewed externally, Krihsna Consciousness and hardcore punk is a rather congruous relationship with both positive and negative influences and experiences.

In some ways, this chapter may differ from the other scholarly approaches contained herein in their analyses of aggression in contemporary music in that it will not explore the aggression as much as it will explore the "peace" projected from the Krishna Conscious movement. While it should be clear that punk—along with its American cousin, hardcore,—is an aggressive form of music in which aural aesthetic aggression (overdriven guitars playing barre chords atop heavy drum and bass lines) is coupled with verbal/vocal aggression (screamed rather than typically *sung* lyrics celebrating opposition, "antiestablishmentarianism," and "whatever you got"), the nature of a "Hare Krishna Hardcore" can be confused by the seemingly incongruent messages of punk and the Hare Krishna movement. While an in-depth analysis of the lyrical, spiritual, and cultural context of the Krishnas' relationship with hardcore music in the 1990s is needed to better understand the culture, I believe an initial focus on this scene requires an understanding of the scene, genre, and culture in the historical context of the Hare Krishna movement's relationship to subculture, popular music, and Western culture at large.

Krishna, the West, and the Counterculture

In the mid-1960s, His Devine Grace A. C. Bhaktivedanta Swami Prabhupada brought Krishna Consciousness to the West with the founding of the International Society for Krishna Consciousness (ISKCON) in New York City. Prabhupada, "a descendant in a line of gurus in India, carried on an ancient tradition of Krishna worship and already had disciples in his homeland."[8] He quickly became a "fixture of the hippie scene in New York."[9] It could be viewed that Prabhupada's timing worked well in his favor and in the success of ISKCON. As Robert S. Ellwood notes, his "timing caught the powerful rising tide of what was called the counterculture, which included within its spectrum of concerns a fascination with India and an exceptional openness to exotic, consciousness-expanding spirituality."[10] Ellwood further notes that though the countercultural movement could be traced back to before the "rise of the hippies" in the 1960s, to the beatniks of the 1950s, or the Transcendentalists of the nineteenth century, both of whom shared an interest in Eastern philosophies, mysticism, and exoticisms—the nature of the baby boomers' coming of age in a time in which psychedelic drugs, "tribalism," and a notion that the generation "sensed itself to be profoundly different" coupled with a "new view of the human self as full of potential for radical self-expression and life construction" greatly aided in Krishna Consciousness's rise in popularity.

At the risk of oversimplification, the devotees of Krishna, an incarnation of the Hindu god Vishnu, follow "four regulative principles: no meat-eating, no intoxication, no illicit sex, and no gambling."[11] Prabhupada's desire was to "systematically propagate spiritual knowledge to society at large and to educate all people in the techniques of spiritual life in order to check the imbalance of values in life and to achieve real unity and peace in the world" and to "a simpler, more natural way of life."[12] Amid the countercultural movement of the late 1960s, ISKCON's mission of spiritual knowledge, togetherness and "a simpler, more natural way of life" seemed to appeal greatly to a subgroup of the counterculture of the hippies. J. Stillson Judah cites an unnamed devotee who claims "[Prabhupada] once said that [ISKCON's] best customers are hippies" because "they are frustrated with material life" and that was the "prime qualification." "[I]f you're thinking you are happy in this material life, then you're a fool, and you're not well qualified for spiritual life."[13] As well as being a student of Vedic culture, Prabhupada was also well versed in Western culture, having been educated at Calcutta's Scottish Church College, India's longest running Christian educational establishment.

Although the surface relationship between the Krishna movement and "hippiedom" seems to "make sense" on some sort of aesthetic, spiritual, and/or activity-based level, there are large oppositional issues at hand. Primarily, Prabhupada preached that in order to reach spiritual enlightenment, one had to seek to reject sense gratification in favor of self-realization. This self-realization included a rejection of material culture already common to the hippie movement, but also included a rejection of drugs and alcohol, tobacco, and casual sex. "Krishna Consciousness [is] a substitute for [the] material bondage" of drug use.[14] To illustrate this, [Judah's] conducted a focus group on the lifestyles of several devotees and found that 93 percent of those questioned were "using drugs" prior to joining the Hare Krishnas, 32 percent were "practicing a spiritual discipline, but were using drugs," and only 1 percent "was practicing a spiritual discipline, but were not using drugs."[15] For the drug-addled hippies, ISKCON answered with the promise that one could, through Krishna, "stay high all day."

ISKCON and Popular Music

As well as attracting general, everyday "hippies," ISKCON also attracted celebrities and public personalities. Ellwood notes an October 1966 article in *The East Village Other* observing poet Allen Ginsberg as one of the Swami's "disciples."[16] Members of the Beatles (specifically guitarist George Harrison), following an extended relationship with the Maharishi Mahesh Yogi's Transcendental Meditation movement, became associated with Krishna Consciousness. Harrison donated property to ISKCON, John Lennon "hosted the guru for two weeks at his own mansion in Tittenhurst, England," and "Prabhupada even starred in a San Francisco rock concert featuring the Grateful Dead, Jefferson Airplane, and Big Brother and the Holding Company, fronted by Janis Joplin."[17] Even the not-yet-famous founder of Apple Computers, Steve Jobs, "regularly attended the Sunday Feast at an ISKCON temple" in his younger years and "recollected that special time [. . .] while delivering the commencement address at Stanford University in 2005."[18]

In addition to spiritual influence, Eastern music and Indian culture crept into the compositions and creations of Western musicians and artists as the counterculture's infatuation with Eastern philosophies began to cross with non-Western aesthetics. George Harrison's exposure to the Indian sitar while filming the band's second film, *Help!*, led to an incorporation of the instrument into future Beatles and solo recordings, most famously "Norwegian Wood." The Rolling Stones, specifically by way of multiinstrumentalist Brian Jones's interest, also incorporated Eastern musical aesthetics and philosophies into their mid-to-late 1960s sound, albeit with a seemingly less "authentic" relationship to the philosophy than George Harrison. Songs like the Stones's 1966 song "Paint it

Black" feature the sitar prominently and, amid the lyrical "stretching out" of the 1960s psychedelic movement, the tone of the song could be mistaken as having a relationship to Eastern culture both philosophically as well as aesthetically, but upon closer inspection, no lyrics seem to hint toward an inspiration of Eastern culture beyond the inclusion of the Jones's sitar and the vaguely "Eastern" minor key of the song.

In all, the incorporation of Eastern philosophy and culture into Western music may not extend too far beyond the introduction of non-Western instrumentation, adoption of non-Western time and key signatures, and the occasional referential allusion to Hindu and other Eastern cultures in lyrics, song titles, and imagery. Even this later allusion seems to have less to do with an "authentic" interest in Eastern cultures, philosophies, and religions, and more to do with the following of the trends and fads of the "othering" in 1960s culture. Insofar as he had an interest in Hindu and Krishna consciousness beyond a purely aesthetic creative tool, George Harrison, particularly in his post-Beatles career, may have been of a small minority if not an anomaly in the culture of the bloated rock star of commercially successful mainstream music.

Away from the pop charts, jazz musicians Alice Coltrane and Tony Scott each musically incorporated Eastern music and philosophies in compositions dedicated to Krishna. Alice Coltrane, following the death of her husband, saxophonist John Coltrane, "converted to Hinduism and moved to more direct forms of religious engagement [and] became the swami of [a California] Hindu temple."[19] Her 1971 album, *Universal Consciousness*, features a song titled "Hare Krishna," a wordless devotional to spirituality. As Jurek notes in his *AllMusic* review of the album, "Hare Krishna" is "easily the most beautiful and accessible track in the set, in that it sings with a devotion that has at its base the full complement of Coltrane's compositional palette."[20] Tony Scott's "Homage to Lord Krishna" from his 1970 album finds the composer combining his clarinet with Indian instruments and compositional structures for what could be seen as an "utterly schizophrenic and [. . .] frustrating listen."[21] While "Homage to Lord Krishna" is a rarity in Scott's catalog in that it directly references Krishna in title, theme, and musicality, Scott remained a philosophical force in avant-garde jazz throughout his life, following a brief period of fame and success in the heyday of the clarinet in popular Western music performing with Charlie Parker and Dizzie Gillespie, among others. Following the "death of the clarinet,"[22] Scott devoted his life to the spiritual quest to be "a jazz musician [rather] than rich and famous."[23] This quest, like Coltrane's, was coupled with a spiritual devotion to Hindu philosophies, if not directly to Krishna Consciousness.

Other Western popular musicians have lyrically or musically referenced and alluded to an exotic "other." Musical genres like the "exotica" movement of bandleaders Les Baxter (*Ritual of the Savage*, 1952) and Martin Denny (*Exotica*, 1957) have dangerously straddled the fence of cultural appropriation and "authentic" and respectful incorporation of other musics in Western music, but it would be difficult to associate such aesthetic appropriation as having a more than passing cultural interest in the cultures. In the appropriation of Eastern aesthetics in the creation of "Hare Krishna" music (and related music) in the West, the movement could be categorized as: Western music incorporating Eastern aesthetics, Western music incorporating Eastern philosophies in lyrical content, and Western music incorporating both Eastern philosophies in lyrical content as well as Eastern aesthetics. So, though there was music that directly quoted or referenced Vedic culture and scriptures, or the subculture of "Hare Krishnas" sprouting up specifically in the late 1960s, it seems to be rather rare that that music also did not sound vaguely "ethnic." This is evident in Scott and Coltrane's music, as well as the usage of "exotic imagery" in the music of the Beatles or Rolling Stones. It would be far more common for the nature of a song's "Eastern exoticism" to be musically based and not lyrically based than the opposite. For example, the Rolling Stones' usage of a sitar in "Paint it Black," a song that lyrically references Kennedy and the Judeo-Christian concept of the Devil or the Beatles' usage of the sitar in a song about lumber from Norway may aesthetically appropriate the sounds of India, but the resulting effect is far more a "generic mysticism" rather than a direct reference to Hindu philosophies. Similarly, "Be In (Hare Krishna)" from *Hair: The American Tribal Love-Rock Musical* utilizes the Hare Krishna Mantra in reference not directly to the philosophies of Prabhupada, but to the "beads, flowers, freedom, [and] happiness" of the hippies.

Largely, the adoption of a devotional life and an "authentic" acceptance of the principles of Prabuphada's message, requires a life away from fame, success, and popularity in favor of a pious and austere existence. For example, John Richardson—drummer and vocalist for the Rubettes, a British glam rock band who scored a hit with "Sugar Baby Love" in 1974—turned to Krishna Consciousness when he found himself unfulfilled spiritually amid musical success. Now known as Jayadeva das Prabhu, Richardson did not abandon creative pursuits, leading choirs of Krishna devotees and the penning a "pop opera based upon Lord Shri Krishna's instructions to the dejected Arjuna," he did largely turn away from the *maya* (or "illusion") of secular professional music.[24] It has been rare for one to exist in both words, though others have tried.

ISKCON after Prabhupada

Following the passing of Prabhupada in 1977, the International Society for Krishna Consciousness entered into several years of turmoil, upheaval, and unrest. Now a decade old as a Western phenomenon, Krishna Consciousness was left without its spiritual leader and founder. The leadership of ISKCON was placed in the hands of eleven successors chosen by Prabhupada.

The new gurus were accused of being too authoritarian, too immature spiritually, or simply too insensitive to their peers who had also been initiated by [Prabhupada]. Very quickly, stories began to emerge about the misconduct of one guru after another. Defections by [Prabhupada's] disciples increased and conflicts arose between many who remained.[25]

By the time of their writing, Shinn and Bromley note that in the years that followed the appointment of the eleven gurus, "six of the eleven gurus appointed to succeed Prabhupada [had] been expelled from the movement by the GBC [Governing Body Commission of ISKCON]."[26] The reasons for expulsion ranged from drug use and moral violations, to accusations and legal battles regarding "child abuse and murder."[27] "The decline of the movement began in part with revelations of child-abuse scandals at boarding schools in the U.S. and India in the 1970s and 1980s. Money troubles followed, and their world changed."[28] While it seems that the intention of Prabhupada's appointments was to carry on his legacy in a unified and collective manner, in keeping with his initial statement to "bring the members of [ISKCON] together with each other and nearer to Krishna,"[29] a splintering occurred. "Although ISKCON has been an international religious movement from its inception, temples are incorporated separately and geographical zones vary in policies and procedures that apply to various spiritual, economic, and institutional activities."[30]

So, whereas music is an important aspect to all of Vedic worship in the United States, music, particularly popular music, was more important in locations already connected to popular music. In *Monkey on a Stick*, authors John Hubner and Lindsey Gruson tell the story of two California devotees purporting to work for "Radio KSNA" raising money to "fight hunger in Africa."[31] According to the authors, this was a scam helmed by the duo's spiritual leader. To believe the account of Hubner and Gruson, Hansadutta, a "pure devotee" and one of Prabhupada's original eleven disciples, was an egomaniacal megalomaniac with delusions of stardom and superiority. Because he was a "pure devotee" (one who is infallible by nature), his drug use, inappropriate sexual relations with his followers, and superiority complex may have presented those under his leadership that even his indiscretions must be "Krishna's will."[32] The primary vehicle in which Hansadutta sought to spread "Krishna's will" was by way of popular music. According to Hansadutta: "Western society is so obsessed with rock 'n roll, I thought [the recording of a rock album] might be a perfect way to spread Krishna Consciousness."[33]

Despite this seemingly rational and devotional evangelical method, a method employed by many others of varying faiths and beliefs, this was likely not Hansadutta's sole purpose for entering the music industry. According to Muster, Hansadutta[34] was less interested in spreading Krishna Consciousness through music than he was "for a career as a rock star."[35] This career, it can be assumed, was complete with fantasies of celebrity, fame, groupies, and drugs. In all, Hansadutta recorded at least three albums: *Nice But Dead* (1978), *Nothing to Lose But All to Gain* (1978), and *The Vision* (1979). Devotees sold his records across the United States and the world, "violating zonal gurus' boundaries."[36] Despite the efforts of his followers, and the violations of his associates, all three self-releases proved rather unsuccessful. In all, only the song "Guru Guru, on the Wall"[37] from *Nice But Dead* achieved a minor success in the Philippines.[38] According to Hubner and Gruson, Hansadutta's assistant Michael Pugliese informed a drugged-up Hansadutta of the manner in which "Guru, Guru, on the Wall" achieved its success in the Philippines

> We met a Filipino disk jockey in Cebu who likes Krishna Consciousness, Pugliese said. "He had you on his show and played cuts from the *Nice But Dead* album. As soon as he played 'Guru, Guru, on the Wall,' the request lines lit up. He played it again, and he played it the next night and every night after that. Before long, stations all over the Philippines were playing it.

In 1980, Hansudatta's Northern California ranch was raided in search of illegal guns and ammunition. Though only legal weapons were discovered (the illegal items had been hidden the night before), the German-born Hansdatta was charged with passport fraud.[39] Eventually, the governing board of ISKCON removed Hansudatta from his leadership role, ostensibly ending his official relationship with ISKCON.[40] It also seemed to mark the end of ISKCON's official relationship with the mainstream music industry.

Punk Krishnas

In a 1989 article in *Back to Godhead*, Madhumangala Dasa (an Irishman born Maurice Foley) recounts the path that led him from soccer hooligan to punk musician to Hare Krishna devotee.[41] In his words, he went from caring for nothing aside from Manchester United and girls, to caring for *nothing*, to a socially conscious punk, to an afternoon on the tail end of an acid trip when he unintentionally found himself among a group of devotees. Although he makes little allusion to his music career in the article, Foley's band, the Threat, achieved limited local success in the Irish punk scene of the late 1970s and were early contemporaries of U2 before disbanding in 1981.[42] For him, adoption and interest in Vedic philosophy was an escape from an increasingly violent punk scene in the early 1980s. As Foley states: "I joined the Hare Krishna's [sic.] . . . I gave up the world . . . I sold my instruments and gave away all my records and everything and I just got into spiritual life . . ."[43]

In a similar path, British vocalist Poly Styrene (born Marianne Elliot-Said), who fronted the short lived yet influential X-Ray Spex, became involved with the Hare Krishna movement, adopting the spiritual name Maharani Dasi, and moving into a temple in Hertfordshire, England following the release of the band's debut album and subsequent breakup in 1980.[44] Although Styrene all but retreated from the music industry and adopted a devotional lifestyle, she did emerge periodically to record with musicians such as Boy George (also a self-purported devotee of Krishna) and others she thought were "cool" and "liked what they were doing,"[45] as well as reformed incarnations of her band X-Ray Spex.

Though many artists dabbled in the grab bag of Eastern mysticism, only a handful actually adopted Krishna Consciousness to the level of conversion and the adoption of a monk's life. Because the adoption of such a life requires a strong commitment to the rejection of *maya*, or the illusion of life, presumably musicians whose interest in Krishna Consciousness may grow to a level of devotion in which one would have to reject the "sense gratification" of popular music production in favor of "self-realization," it seems unavoidable to this spiritual development would require one to leave professional music.

The overly materialistic nature of mainstream popular culture and music of the 1980s suggests a continuation of the incongruous relationship between the antimaterialistic teachings of the *Bhagavad Gita* and the "trappings" of rock and roll stardom. In light of this troubled relationship, the almost inherent rejection of such "trappings" by punk and others outside the mainstream music industry suggests a potential for a more congruous relationship between Krishna Consciousness and punks musicians. Despite this, the aggressive, often violent nature of punk, specifically American hardcore music, creates a potentially troubling dichotomy of a quest for peaceful self-realization on one hand and an outward expression of ego, individuality, and aggression on the other.

Unlike the Krishna movement's social attraction to the already largely spiritual hippie movement, the aggressive and often violent punk movement may not seem a "natural" ally. Despite this, the charitable activates of the New York ISKCON temple seemed to fit with the dissension of drugs as a mind-opening tool to addiction and ugliness. The East Coast Krishnas stayed and fed the poor, sought to enlighten the unenlightened, offer solace for the addicted, and house the homeless, runaways, and otherwise disenfranchised youths. One of these disenfranchised youths was named John McGowan, but became better known as John Joseph with his band Cro-Mags. According to Joseph's 2007 autobiography, he was a common thug on the streets of Rockaway Beach as likely to sell you acid as he was to jump you for your wallet. McGowan found solace in a local Krishna temple, assisting him in cleaning up his act, and refocusing his efforts on music.

Though coverage of the Cro-Mags in mainstream media was scattered at best, the band's involvement with Krishna Consciousness was potential fodder for a discussion of the band in similar fashion to how mainstream media treated the Beatles' involvement with LSD or Eastern mysticisms, a point of cultural dismissal. Mark Jenkins wrote in 1987 for *The Washington Post*, that Cro-Mags are "under the influence of Hare Krishna guru A.C. Bhaktivedanta Prabhupada." In an earlier article, Jenkins makes a note of Cro-Mags's incorporation of Krishna themes in their lyrics similarly using the term "under the influence of Hare

Krishna teachings."[46] Rather than focusing on the specifics of Joseph and fellow member Harley Flannigan's incorporation of Krishna themes in their lyrics, Jenkins makes note of the band as a representation of the non "monolithic" nature of punk music. Herein, Krishna Consciousness, or one can assume any clearly *not* punk rock influence on music otherwise observed and even dismissed as "monolithic punk," is another splinter in punk on par with aesthetic values like "funk, metal, acid-rock, and other styles."[47] Despite the influence of Krishna Consciousness into their music, Jenkins notes that the band doesn't "deviate much from the hardcore norm: double-time rhythms, hard-edged guitars and refrains shouted in unison" and that, despite the Krishna Conscious lyrical and visual imagery of Cro-Mag's 1986 debut, *Age of Quarrel*, "Doug Harris and Parris Mayhew's crunching guitars have more impact than Joseph's testimonials." Herein lays an interesting phenomenon in assumptions regarding Krishna influence in popular music and the assimilation of non-Western philosophy and religion in general. There exists an assumption that music influenced by Eastern philosophy, music in which the primary method of delivery of this influence is by way of lyrical content *should*, in some way, also sound "Eastern."

Cro-Mag's debut album, titled *Age of Quarrel*, was released by Profile Records in 1986. The "age of quarrel" is, in Hindu tradition, the "age of Kali" following the 125 years of "Krishna's lila (pastime) on Bhumi Loka (earth)."[48] The cover of the album features an apparent visual and violent representation of an end to this era: the famous mushroom cloud image from the 1954 Bikini Attol nuclear bomb test.[49] While Joseph is the vocalist for the band on *Age of Quarrel*, the songs on the album are penned by bassist (and occasional vocalist) Harley Flannigan and guitarist Parris Mayhew. Allusion to a quest for answers presumably inspired by Flannigan and Joseph's relationship with ISKCON exist in the lyrics, but the only outright mention of Krishna Consciousness comes by way of the album's acknowledgments which include "Special thanks from Harley and John to A.C. Bhaktivedanta Prabhupada for his inspiration"[50] suggesting that the other three members of the band wish to distance themselves from the Krishnas.

While the heavily tattooed and visually "thuggish" members of Cro-Mags employed Vedic philosophy, incorporated visual and lyrical references to the *Bhagavad Gita*, and (at least partially) professed an allegiance and reverence to ISKCON and Krishna Consciousness, they *still* presented the image of punk influenced by Eastern philosophies rather than an outright Krishna Conscious band. As Equal Vision Records owner Steve Reddy recollects, "If you were to ask me what a Hare Krishna was in 1987, I would have said it's a dude with lots of tattoos who beat the crap out of people."[51] To label the Cro-Mags era of hardcore as a "First Wave of Krishna Conscious Hardcore" would be a misnomer on par with the labeling of Minor Threat–era straightedge hardcore as a the "First Wave of Straightedge Hardcore" to the youth crew–era (Youth of Today, Bold, Judge, Gorilla Biscuits) "Second Wave of Straightedge Hardcore." Though Minor Threat may have penned the concepts and tenets of a straightedge lifestyle, thereby possibly inadvertently launching the straightedge hardcore subculture, there was no real scene to speak of beyond a handful of supportive allies. Similarly, although others in the 1980s New York City hardcore scene began to explore Krishna Consciousness in their personal and creative lives, including Keith Burkhardt (Cause for Alarm) and "members of Antidote,"[52] beyond Cro-Mags, there was no substantial scene to speak of.

Even today, the history of Cro-Mags is presented in different manners stemming from extensive infighting within the band. One history is authored by Parris Mayhew at "The Official Cro-Mags Website" (cro-mags.com). The other history is located at cromags.com (without the hyphen), a site owned by former guitarist Harley Flanagan, and is also titled "THE OFFICIAL CRO-MAGS WEBSITE," but does so in all capital letters. Both Flanagan and Mayhew's sites operate as archives for a disbanded band, but a third representation of the band, the Cro-Mags' Facebook page (facebook.com/pages/Cro-Mags) presents a still active band helmed by Joseph. Flanagan's site refers to Joseph's incarnation of the band as the "No-Mags."

> Harley Flanagan WILL NOT be touring with John Bloodclot and his FAKE Cro-Mags. This is misleading information put out by John Bloodclot and his booking agent Matt Pike to deceive fans and MAKE MONEY. They are not presenting the CRO-MAGS since Harley Flanagan WILL NOT be appearing.
> There are currently NO CRO-MAGS gigs booked. Harley Flanagan WILL NOT be touring with John Bloodclot and his NO-MAGS. Keep checking back for updates.[53]

Joseph's autobiography goes into greater detail regarding this split and disagreement between the members of Cro-Mags,[54] but the more relevant confusion regarding the history of Cro-Mags and their positioning within the greater subculture of music related to ISKCON and the Krishna Conscious movement is that Mayhew's history[55] makes no mention of the influence of Krishna Consciousness and ISKCON throughout the history of the band, whereas Flanagan's history,[56] as well as Joseph's history, does.

Straightedge Hardcore and the Krishnas

The heyday of Krishna Conscious hardcore music in the 1990s could be boiled down to two intertwined bands, Shelter and 108, and the groups' respective leaders, Ray Cappo and Vic DiCara. Though both commonly understood to be hardcore bands, the two bands represent two varying extremes of hardcore in the 1990s. Shelter's music is far more melodic, while 108's musical output has leaned toward the darker, more aggressive end of hardcore music

By the late 1980s, Ray Cappo's band, Youth of Today, was beginning to wane. With Youth of Today, Cappo and his allies built a scene on the tenets (née lyrics) of Minor Threat's "straightedge" lifestyle. By the time of Youth of Today's forming, Cappo was already an established personality in the New York

City and suburban Connecticut scenes, having formed bands and recorded a handful of releases under the monikers of Reflex from Pain and Violent Children while still a teenager. When Cappo formed Youth of Today with John Porcelly, the charismatic and athletic Cappo stepped firmly to front of the band as a vocalist, leader, and mouthpiece of a movement. Drug-free, alcohol-free, vegetarian, and a move so "punk" it eschewed established norms of "punkness," unapologetically unhip and more akin to a varsity gymnastics squad (complete with varsity-style jackets) with guitars than a leather-clad, mohawked punk band. "Contrary to the 1960s and 70s, where kids rejected parental dogma by embracing drugs and free love, decades later, Straightedge punks were practicing defiance by rejecting the very freedoms for which their Flower Power parents so valiantly fought."[57]

Youth of Today made several releases between 1985 and 1990. The music was aggressive, featuring a smattering of heavy metal influences beside traditional fast-paced hardcore aesthetics. Cappo's lyrics, barked and growled at listeners, spoke of friendship, loyalty, and other increasingly standardized tropes of the scene. If straightedge hardcore was a movement, Ray Cappo was a venerable leader at its helm. "Yet with [straightedge's] strict and puritanical rules, one could draw many similarities between an austere monk and a Straightedge punk. They are both intoxicant free, sacrificing, indoctrinated (whether good or bad), and giving their life path up to a sort of higher purpose in exchange for a higher taste. A more important distinction would be served by grouping all these aspirants, monks and punks together into one, and you could better divide them not by way of ideology, but rather by underlying intention."[58]

As Youth of Today began to draw to an end, Cappo was forming the basis for a new band called Shelter inspired by his growing interest in the teachings of Prabhupada. Shelter's debut releases *No Compromise* (Equal Vision Records) and *Perfection of Desire* (Revelation), and Youth of Today's final release, a self-titled seven-inch on Revelation Records, were all released in close proximity to each other in 1990. Though this may have created a sense of overlap, or coexistence, of the two bands, Youth of Today was finished and Shelter was the new band. Similarly, if viewed as chronological representations of "real life," the two releases could suggest an "overnight" (or several- month) transformation from "Ray Cappo" to "Raghunath Das," his new spiritual name. In fact, by the time the Youth of Today record was released, Cappo was already in the beginning stages of his spiritual education. This is confirmed in a liner notes photo showing Cappo with a copy of *India's Spiritual Renaissance: The Life and Times of Lord Chaitanya* by Steven J. Rosen, a prolific scholar of Krishna Consciousness, Hindu culture, and vegetarianism. On Shelter's second release, *Perfection of Desire* on Revelation, a conversation between Rosen and Cappo is included in the liner notes, providing a spiritual and intellectual context for the album. Likewise, on the biography page of the now-inactive site for Cappo's *Raw Yogi*, a site on the benefits of a largely raw foods diet coupled with yoga and Eastern philosophy, Cappo seems to suggest that the adoption of Eastern philosophies into his life began before the release of the final Youth of Today and first Shelter records.[59] According to the page, Cappo started to practice yoga in 1987 and his first trip to India was in 1988. Despite this evolutionary timeline, the release of Youth of Today's (a band synonymous with New York's late 1980s "youth crew" straightedge scene) final release on a label founded by Cappo with partner Jordan Cooper (Revelation Records) occurring in quick succession with a release on Cappo's new label founded with Steve Reddy (Equal Vision Records) by a band that would come to embody "Krishnacore," reinforced ideas of cult-like brainwashing.

While the Cro-Mags had employed lyrical and visual reference to Krishna Consciousness years earlier, Shelter's releases clearly mark themselves as more than a punk band *inspired* by Eastern philosophy and culture. They are "Hare Krishna records." Cappo was not a musician with passing interest in Eastern philosophies, he was a celibate monk and Shelter was his mission. The notion of finding shelter in devotion to Krishna is present throughout Prabhupāda's translation of the *Bhagavad-Gita*. In text 19 of chapter 1, the "purport" of the text is conveyed: "[o]ne who takes shelter of the Supreme Lord [Krishna] has nothing to fear, even in the midst of great calamity."[60] This is merely the first of dozens of appearances of the word "shelter" throughout Prabhupāda's English passages in the *Gita*. With this understanding, one can understand Shelter, the band, as a musical representation of Cappo's finding shelter in Krishna.

Cappo established Equal Vision Records first at an ISKCON temple in Potomac, Maryland,[61] then at the Philadelphia temple. As Shinn and Bromley note, "book publishing and distribution was stressed as the central mission and economic activity" of ISKCON, but regional temples also established "private business ventures [. . .] to provide acceptable means of raising funds."[62] While historically, these ventures leaned towards "vegetarian restaurants and incense manufacturing," other temples ventured further away from stereotypical Krishna Conscious activities to raise funds. Cappo's contribution to fund-raising was Shelter and Equal Vision Records (at least until the company was sold to Steve Reddy and his wife Kate). Equal Vision would release many of the first "Krishnacore" albums and seven-inches, including releases by Shelter and 108.

No Compromise and *Perfection of Desire* marked not only a new spiritual direction for Cappo, but also a new musical direction. "Turn it Around" from *Perfection of Desire* features samples from a news report and *Star Trek* ("Captain, we've got to do something") throughout the song. The standard *palm-muted* "chugging" rhythms of guitars are interspaced with tremolo bar guitar dives, and the common "d-beat" drums are accompanied with a little bit of a swing. *Perfection*'s songs move through a variety of genre influence. "In the Name of Comfort" features droney, no wave–style, tension-building spoken vocals with a pain-filled, orgasmic release. "Enough" begins with a surf rock–style descent down the guitar neck before continuing into the album's most stereotypically punk song. Portions of "Society Based on Bodies" sound mechanical and mathematical.

The band, at the time of *Perfection's* recording, consisted of a group of musicians who, though not directly related to the Krishna Consciousness movement, had been longtime friends and collaborators of Cappo. For the purposes of recording, the band consisted of guitarist Tom Capone (Bold, Beyond) and three members of Connecticut's 76% Uncertain (who previously recorded a seven-inch record with Cappo as Reflex from Pain). 76% Uncertain bassist Dave Ware recollected in a 2005 Amazon.com comment for the album: "So different from what I expected. It could have been as simple as a RFP [Reflex for Pain] reunion plus Tom. It wasn't."[63]

For the recording of *No Compromise* (which also produced *Perfection's* eponymously titled "bonus" track) at famed hardcore producer Don Fury's New York City studio, Cappo was joined by devotees "Bhakta Graham" and "Yaso-matinandana das" on guitar and bass, respectively. Also joining the group for recording were Youth of Today members Sammy Siegler on drums and John "Porcell" Porcelly on "2nd guitar." Like Cappo, Porcell grew up in the Connecticut straightedge hardcore scene, accumulating an impressive pedigree of bands including Shelter, Youth of Today, Project X, Judge, an electronic collaboration with Cappo called Ray and Porcell, and Bold.

At the time of his early assistance with Shelter, Porcell was neither an "official" member of the band nor a devotee of Krishna. Much in the same way Steve Reddy's perception of Krishna Consciousness was influenced by the violent nature of Cro-Mags, Porcell processed a similar stance regarding what he initially saw as the brainwashing of Ray Cappo.

> [W]hen you live in New York and you grow up in the New York hardcore scene, the representation of Krishna wasn't [ISKCON guru] Romapada Swami and it wasn't Dhanurdhara Swami [who was involved in an alleged child abuse scandal that may have led to the suicide of a former student, but who at the time was a well-respected leader and scholar]. It was Harley [Flannagan and. . .] John Bloodclot [of Cro-Mags]. So I always thought that Krishnas had a violent edge. Even though I used to go to the Greenwich Avenue programs and I thought that anti-materialism and vegetarianism were really cool, I never really trusted them. Anyway when [a *Maximum Rock'n'Roll* article on Cappo's conversion to Krishna Consciousness] came out, I was telling [Youth of Today bassist] Walter [Schreifels], "Dude! We gotta deprogram Ray! We gotta get him back; he's brainwashed!"[64]

As the story was told to *Anti-Matter* editor Norman Brannon (onetime guitarist for Shelter and co-founder of Texas is the Reason) Porcell and Schreifels's decision not to "deprogram" Cappo was based primarily in the fact that the two could not afford the deprogramming counseling. Eventually, Porcell would become a member of Shelter, moved to an ISKCON farm, and become a Krishna devotee.

Before Porcell became an official member of Shelter, Cappo brought guitarist Vic DiCara onboard to join the band during the recording of Shelter's third release *In Defense of Reality* and subsequent live performances. While Porcell may have come to Krishna Consciousness through Ray Cappo and Steve Reddy, DiCara's interest in Eastern philosophy and Krishna Consciousness creates a parallel to Cappo's interest. Like many, DiCara's first exposure to Krishna Consciousness was by way of Cro-Mags, but his interest in the marriage of spirituality and music may have may have also been fueled by Bad Brains.

> Another real important band in my life was Bad Brains, and they were spiritually oriented with the Rasta[farian] stuff. They had so much energy and I wanted to find a way to tap into that. I remember I pulled a Bible out and I was like, "This isn't making any sense at all and it's not even really telling me anything." For me, there wasn't much in the Bible other than some moral stories and history but nothing that was scientific or philosophical. The deal with the Krishnas was that they dealt with supernatural stuff in a scientifically logical way. [. . .] I was interested in spiritual stuff, but I was also a punk, so it was kind of against my grain to be into a mainstream religion. But here was an opportunity for a religion that was taboo, so it was a real mesh. It was a one-two punch that knocked me out.[65]

DiCara's first band of note, Beyond, also featured future Shelter collaborator Tom Capone, but it was DiCara's second band of note, the California-based Inside Out, that began to explore his common interest with Cappo in Krishna Consciousness and hardcore. It also began to hint at DiCara's similar, yet differing approaches to music, spirituality, and the presentation of a Krishna Conscious image. Inside Out's sole release, *No Spiritual Surrender*, also released on Revelation Records in 1990, marks a more conceptual and aggressive approach than Cappo's melodic and overt approach. The seven-inch contains no conversations with noted scholars on Vedic philosophies, no personal accounts of coming to Krishna, no reproductions of Krishna-related imagery, no dedication to Prabupāda, and no clear indication that this was a Krishna Conscious record. Despite this, when viewed retrospectively and with knowledge of DiCara's personal beliefs, it most certainly is.

For example, the release's leadoff track, "Burning Fight," could be interpreted as a common straightedge lyrical trope ("I will never choose a different path; I will never turn away from you") just as easily as it could be interpreted as a song of spiritual awakening. Whether this is an ode to a friend in celebration of loyalty, or homage to a new spiritual leader is unclear and potentially open to the interpretation of the listener. But, in understanding the nature of Inside Out, DiCara's spiritual interest, the benefit of hindsight in viewing Inside Out as DiCara's move "beyond Straightedge" toward Krishna Consciousness, "Burning Fight" is more a unflinching celebration of and devotion to Krishna as the "you." In a similar manner, the lyrics to the release's title track, "No Spiritual Surrender," present a deeply philosophical questioning of devotion, spirituality, and surrendering to the will of a higher power ("Try to make me bow down to you. Try to take my identity. Try to make me just another pebble on the beach.") rather than a repackaging of direct quotations from Prabupada's writings.

Though it is widely understood that Shelter is Cappo's vehicle, the under-standing of Inside Out as DiCara's vehicle may be confused by the fact that DiCara was not the vocalist and therefore "mouthpiece" or front man of the group. And while it can be assumed that the lyrics of *No Spiritual Surrender* are DiCara's words, the voice is not his. This fact becomes all the more interesting with the knowledge that the vocalist was a twenty-year-old Californian named Zack de la Rocha. de la Rocha would, in the years following the short career of Inside Out, rise to commercial and critical success as the outspoken vocalist for Rage Against the Machine, driven strongly by de la Rocha's lyrics. In the hands of de la Rocha, DiCara's lyrics are somewhat depersonalized and, in their avoid-ance of direct reference, applicable to any number of interpreted meaning. Un-like Cappo's move toward a more melodic brand of hardcore in Shelter, Inside Out is aggressive and driven, utilizing, among other techniques, the use of short repeated refrains and chorus. DiCara would continue this approach following his short tenure with Shelter following Inside Out's demise.

From Straightedge to Krishna

Throughout straightedge hardcore's existence, there has existed a strong disdain for "losing one's edge," or the breaking of the "rules" of straightedge (no drugs, no alcohol, no promiscuous sex), even inspiring the launching of a controversial "Edge Breakers List"[66] (no longer active) on the website howsyouredge.com in which users "outed" formerly straightedge individuals. But, unlike these notions of one "losing the edge" by experimenting with drugs and alcohol, the tenets of straightedge are rendered as entry-level in favor of following the more strict tenets of Krishna Consciousness (additional vegetarianism, antimaterialism, etc.). Therefore, while still "straight," association with Krishna Consciousness seemed to supersede and render needlessly redundant an identity as "straight-edge" for Cappo, DiCara, Porcell, and others. Porcell has noted that prior to joining Shelter and becoming a devotee, he *was* straightedge,[67] suggesting that he no longer held allegiance to a scene he helped to create with Cappo and oth-ers in the era of Youth of Today upon joining the Krishnas.

Vic DiCara's tenure with Shelter ended in the fall of 1991.[68,69] The follow-ing spring, Equal Vision Records released *Holyname*, an EP of highly aggres-sive, emotional, somewhat conceptual music. The album[70] was the label's first compact disc release.[71] Possibly as a result of naïveté regarding the new medi-um, the compact disc, "[d]ue to a technical error, [. . .] came out as one track only, clocking in at 43:51."[72] Because of the "technical error," an interesting listening situation presents itself: the album's listed ten tracks, contained on a single compact disc track, must be listened to as a collective album adding to an almost "concept album" situation.

108's follow-up, *Songs of Separation*, was released in 1996. Soon after the release of *Songs of Separation*, in 1996, 108 embarked on a tour that would mark the band's end until a 2005 reunion. Documentarian Evan Jacobs joined the band for a two-week U.S. tour followed by a month long European tour to produce a video called *Curse of Instinct: 108's Final Tour*. For the recording of *Songs of Separation*, the band had grown from a project featuring DiCara and a group of collaborators, to a cohesive unit with the core membership of Chris Daly on drums and Rob Fish on vocals (both formerly of Ressurection), Franklin Rhi on bass, and Kate Reddy (wife of Steve Reddy and co-owner of Equal Vision Records) on second guitar. But, by the time of the "final tour," Reddy had left to concentrate on her own music and the running of Equal Vision Records, Rhi left to play with Shelter, and Chris Daly left to form Texas is the Reason with former members of Shelter and Copper.

Bassist and Krishna devotee Tim Cohen (Trivikrama dasa) replaced Rhi as a full-time member on bass. For the tour, drummer Mike Paradise (Downside, Bloodline) and guitarist Dan Hornacker (Ressurection) joined 108 for the tour. The band is presented as not entirely healthy, physically whole, or spiritually whole. DiCara was recovering from malaria and drummer Mike Paradise had contracted the chicken pox. While Fish, DiCara, and newcomer Cohen were practicing Bhakti Yoga and were associated with ISKCON, Paradise and Hornacker were not. In viewing *Curse of Instinct*, 108 is not a cohesive band and the tour seems to be the "death rattle" of the band, albeit an aggressive "death rattle." On camera, the band members seem content with the tour as the "end of 108." Fish states, "we did what we wanted to do," citing the band's records and "seven tours."[73] Paradise states, "I think this is the most cynical group of people I've ever hung around with in my life."[74]

"Who the Hell is the Blue Guy?"[75]

In a comment on his *Stuck in the Past* blog, xCHIPxSEM (Chip Walbert) notes the strange acceptance the larger hardcore scene had of Krishna Consciousness. Despite this, he notes, more "conventional" Western religions like Christianity are met with strong opposition. Walbert continues, "Kids supported Shelter, 108 and Equal Vision Records but as soon as the topic of Christian hardcore came to the forefront, it was as if that certain elephant was in the room and everyone was glaring at it."[76] Clearly, while there was a general camaraderie and support from within the culture of Hare Krishna hardcore, the scene was certainly not without its critics.

Early on, *Maximum Rock 'n' Roll* published an article titled "The Truth, The Whole Truth, And Nothing But the Truth, So Help Me Krishna?" in the same 1989 issue that featured Ray Cappo on the cover under the headline "Inside Ray Cappo and the Krishnas." According to Porcell, it was this issue that sparked his desire to "deprogram" Cappo. The article, credited simply to "Annabella," delivers a lengthy and detailed explanation of the Hare Krishna move-

ment's history, controversies, and involvement with punk and hardcore. As Porcell and others noted, Krishnas were prevalent in the subcultural scenes since the
days of the hippies, and since the relative principles of Krishna Consciousness
were not too far off from common lifestyle choices of straightedge hardcore
scenesters, the presence of devotees in and around shows and local hangouts
may not have seemed out of the ordinary. Similarly, for many, Cro-Mags's involvement with and outright lyrical and visual celebration of Krishna Consciousness, and other musicians' more subtle interest in Eastern philosophies,
meant that it was not unusual that Krishna Consciousness and ISKCON were a
part of the cultural lexicon of punk and hardcore. But, it was the high level of
involvement by people like Ray Cappo, already in an advanced stage beyond
initial interest symbolized by the adoption of his "spiritual name" Raghunatha
Das, and his devotion to be a monk whose mission was his music, rather than a
musician with a spiritual interest in Krishna Consciousness, that may be reason
for increased concern.

   Annabella's article begins with an account of the author's involvement with
ISKCON, and the eventual deprogramming process of her husband. Although a
portion of the article goes into "Hare Krishna and the Hardcore Scene Beyond
Straightedge," it assumes that the readers of *Maximum Rock 'n' Roll* already
know the basics, know Cro-Mags's relationship with Krishna Consciousness,
are aware of who Ray Cappo and Youth of Today are, and understand their influential position as "underground heroes for kids not wanting to go along with
their peers regarding drinking, drugs, and sex." The article is neither a celebrato-
ry support of the positives of a Krishna-centric lifestyle nor an in-depth account
of the spiritual awakening of moving "beyond straightedge" to a devotional life
of Krishna Consciousness. Beyond the personal story of deprogramming, the
majority of the article is focused on the incongruent relationship between the
internal history of the Krishna Conscious movement (an unbroken lineage 5000
years old) with evidence showing numerous breaks and splintering, gender inequality, and immoral and illegal practices of ISKCON in an apparent effort to
discredit the movement's influence on the scene. As a word of caution to others
showing interest in the "cult," Annabella offers advice for those seeking assistance in the deprogramming of "brainwashed" individuals and a listing of available resources. Unapologetically biased against Krishna Consciousness, and
specifically ISKCON, the article, appearing early in the rise of the strongest
wave of Krishna Conscious hardcore music, may have influenced some to steer
clear of the organization, but it did little to quash the rise of Shelter, 108, and
Equal Vision Records, who, for a short time, became the torchbearers of a small,
yet devoted and focused, movement.

   In 1993, *Trustkill Fanzine* published an "interview" with Krishna by Josh
Grabelle. Grabelle, careful to cue the intended biting humor of the article, pref-
aces the article with the statement: "Yeah, yeah, some people interview Shelter,
some people interview 108, but I decided to go straight to the man himself. I
now present to you a little chat I had at the temple with . . . Krsna."[77] Throughout the article, Grabelle takes none-too-subtle jabs at spiritual names (Haagan

Das), abstinence, gender inequality, Shelter (Krishna is not aware of them) and Krishna's "blueness." When *Stuck in the Past* made a download of the interview available in January of 2011,[78] it was accompanied by a disclaimer by Grabelle

> I'm not all that proud of this to be honest. I wrote it when i was 19 and I thought it was hilarious back then in 1993, but looking back on it, it's just kinda mean. Ha Ha. No wonder Rob Fish, Vic Dicara, Steve Reddy, and everyone else wanted to beat me up. What did I even KNOW about Krsna back then? What I learned from Shelter albums? Seriously uneducated about it. Granted, the 36 year old me still hates all religions and think (know) they are the root of all wars, but you gotta respect whatever makes people happy right? As long as you aren't killing anyone or impeding on anyone else's rights, more power to ya.

Shelter achieved a limited spurt of relative success (when judged against the concentrated, yet humble success of the band's predecessors) toward the end of its first decade as a band. Over the course of its existence, the band had gone through several incarnations of devotee musicians and sympathetic secular collaborators. As is often the case with "crossover" success, the music had also changed. While never as aggressive or "hardcore" as 108, Shelter's sound began to verge more on a more accessible "pop punk" sound. In 1998, the band achieved a short-term level of commercial success in South America, brought about in part by a video produced for "Here We Go," a song originally contained on Shelter's 1995 album for Roadrunner Records, *Mantra*. According to the Shelter biography on Victory Records' website: "Their video for "Here We Go Again" hit #1 on the MTV Top 20 Countdown in Brazil in 1998 for 3 weeks in a row, catapulting the band to short term super status there."[79]

Though Shelter's popularity and success increased, its identity as a "purely" Krishna Conscious band was waning. Longtime collaborator Porcell left Shelter around the turn of the century.[80] In an interview, Porcell admits that he left the band "because [he] felt the spirituality of the band had been lost over time" and that the past few tours, presumably including tours in larger venues opening for more commercially successful bands such as No Doubt, were "disheartening."[81] Similarly, though Shelter still employed Vedic references in lyrics and Krishna-related imagery in its visual representation, there was a move away from the governing organization of Krishna Consciousness in the West, the International Society for Krishna Consciousness. At the time[82] of the aforementioned interview, Porcell makes numerous mentions of "spirituality," but none specifically of Krishna, Prabupada, ISKCON, or related Vedic culture.

Like Porcell, Cappo had grown to be far less militant than he was in his youth. In an essay appearing at various places[83] on the Internet, titled "Ray Cappo on Straight Edge, Community, Love, and Fanaticism," Cappo attempts to clear many of the rumors that had spread surrounding him by stating: "My crime was when I was in Italy, in wine country, in a particular village in front of the entire band I had a glass of wine with my meal."[84] While Cappo notes that he still loves "natural foods, healthy living, working out, natural medicine martial arts, yoga, enlightening literature and good friends," he has grown to be less militant in his association with the straightedge label and has learned to become "very accepting of people that do drink, smoke or whatever."[85]

In a similar manner, though some may have seen this "softening" of the once youthfully brash Cappo being brought on by his turn toward a more "pop oriented" sound, it was not the first move toward a pop sound by those who identified as Krishna Conscious, nor the first by the scene spurned by IS-KCON's relationship with the straightedge hardcore scene. The Hare Krishna hardcore subculture also saw releases by two bands that not only broke the ste-reotypically male-centric culture of hardcore music, and the perceivable inequal-ity of women in ISKCON, but also the highly structuralized standards of Ameri-can hardcore music in the 1990s. As "Kate 08," Kate Reddy was a member of 108 for the release of *Songs of Separation* and several live performances. Upon her exit from the band, Equal Vision Records released . . . *the way the birds fly* by her band, Project Kate. Though elements of Reddy's hardcore pedigree are evident, the more pop-oriented, even singer-songwriter-oriented album presents a far less aggressive collection of music. But, despite the fact that the overtly noticeable aesthetic allegiance to hardcore music may not be evident, the culture of the album is. As Reddy explains the process in the album's liner notes, the album was recorded with one group of musicians, forgotten about, lost, and re-recorded with a new group of musicians including members of Quicksand and Texas is the Reason.[86]

In addition to her role as a musician, Reddy continues to run Equal Vision Records with husband Steve Reddy, since 1991 when Cappo "basically gave [the Reddys their] first record and an old fashioned Apple computer" when he sold the couple the label.[87] The Reddys oversaw Equal Vision Records' depar-ture from the Philadelphia ISKCON temple, eventually to a permanent home in Albany, New York; and the growth from a niche label releasing solely Krishna Conscious hardcore artists to a "legitimate" independent label releasing albums by Saves the Day, Coheed and Cambria, and dozens more. Additionally, the couple runs sister company MerchNow, manufacturing band merchandise. Though the music may have grown away from Krishna Consciousness, as well as the marketed identity of the label, the Reddys' spirituality remained. Reddy explained in a 2012 article, "We practice Bhakti yoga. The main practice is sing-ing and dancing. The force behind this idea is that you can experience the divine through sound vibration. Everything we do is divine by that principle."[88]

1996 also saw the release of the eponymously titled album by Baby Gopal[89] on Victory Records, a Chicago-based record label that, like Equal Vision, was growing from a solely hardcore record label to releasing a wider variety of art-ists. Boby Gopal's sound was "a combination between British pop, American punk and hardcore. Really crunchy guitars with girlie pop melodies."[90] Where Project Kate's release is introspective, minimally produced, and acoustic, Baby Gopal's release is high energy, in keeping with contemporaneous "alternative music," and overly produced. Where Project Kate contains no blatant Krishna-related imagery (lyrically or visually), everything from Baby Gopal's name, to its lyrics, to its visual imagery seems to be an amalgam of Shelter and No Doubt. Clearly targeted toward a potentially larger, more "crossover" audience, complete with a video for the leadoff track, "Shiva," the connection to hardcore, and therefore Hare Krishna, may not appear evident. Aside from the Victory Records connection, Baby Gopal was a vehicle for front woman Sri Kesava, an Australian-born Krishna devotee and wife of Ray Cappo, who also coproduced the album.[91] Baby Gopal would eventually leave Victory for Tommy Boy Records before disbanding.[92] Today, Kesava is a Los Angeles-based real estate agent[93] and contributor to *Washington Times*[94] and *Yogi Times.*[95]

Conclusion

There certainly are many contentious issues regarding the Hare Krishna movement: gender inequality, brainwashing, legitimacy, and well-documented scandals involving child abuse, drugs, and illegal weapons. Similarly, there are issues with placing too large of a sense of retaining militant allegiances to the decisions of youth. And, while it seems that many of the afore mentioned players in the Hare Krishna hardcore movement have severed official ties with IS-KCON, many of the individuals remain spiritual persons. Perhaps it *actually is* the incongruous reality of living a monk's life in the unavoidably materialistic world of popular music. It could be understood that this problematic relationship is the reason why Foley largely left the materialistic world in favor of a devout life, Hansadutta became so embroiled in such corruption, and Cappo and DiCara chose to embrace the liminal existence of commingled spirituality and materialism as they sought to move away from ISKCON and a chaste lifestyle.

And, while it is important to note that though there is a devotional progression from those who may have dabbled in Krishna-related philosophies in the 1960s and 1970s to the time Cappo and DiCara live as monks who played music, their music presents a situation in which the authentic philosophical interest is not coupled with a potentially dismissible cultural theft of the aesthetics of Eastern culture. This creates an interesting inverse relationship existing in regards to the purely musical presence of Eastern aesthetics to the adoption of Eastern philosophies. The hardcore of Shelter, 108, Refuse to Fall, Prema, or Inside Out was Western and, in relationship with the music of the surrounding subculture(s), rather conformist to the genre's unwritten standards: short simple songs, distorted guitars, largely simplified barre chords over fast and aggressive drums and vocals. The almost inherent presence of "Eastern sounding" music to accompany vague allusion in earlier music led to purely "Western sounding" music accompanying the lyrics of devoted and committed scholars and students.

Despite the seemingly incompatible worlds of the punks and the Krishnas, there do exist two very strong connections to becoming a punk (in some sort of "authentic" manner) and becoming a Krishna: tribalism. Paul Rachman's 2006 documentary *American Hardcore*, based on the book of the same name by Steven Blush, suggests this idea of "tribalism" in the subcultural identity of hardcore music. It could be argued that this seeking of subcultural identity could be inspired by an individual's dissatisfaction with mainstream culture, the commercial or corporate world, or other aspects of "everyday life." Steven J. Gelberg notes a similar occurrence in a devotee's often slow passage from a "normal" secular life to a devotional life. As he explains, for the ISKCON devotee, "the material world and society [. . . are] not quite fully real—dreamlike in its temporality and insubstantiality."[96] Though the outsider may see a person's move away from "normal" society, the insider may view the move toward a "better" reality, community, or existence. And, like the subcultural sense of a "punk scene" offering a certain level of communal or tribal camaraderie and identity, the ISKCON devotee sees his/her "communal lifestyle of fully committed devotees, who view their ashrams—communal religious centers—as 'outposts' of the spiritual world and as 'bases for fighting *maya* [illusion].'" Just as the punk's seemingly nihilistic stance aggressively against the "normal" world is far more complex and far less nihilistic when viewed from within, the devotee's conversion to Krishna Consciousness is one based not only in their own spiritual interest in an "otherworldliness," but is actually a "rejection of the world" in a "protest against society."[97]

Notes

1. Dasa, Satyaraja. "The History of Back to Godhead Magazine." http://btg.krishna.com/history-back-godhead-magazine. Accessed April 16, 2013.
2. Swami, Jayādvaita. "From the Editor: Gifts and Gathering" *Back to Godhead.* vol. 25, no. 5. September/October 1991.
3. I attended Pennsbury High School from 1990 until 1994. As unexceptional as the high school seemed while in attendance (as, I assume, is common to many people's high school experience), coupled with a healthy dose of nostalgia, I have come to find it to be rather exceptional. In addition to running a cable access television station, actually containing the normally *figurative* railroad tracks of which someone could be "from the other side" of, and providing the setting for Michael Bamberger's *Wonderland: A Year in the Life of an American High School* (2002), Pennsbury in the early 1990s had, for lack of a better word, a Hare Krishna clique. And though the number of *actual* students living a serious, devotional existence was dwarfed by the eight hundred students in a graduating class, it seemed that most people were aware that "Hare Krishna hardcore" was "a thing."
4. This may be more commonly referred to as the Hare Krishna "smile" image.
5. In my short time regularly hanging out with those associated with the Philly ISKCON temple, I found Shelter guitarist John "Porcell" Porcelly and drummer Ekendra Das to be extremely nice and warm people. Contrarily, I was intimidated by Ray Cappo. I

realize that this was likely self-imposed by adolescent fandom, but Cappo seemed to possess a seriousness beyond other devotees.

6. Several people have been working to preserve the history of City Gardens and the Trenton, New Jersey, scene including the people running the "No Slam Dancing, No Stage Diving, No Spikes" site at http://citygardensnj.com. Among other memories, the site contains a detailed calendar archive. This particular show can be found in the January 1992 calendar at http://citygardensnj.com/pdf/1991-1992.pdf. I also have a collection of "punk cards" (mailers sent out as postcards) at http://cornslaw.net/city-gardens.

7. There exists an alternate spelling of "Krishna." Often stylized as "KRSNA" with small dots below the "RSN," there does exist some debate regarding the proper usage of each spelling. I will usually default to the more common, Western spelling, "Krishna," herein except when the "KRSNA" spelling is used in a direct quote. Even within the Krishna Conscious community, there seems to exist a fair amount of confusion and debate: http://www.indiadivine.org/showthread.php/445383-KRISHNA-or-KRSNA-Which-is-better-Is-there-a-subtle-difference

8. Muster, Nori J. *Betrayal of the Spirit: My Life behind the Headlines of the Hare Krishna Movement*. Urbana, IL: U Illinois P, 1997, 8.

9. Muster, Nori J. *Betrayal of the Spirit: My Life behind the Headlines of the Hare Krishna Movement*. Urbana, IL: U Illinois P, 1997, 8.

10. Ellwood, Robert S. "ISKCON and the Spirituality of the 1960s." *Krishna Consciousness in the West*. Eds. David G. Bromley and Larry D. Shinn. Cranbury, NJ: Bucknell University Press, 1989.

11. Muster, Nori J. *Betrayal of the Spirit: My Life behind the Headlines of the Hare Krishna Movement*. Urbana, IL: U Illinois P, 1997, 8.

12. http://iskcon.org/philosophy - .ULTRdaU9-Cg

13. Judah, J. Stillson. *Hare Krishna and the Counterculture*. New York: John Wiley & Sons, 1974, 16.

14. Judah, J. Stillson. *Hare Krishna and the Counterculture*. New York: John Wiley & Sons, 1974, 127.

15. Judah, J. Stillson. *Hare Krishna and the Counterculture*. New York: John Wiley & Sons, 1974, 129.

16. Ellwood #

17. Clark, Dorie. "Where have all the Krishnas gone?: More cash-conscious than counterculture, the Hare Krishnas are changing their marketing plan and going mainstream." *The Ross Institute Internet Archives for the Study of Destructive Cultus, Controversial Groups and Movements*. http://www.rickross.com/reference/Krishna/krishna34.html. Accessed 8 mar 2013.

18. Chander, Vineet. "Steve Jobs and the Krishna Connection." *ISKCON News*. 7 Oct 2011 http://news.iskcon.com/node/3939 - ixzz2MySQhfHd. Accessed 8 Mar 2013.

19. Fordham, John. "Alice Coltrane: Skilful modern jazz pianist who developed her own musical spirituality from her husband's legacy." *The Guardian*. 16 January 2007. http://www.guardian.co.uk/news/2007/jan/17/guardianobituaries.obituaries. Accessed 8 Mar 2013.

20. Jurek, Thom. "Review: *Universal Consciousness*." *AllMusic Guide*. http://www.allmusic.com/album/universal-consciousness-mw0000219859 Accessed 8 Mar 2013.

21. Collar, Matt. "Review: *Homage to Lord Krishna.*" *AllMusic Guide.*
http://www.allmusic.com/album/homage-to-lord-krishna-mw0000696368 Accessed 8
Mar 2013.
22. This is Scott's idea. He believed that popular music moved away from the
clarinet throughout the 1950s, leaving him the option of either abandoning the clarinet in
favor of "selling out," or pursuing a spiritual commitment to the clarinet. He chose the
latter.
23. Scott, Tony. "Recent years." *The Musical Universe of Tony Scott.*
http://web.archive.org/web/20070202015959/http://www.tonyscott.it/ Accessed 8 Mar
2013.
24. Adhikary, Patita Pacana das. "Book Review: The Beat of Different Drums."
The Sampradaya Sun. Sept 2011. http://www.harekrsna.com/sun/editorials/09-
11/editorials7714.htm Accessed 6 Mar 2013.
25. Shinn, Larry D., and David G. Bromley. "A Kaleidoscope View of the Hare
Krishnas in America. *Krishna Consciousness in the West.* David G. Bromley and Larry
D. Shinn, Eds. Lewisburg, PA: Bucknell UP, 1989, 15.
26. Shinn, Larry D., and David G. Bromley. "A Kaleidoscope View of the Hare
Krishnas in America. *Krishna Consciousness in the West.* David G. Bromley and Larry
D. Shinn, Eds. Lewisburg, PA: Bucknell UP, 1989, 16.
27. Shinn, Larry D., and David G. Bromley. "A Kaleidoscope View of the Hare
Krishnas in America. *Krishna Consciousness in the West.* David G. Bromley and Larry
D. Shinn, Eds. Lewisburg, PA: Bucknell UP, 1989, 16.
28. Rush, Curtis. "Where did the Hare Krishnas go?" *Toronto Star.* 24 Oct
2010. http://www.thestar.com/news/gta/2010/10/24/where_did_the_hare_krishnas_go.
html Accessed 8 Mar 2013.
29. http://iskcon.org/philosophy
30. Shinn, Larry D. and David G. Bromley. "A Kaleidoscope View of the Hare
Krishnas in America. *Krishna Consciousness in the West.* David G. Bromley and Larry
D. Shinn, Eds. Lewisburg, PA: Bucknell UP, 1989, 18.
31. Hubner, John and Lindsey Gruson. *Monkey on a Stick: Murder, Madness,
and the Hare Krishnas.* San Diego, CA: Harcourt Brace Jovanovich, Publishers, 1988,
217.
32. Hubner, John and Lindsey Gruson. *Monkey on a Stick: Murder, Madness,
and the Hare Krishnas.* San Diego, CA: Harcourt Brace Jovanovich, Publishers, 1988,
219.
33. Hubner, John and Lindsey Gruson. *Monkey on a Stick: Murder, Madness,
and the Hare Krishnas.* San Diego, CA: Harcourt Brace Jovanovich, Publishers, 1988,
221.
34. Muster refers to Hansudatta as "Hamsudatta."
35. Muster, Nori J. *Betrayal of the Spirit: My Life behind the Headlines of the
Hare Krishna Movement.* Urbana, IL: U Illinois P, 1997, 68.
36. Muster, Nori J. *Betrayal of the Spirit: My Life behind the Headlines of the
Hare Krishna Movement.* Urbana, IL: U Illinois P, 1997, 69.
37. https://soundcloud.com/ccr2k/nice-but-dead-track-1-guru-guru-on-the-wall
38. Muster, Nori J. *Betrayal of the Spirit: My Life behind the Headlines of the
Hare Krishna Movement.* Urbana, IL: U Illinois P, 1997, 68.
39. Muster, Nori J. *Betrayal of the Spirit: My Life behind the Headlines of the
Hare Krishna Movement.* Urbana, IL: U Illinois P, 1997, 67.
40. Although it was assumed that Hansudatta was expelled from ISKCON, a
1993 letter from Hansudatta and his attorney claims that of "27 references to Hansadutta

or Hamsadutta" in published GBC resolutions "[n]one of them indicated that he is or has been 'excommunicated' from ISKCON." (http://www.harekrsna. org/pada/documents/ex communication.htm).

41. http://backtogodhead.in/from-punk-to-monk-by-madhumangala-dasa/

42. http://irishrock.org/irodb/bands/threat.html

43. Boz. "HIGH COST OF LIVING — PUNK GOES UNDERGROUND - THE THREAT '78–'81 (Originally appeared in Riot 77 Magazine)" *Riot 77*. http://w ww.wretchfalafel.com/2009/02/interview-with-seminal-dublin-punk.html - comment-form Accessed 5 July 2012.

44. [no author]. "Punk icon Poly Styrene dies at 53." *BBC News.* 26 April 2011. http://www.bbc.co.uk/news/entertainment-arts-13193968 Accessed 9 Mar 2013.

45. "Poly Styrene (Maharani Dasi) talks of her Hare Krishna devotion." http://www.youtube.com/watch?v=sEme4f7d_Wg

46. Jenkins, Mark. "The Cro-Mags, Clubbing Away." *The Washington Post.* STYLE; PAGE D7. November 29, 1986. Accessed June 28, 2012 via LexisNexis.com.

47. Jenkins, Mark. "The Cro-Mags: Krishna Crushya." *The Washington Post.* WEEKEND; PAGE N17; SOUNDS. June 26, 1987. Accessed June 28, 2012 via Lex-isNexis.com.

48. "The celebration of Janmashtami." *New Strait Times (Malaysia).* People; PAGE 11. September 3, 1997. Accessed June 28, 2012 via LexisNexis.com.

49. The original image is available via Wikimedia at http://en. wikipedia.org /wiki/File:Castle_Romeo.jpg. Accessed 9 Mar 2013.

50. Cro-Mags. *The Age of Quarrel.* Rock Hotel Records/GWR Records. [1986]. Probable bootleg of original album which is out of print.

51. Peterson, Brian. *Burning Fight: The Nineties Hardcore Revolution in Ethics, Politics, Spirit, and Sound.* Huntington Beach, California: Revelation, 2009. 115.

52. "Krishnacore in 90s." *XStuckInThePastX: 90s hardcore webzine.* March 17, 2009. Accessed August 31, 2012. http://xstuckinthepastx. blogspot.com/ 2009/03/Krishna core-in-90s.html

53. http://www.cromags.com/shows.html Accessed 9 April 2012.

54. This disagreement came to a head when in the summer of 2012, Flanagan attacked current members of Joseph's incarnation of Cro-Mags with a knife.

55. http://www.cro-mags.com/history.htm Accessed 12 April 2012.

56. http://www.cromags.com/history.html Accessed 9 April 2012.

57. Keshava, Sri. "From the White House to Straightedge punks: Contrarianism is uniquely American." *Washington Times Online.* 30 Dec, 2010. http://communities.washingtontimes.com/neighborhood/omkara/2010/dec/30/white-house-straightedge-punks-contrarianism-uniqu/ Accessed 7 Mar 2013.

58. Keshava, Sri. "From the White House to Straightedge punks: Contrarianism is uniquely American." *Washington Times Online.* 30 Dec, 2010.http://communities .washington times.com/neighborhood/omkara/2010/dec/30/white-house-straightedge-punks-contrarianism-uniqu/ Accessed 7 Mar 2013.

59. Cappo, Ray. "About Us." *Raw Yogis - Take command of your life with the Raw Yogis' Detox!* Accessed September 15, 2012. "http://web.archive.org/web/2 006102 6052423/http://www.rawyogis.com/6/ABOUT_US.htm

60. Prabhupada, A.C. Bhaktivedanta Swami. *Bhagavad-Gita As It Is.* 2nd Ed. Mumbai: Bhaktivedanta Book Trust, 1986.

61. Equal Vision Records' first release, *No Compromise*, contains a Potomac, Maryland PO Box, presumably used by the Hare Krishna Temple of the Washington DC Area, located in Potomac.

62. Shinn, Larry D. and David G. Bromley. "A Kaleidoscope View of the Hare Krishnas in America. *Krishna Consciousness in the West.* David G. Bromley and Larry D. Shinn, Eds. Lewisburg, PA: Bucknell UP, 1989. 17.

63. http://www.amazon.com/Perfection-Of-Desire-Explicit/dp/B0013GHA5I

64. Norman, Brannon. "Shelter: John Porcelly." *The Anti-Matter Anthology: A 1990s Post-Punk & Hardcore Reader.* Huntington Beach, CA: Revelation Records, 2007. 122

65. Burning Fight 117-8

66. http://shzine. proboards.com/index.cgi?board =general&action=print& thre ad =4524

67. RF. "Porcell and Daniel of Last of the Famous..." ThePlaylist.net. [Date of Publishing Unknown.] Accessed September 15, 2012. http://theplaylist.net/interviews /lastofthefamous.htm

68. DiCara identifies the October 13th, 1991 show at The Revival in Philadelphia as his final show with Shelter. DiCara, Vic. "Shelter Tour Report." *Enquirer #6.* Potomac, MD: self-published, 1992.

69. DiCara apparently rejoined Shelter for their 1992 European tour, presumably sharing guitar duties with Porcell, as suggested by Porcell's "Realizations on the road: A Peek into Porcell's tour diary" in the first issue of the *Equal Vision Fanzine.* Porcell states, "Me and Vic took our setlists backstage to get ourselves psyched up." (Porcelly, John. "Realizations on the road: A Peek into Porcell's tour diary." *Equal Vision Fanzine & Journal.* Equal Vision Records. No. 1. [1993].)

70. http://www.equalvision.com/releases/show/126 Accessed 6 Mar 2013.

71. Shelter's *No Compromise* (EVR001), Refuse to Fall's *Soulfire*, and Shelter's "In Defense of Reality"/"The News" (EVR004) were released as seven inch records. According to the *Fonorama* label catalog page for "Equal Vision Records" (http://www.fonorama.cz/firmy/E/Equal%20Vision.htm), there is no record for EVR003 or EVR005. *Holyname* was released as both EVR005 and EVR006 to account for the release of the album on both twelve inch record and compact disc. In a July 2012 email to me, a representative from Equal Vision Records (Paul) suggested that EVR003 "could have been a book or zine." This may be the first issue of *Equal Vision Fanzine & Journal.*

72. http://www.equalvision.com/releases/show/126

73. Jacobs, Evan. *Curse of Instinct: 108's Final Tour.* http://www.youtube.com/watch?v=jK7J6LqEJmQ. Accessed 7 Mar 2013.

74. Jacobs, Evan. *Curse of Instinct: 108's Final Tour.* http://www.youtube.com/watch?v=jK7J6LqEJmQ. Accessed 7 Mar 2013.

75. This is a lyric from the Hold Steady's song "Barely Breathing" in which the singer recounts meeting Ray Cappo after a Youth of Today show in 1988.

76. http://xstuckinthepastx.blogspot.com/2010/12/xdisciplex-interview-i-stand-alone-zine.html

77. http://2.bp.blogspot.com/_M2cfrX-qTqM/TTC20LqXHUI /AAAAAAAAC uI/FsUpgP36U44/s1600/Krsna1.jpg

78. http://xstuckinthepastx.blogspot.com/2011/01/krishna-interview-trustkill-zine-2-1993.html

79. http://www.victoryrecords.com/shelter

80. Jaschke, Magnus. "Interview Porcell (Shelter, Youth of Today)." *Creative Eclipse PR*. 2008. Accessed September 12, 2012. http://www.creative- eclipse.com/file/interviews2.htm

81. Jaschke, Magnus. "Interview Porcell (Shelter, Youth of Today)." *Creative Eclipse PR*. 2008. Accessed September 12, 2012. http://www.creative-eclipse.com/file/interviews2.htm

82. An exact date of the interview is unknown, but the mention of George W Bush's reelection seems to place it sometime in late 2004 or early 2005.

83. While the exact origin (likely one of Cappo's blogs) of this statement has been lost to the fluxing nature of in active URLs and site redesigns, the statement is believed to be accurate and legitimately written by Ray Cappo early in the 21st Century. The interview is contained in essentially the same format at http://forums.livewire-records.com/v5/read.php?1,102169,102214, http://bestoftimesoc. blogspot.com/ 2009/ 11 /ray-cappo-explains-straight-edge.html, http://www.reocities.com/southbeach/breakers/42 88/raystatement.html, and http://www.myspace.com/screamingslave28/blog/392565986

84. http://www.myspace.com/screamingslave28/blog/392565986

85. http://www.myspace.com/screamingslave28/blog/392565986

86. Project Kate. *...the way the birds fly*. Equal Vision Records. EVR 28. 1996. CD.

87. Connally, Siobhan. "MerchNow." *All Over Albany*. Mar 26, 2012. http://alloveralbany.com/archive/2012/03/26/merchnow Accessed 6 Mar 2013.

88. Ibid.

89. "Gopal" is a common name for the infant form of Krishna.

90. de Fontenay, Sounni. "An Interview with the former Baby Gopal front lady Sri." *MusicDish e-Journal*. 16 Dec 1998. http://www.musicdish.com/mag/index.php3?id =730 Accessed 7 Mar 2013.

91. Baby Gopal. *Baby Gopal*. Victory Records. VR46CD. 1996. CD.

92. McGrath, Jay. "Baby Gopal Biography." *Baby Gopal - Victory Records*. http://www.victoryrecords.com/babygopal Accessed 7 Mar 2013.

93. http://www.trulia.com/profile/SriKesava/

94. http://communities.washingtontimes.com/neighborhood/omkara/2012/jan /31/dylan-ratigans-greedy-bastards-american-traitors-e/

95. http://www.yogitimes.com/article/living-green-sustainable-recycling-home-voc-free-solar-power/

96. Gelberg, Steven J. "Exploring an Alternative Reality: Spiritual Life in IS-KCON." Eds. David G. Bromley and Larry D. Shinn. Cranbury, NJ: Bucknell University Press, 1989. 142.

97. Ibid. Citing Max Weber.

Chapter 10
The Cult of Hellmouth:
The Success of Contemporary Hardcore
Eric James Abbey

Within aggressive and harsh music, there may be a distinction made between music that is created to be technically proficient and music that vents frustration and moves the audience. The success of both manifestations greatly relies on the musicianship and talent of the members of the band. When the music and the motivation are focused on an aggressive output with the audience in mind, success is almost always in sight. The definition of success is greatly subjective, but for hardcore punk, metal and other aggressive music styles, the audience moving and sharing a commonality of release is success. Detroit's Hellmouth is the contemporary equivalent to the hardcore of the past with their motivation, drive and aggression. As they are consistently referenced with Cold as Life, Negative Approach, the Meatmen and many others, Hellmouth have reclaimed a past that was somewhat lost. The focus of the group comes from a disdain with the contrived notions of the music community and with everything that has previously existed. This attitude is vulgar to the masses and allows Hellmouth to reconfigure the hardcore from the past into a contemporary statement that is powerfully focused on community. As they continue to play shows around the country, the group espouses a mentality of resistance and destruction to the contrived norm. While this is not inherently different from other groups, Hellmouth drives the audience with their sound first, their ideals second, and their marketing third. The reasons behind the group's formation are the basis of their popularity.

Hellmouth formed when the lead singer, Jay Navarro, decided that he was fed up with the corporate music scene and wanted to vent his frustration. As someone who led the Detroit band The Suicide Machines who achieved success, he knew full well the downfall of "selling out." the Suicide Machines, originally called Jack Kevorkian and the Suicide Machines in 1991, contributed to the third wave of punk/ska and went on to sign with Hollywood Records. With this signing, the band changed its sound and focus and would go on to great success, touring with No Doubt, the Specials, and other major-label acts, gaining fans around the country and the world. The formation of Hellmouth occurred after the breakup of the Suicide Machines in 2006 when Jay was determined to "get back" to something that he felt he lost. He stated, "I was part of selling out what I originally believed in with the Suicide Machines . . . . not by going to a major, but by playing out of the community that was a part of it."[1]

The community aspect of Jack Kevorkian and the Suicide Machines was rooted in the punk elements of giving back to the community and espousing ideals that were predominately left wing and underground. By working with groups such as Food Not Bombs and Anti-Racist Action, the band gained a very dedicated and large underground following. This occurred throughout the United States with the nineties wave of punk, but in Detroit there were only a limited number of groups doing this. Through the formation of a community around the group, Jay and the rest of the original members of Jack Kevorkian and the Suicide Machines gained their success. According to Navarro, Hellmouth is attempting to get back to this feeling.

It is the similarities away from the norms of society that drive the listeners of Hellmouth to react and become immersed in an experience where they feel connection. While these shared experiences are often viewed as disturbing to outsiders they are what create and define the community. In, *Subcultural Identity in Alternative Music Culture,* Holly Kruse suggests that, "Indeed, as much as the word 'identification' seems to imply a sense of belonging, perhaps even more it describes a process of differentiation."[2] This difference is the key to the community surrounding Hellmouth. As Navarro attempts to "get back" to something, he and the band have created a community formed through going against contrived norms. Kruse continues, "Senses of shared identity are alliances formed out of oppositional stances."[3] The opposition is the key to Hellmouth and the community's success.

Before Hellmouth began, Navarro created a booking and promotions company called Defiant Culture, the main goal of which is promoting bands in nontraditional venues. Defiant Culture still exists and is creating opportunities for bands from around the country to play in Detroit and Flint, Michigan, without the constraints of bars. This has also led to the promotion of social ideals and concepts that Jay himself feels have been lost within the scene. The group runs clothing and coat drives at shows held at the Trumbellplex, an anarchist house in the heart of Detroit, and are bringing back the importance of social ideals that were once prevalent within the scene. The main difference with this contemporary assertion is that there is not a demand to follow a set agenda, only to be a conscious individual. When you set the music and message of Hellmouth alongside these social ideals the true essence of hardcore and underground music is shown.

The Formation of Vulgarity

Hellmouth consists of Justin Malek on drums, Alex Awn on Guitar, Jeff Uberti on bass, and Jay Navarro on vocals. With this lineup, an immense amount of power is created with music. Through their two full-length albums they have distinguished themselves within the hardcore world by signing to Ferret Records, one of the most prolific hardcore and post-hardcore labels in contemporary times, for their first album, and Paper and Plastick for their second. From Hellmouth's bio, "Our goal for existing is to take the people back to the glory days of the underground and remind people of the fear, anger and honesty that once existed in a music scene that's since gone soft and has lost all integrity."[4] This statement starts the bio of the band and captures what the new hardcore is all about.

The group's musical power is displayed at any concert through the crowd. As the music starts, the crowd becomes a moving entity responding to the sound as aggressively as possible. For many concertgoers this is the point of the band, to release aggression and to "get away" from the problems of the world. Why then has Hellmouth captured the success of the underground so quickly? Are they simply graced with a great lead singer and musicians or is it because of Jay's familiarity with the music business that they succeed? The answer lies in all of these factors but particularly in the way the message of total self-fulfillment without outside influence is expressed. Herein is the importance of the band for the audiences and people that are not directly involved musically with the group. The message of total fulfillment through self is the key. This is nothing new, but being packaged in such a way with a band and singer that can express it is. The examples of these ideals are throughout the many lyrics that are recorded but more directly within the band's manifesto, that can only be found on a record sleeve or at a live show.

This manifesto appears on a small 8 inch x 10 inch flyer that is passed out at shows. *The True Cult Ov Hellmouth. The Apocalypse and Blasphemy Issue* explains their entire manifesto starting with the front cover statement, "To have a beginning you must first have an ending." It continues with nine sections of "beliefs:"

Metamorphoses: . . .We are hurtling towards obsolescence and gaining momentum at an exponential speed.
Doom: . . . The wheels are in motion and no God nor bastard can provide salvation from the impending apocalypse.
Revelation: . . . Do what thou wilt shall be the law of the land. Walk among us. Destroy Everything. Worship nothing.
Damocles: . . . The river runs red from the lacerated sky while humans trudge on in ignorant bliss.
Death: The misanthrope casts off his robes and shoulders his burden without pity or sorrow.

Truth: The truth wont set you free from damnation. The truth is hemlock.
Peace: Babylon knows little peace.
Contradiction: . . . is everywhere
Ouroboros: The True Cult ov Hellmouth never sleeps.[5]

Each category is further explained for the "initiate" and lays out the band's ideals. This small 8 inch x 10 inch flyer is passed out at every show and has become a way for the crowd to become a part of the band. The construction of the band is based on these elements and the music echoes the themes in the pamphlet for anyone to "get."

The band's focus and outward appearance are full of Hell and damnation but, Jay and the group really consider the message as a positive one. "I just feel that . . . I want to rebuild what I was a part of destroying. I want to take back what is left of punk because there isn't shit left of it. Rethink how to keep it a community."[6] The group continually perpetuates the idea that anyone can be something and someone without constricted guidelines to life. They are not attempting to provide any directions on how to live, just a way to start over. According to Brent Callwood in a review in Detroit's *Metro Times* of their first album entitled *Destroy Everything. Worship Nothing*, "Despite the heavy riffing, though, Hellmouth can very much be defined as a punk rock band. The anti-authority themes alone attest to that. Some will call them hardcore and others, especially those with a taste for overcomplicated genre labels, will call them metalcore or crossover. But make no mistake about it: They're totally punk in the same way that bands like Discharge and Neurosis are punk."[7] These themes of "do it yourself" and "rely on nothing" are throughout the band and remain into their second album.

The second album, *Gravestone Skylines,* asserts the message of the group in every song. Even the way that the album was sold was vulgar to the masses and an attempt to shock the normal notions of record sales. The band, through the Paper and Plastick label, sold thirty-three copies on vinyl that were pressed with the ashes of a nineteenth-century Bible. These editions sold out rapidly and are not playable as records but remain as statements of the band. The records are not playable as the ashes from the Bible used to press the record break up the integrity of the vinyl and force the needle of the record player to skip. The idea continues in the lyrics throughout the record. In "The Calling part II" Navarro screams:

I am a new millennium outlaw, outcast hesh punks one and all, 22 years and I'm still defiant fuck the world, I want to destroy it. But this can never die, it will transcend time, this cult gives everything, when the end is calling. I disappear in a glass of whiskey, a scrap heap of human misery, something broke down deep inside of me, my war, my hate deny everything (PP0066).[8]

Again, this disgust with the mainstream and insistence on destruction form the framework of Hellmouth.

Vulgarity as Power

While all of these statements are viewed in other aggressive music, it is the way the band expresses the message that appeals to people. Hellmouth constructs itself through the concept of vulgarity and is extremely successful because of it. Aggression is one thing, but to completely revolt against the norm of music in an attempt to vent frustration and not simply sell is something else. That something else is vulgar to the masses and is part of the band's motivation. Vulgarity for a positive purpose is extremely important in a world that continues to renege on its promises for many people. Rock music has always been vulgar to some people and the only way for the music to remain vulgar is through punk and hardcore music. Robert Pattison in *The Triumph of Vulgarity, Rock Music in the Mirror of Romanticism*, defines the attitude of rock groups. "Rock disdains polite or correct diction and rejects refined theorizing about society and politics. 'We are the white crap that talks back.' say the Fall. In describing themselves, they describe all rockers."[9] This attitude is taken further Hellmouth in the way the "crap" screams back. The only way for hardcore music and aggressive music in general to reach the masses is to be vulgar and to offend people. Therein lays the point of it all. How much can we offend?

In our contemporary world, this offense is not easily accomplished. We are generally numb to things that shock and appall. The "Satanism" of 1980s bands like Motley Crue and Slayer has become somewhat of a constructed joke to the followers of aggressive music. Even the Norwegian black metal that comes with ritualistic death on stage becomes somewhat of a cultural expectation in the contemporary world. How then can a band like Hellmouth reach people by using the same themes as these past groups? Again, the answer lies in the message, or lack of message, that they perpetuate. Chaos and destruction of everything is not new, but is needed in the contemporary world. "Vulgar pantheism is abysmally indiscriminate—or said another way, it is infinitely tolerant. The vulgar pantheist finds room in his universe for the atheist and the witchdoctor as well as the Pope and the rabbi. Professing no religion, he accepts and rejects them all."[10] It is this thought process that allows for Hellmouth to remain relevant.

Pantheism is the belief that God and the Universe are interchangeable and that nature and the entire world is a divine entity. The term first appeared in 1705 in the writings of John Toland.[11] With this belief, the traditional viewpoint of God becomes linked to everything and God becomes removed as a higher power or deity and is grouped with nature and everything in the cosmos. This philosophy is full of different beliefs and thoughts on religion but the main line of reasoning here is that every religion, every thought or reverent feeling, is valuable and worthy. The belief also maintains that if there is good than there must be evil and that the way to approach life is through existing with nature and the world. "In many traditional religions salvation has been linked to immortality. Against this, it has been common among pantheists to argue that what is distinctive about pantheism is precisely its disavowal of any hope of personal immortality."[12] This thought has been reconstructed in our contemporary time.

The pantheism that occurs throughout the world today is filled with attempts to define self through forms outside religion. What was once considered as an antireligious statement has grown into something that empowers individuals to claim status within a community. It is with bands and groups that champion this thought that the listeners again find solace in being different or outside constructed norms. Throughout the past hardcore movement, bands gained followers by expressing ideals that went against the norms and attempted to establish a way to live outside the societies that they were forced to be a part of.

Representations of Vulgarity in Detroit, MI

In Detroit and other cities that are experiencing a deluge of economic and other problems, the attitude has shifted to a much bleaker one. It is because of this depression that more and more bands are turning toward harder forms of music for expression. Detroit has always been a place for hardcore music and has given many bands a start that constructed the genre. From Negative Approach and the Meatmen to Cold As Life and the Feisty Cadavers, the city of Detroit has pissed a lot of people off and caused them to form bands to vent their frustration. Hellmouth continues this and leads the way by playing shows with all of these bands. Navarro states, "We're not going out there to make money. We're going out there because we're pissed off at everything there is to be pissed off about."[13] The new wave of hardcore consists of bands like the A-Gang, Snakewing, Child Bite, U.D.I., Year of the Pig and many others that are going back to the first and second waves of Detroit hardcore. The popularity of this music is on the rise all over the country with different subgenres.

One of the most influential groups that gave Detroit Hardcore its start was Cold as Life. The band began with Jeff Gunnells and Roy Bates as the aptly titled Apathetic Degenerates, which led to the Mattress Rats and then Cold as Life in 1988. The most controversial figure of the group was their singer, Ron "Rawn" Beauty, who was murdered by his roommate, Richard Werstine. The murder and the stories surrounding Beauty's life are legendary in hardcore circles and form the basis for many fans, entrance into the politics and violence of the underground. "'He was so angry, dude; just burning inside, just so full of hate,' Gunnells said. 'There were many, many people on the receiving end from his dysfunctional upbringing.'"[14] Dougie Toms, "Sir Thomas," states in an interview for *Hardcore Times*, "'When Cold as Life played, it wasn't just a hardcore scene back then. You had the hardcore kids, the punk rockers, the skinheads; even the straight edge kids came out a lot back then,' he said. 'Ron had politicked it that way, where anyone could come to a Cold as Life show and there wouldn't be no fights. That was really cool because nobody wanted to fuck with Ron, so it was like Ron's band, Ron's show, Ron's night to shine basically,' Toms added."[15] That was the intent of the scene at the beginning, to create a family, but through violence and a hatred of life.

The city of Detroit is a working-class town and a "hard" town. To be brought up in, or in the surroundings of, one of America's toughest cities leads to a feeling of disgust toward those that have not had to struggle or work hard for what they have gained. Members of the scene often cling to this feeling and are drawn into it. Larry Kole, currently of the band Ten Second March, previously of the Jobbers, suggests, "Bands like the Bumpin Uglies, Multi Grain, and Malpractice [. . .] played a show like it was the last time they were ever going to be on stage again."[16] The concept of leaving everything on the stage and performing with a hatred for society, as if you would never be able to play a show again, was essential to Detroit hardcore. This feeling of hatred and disgust appears throughout the hardcore scene. The importance here is that the members of this scene treat each other as family and a support network consistently develops because of this. This perpetuates the ideals of Detroit Hardcore and the people that follow the music cling to this concept of family away from the established norms of family.

Many people in the hardcore scene were a part of groups that were created as alternatives to families. These became known throughout the community as groups that controlled the event and the surrounding atmosphere. Many were bouncers at the club where bands performed and the crowd was aware of their presence at every show. Cold as Life had a following that became the center of many discussions throughout the scene with the founding of C.T.Y.C.

The members of C.T.Y.C. or Colder Than You Crew, were the harshest people at the beginning scene of Detroit hardcore. It was these people that ruled the scene through violence and intimidation, but also took care of those that were weaker and needed help. Today, C.T.Y.C. exists but only in fan-based membership. The original intent has passed, and most of the members have grown up and have moved on to other things but remain as a part of the scene. In a recent interview with the newest formation of Cold as Life lead singer Vinnie "Enzo" Dufour, suggested, "For me it was a rite of passage."[17] Roy Bates added, "It's about fucking frustration you know, people joining together to get through their own anger and frustration of life."[18] The foundations of the scene stem from a concept of unity through violence.

The phrase, "unity through violence," receives many interesting responses in interviews and suggests that the current, older members of the scene remember the beginnings with nostalgia and longing. These responses go from laughter to a look of serious concern for the term violence. Unity is a concept that is consistently thrown around within underground music circles, but the hardcore scene is one that truly represents this across the nation. Any challenge to this unity leads members to become violent, and the main difference between the two stems of Detroit hardcore is this unity, of Cold as Life, versus apathy of Negative Approach. Other scenes around the country have similar feelings, but the harshest continue to remain in Detroit and New York City. Bands that play within these scenes rely on the feeling of unity through violence and harshness, and this feeling is growing.

Contemporary vs. Past Vulgarity

Aggressive music that challenges people to think is again reaching out of the underground. Groups like Oceano, Every Time I Die, and The Devil Wears Prada are gaining acceptance on the feeling that society has turned for the worse and needs to be given back to the fans and people of the underground for safekeeping. The political and economic issues in the contemporary world of 2010 and those which led to punk in the 1980s are very similar. But, according to Tony Vegas, guitarist for the A-Gang and Hi-fi Handgrenades, "Things aren't like they used to be. It's not dangerous anymore. There's no conviction."[19] The lack of conviction that is sometimes felt from the members of the scene is offset with the way the music offends people. Again, the vulgarity is shown in contemporary times. Society needs aggressive, violent, and vulgar music to represent the actual feelings of the underground and many others.

If there is any distinction between the contemporary and past hardcore scenes it is the ease of attaining the music. With the advent of iTunes and illegal file-sharing sites it is much easier to find music today. This has also made underground music more accessible to younger generations. The concept that "it is not dangerous anymore" is accurate only in the fact that it used to be much more difficult and potentially dangerous to hear hardcore music. In *Why Be Something You're Not, Detroit Hardcore 1979 – 1985,* Barry Henssler, lead singer of the Necros, states, "I had never been to Cass Corridor before then; it was the land that time forgot. The front stairs of the building had rotted away and people were climbing up on ladders to get inside."[20] This thought of danger continued into the second wave. As Jay and others have often mentioned, it used to be that you had to go to places in Detroit like the Vegan Grocer and The Trumbellplex to hear any form of hardcore music. These venues were the second wave of Detroit hardcore and the music took on a more social context with clothing drives and social politics being put forward.

The social context of hardcore was felt during the first wave, but really took hold in the second wave of hardcore in the early 1990s. This began with the Teen Idles, who would later become Minor Threat, and others perpetuating the Straight Edge agenda and went on to bands like Earth Crisis and Youth Brigade pushing the agenda to the limit of breaking. In *Burning Fight, The Nineties Hardcore Revolution in Ethics, Politics, Spirit and Sound,* Karl Buechner, lead singer of Earth Crisis, states, "Our goal was to be the best vegan straight edge band possible. We wanted to take our time to craft our music and lyrics and forward a message to the people."[21] The pushing of ideals are what eventually would lead to the dissolution of the hardcore scene, but are again being viewed in positive ways by the contemporary groups.

Aggression is also a key motivator of this music and, in Detroit, can be seen from the beginning of the hardcore movement. The energy of the first wave of hardcore in Detroit and the rest of the country came from the underground skateboarding scene, and many of the Detroit bands came out of this desire to mimic bands from the East and West coasts. Negative Approach and others, like Youth Patrol, began at skate parks and by seeing Black Flag at Bookies and the Freezer Theater in the early 1980s.[22] The aggression and vulgarity of youth formed the foundation of hardcore music around the country. John Brannon and Pete Zelewski, the founding members of Negative Approach, went to high school in Grosse Pointe, an upper-class suburb of Detroit, and used punk and hardcore as an outlet for the frustration and aggression of youth. During this time, punk and hardcore music was vulgar to the mainstream community and meant to offend.

A Community of Offense

The community aspect of this music is easily seen within the movements of the crowd during a show. While many people are content to simply listen to the music and sing along, the audience members that dance are literally throwing their bodies into one another in an effort to rid themselves of their aggression and anger that the world has placed within them. In William Tsitsos's *Rules of Rebellion: Slamdancing, Moshing, and the American Alternative Scene,* he states that, "The members of the alternative scene, however, are all attempting to rebel against various aspects of American Life."[23] It is this rebellion against the contrived norms of popular music that sets hardcore music apart from the other forms of underground music. He continues by saying that they, ". . . want to create their own environment separate from the mainstream in which they are free from all controlling forces and rules, even if that results in chaos."[24] The moshing is offensive to some, but members of the scene are driven to offend and take the opportunity at shows to express their disdain for contemporary society.

Offense takes on many forms and with Hellmouth is meant to cause people to rethink their positions in society. This rethinking may mean self-fulfillment without a constructed religion or mandated societal controls. Many of their songs revolve around the concept of removing religion as an answer. In "Amen, Assholes," Navarro rages against the religion of our time:

> The death of gods lies in our heads. Clinics bombed, someone's daughter's dead, 300 hundred years of this bullshit, top kill for a god that does not exist, no gods, no masters, bow down to no bastards, the death of all lies in these books, in synagogues, in temples and church, a boss worshipped by a mindless idiot, lies, lies, your hands and feet bleed it, your god doesn't mean shit to me (PP0066).[25]

This becomes a consistent theme throughout many of Hellmouth's songs and encourages; not only the destruction of religion, but the rethinking of personal control.

The offense is not only in music that is extremely limited in technique, but also the lyrical content and aggression displayed. The contemporary bands are now adding a level of musicality to the style of Negative Approach and the Necros that forces the new underground and some parts of the mainstream to listen. In discussing the concept of vulgarity, Robert Pattison links rock with the Romantic aesthetic and states, "Rock is the aesthetic of Romanticism vulgarized. The first rule of both rock and Romantic aesthetics is that the world will put a negative value on every genuine artistic standard, so that each virtue in the Romantic of rock aesthetics has its double among the vices enumerated by straight, boring middle-class criticism."[26] The way that Hellmouth and others of the contemporary scene construct themselves allows for this double meaning to take place and demands that people listen.

Through listening to hardcore and participating in concerts, the frustration that builds within is allowed to be expressed and usually released as rage and aggression. The singers, bands, and participants share a common goal of freedom that spreads throughout the venue. For many, this is their only means of expression and is the dominant form of release from society. Johan Fornas, in *Moving Rock: Youth and Pop in Late Modernity* places these members into a shared experience. "The subculture counter public sphere protects (*sic*) them from systemic pressures (*sic*) and offers practical and cultural means for alternative communication and meaning production."[27] This protection is key to the band's development and to those that form the underground scene.

In order to develop these forms of meaning, Hellmouth has constructed a way to be and a system of communication that focuses away from the contemporary notions of society. Through a constructed rebellion and the display of power against the social norm they have established a way for participants in the scene to stand apart from the society that they were brought up in. Rebellion is often viewed as fleeting, but with Hellmouth the rebellion leads to a way of living that is outside of the accepted society. The vulgar parts of the world are claimed as beneficial and become ways to stand outside.

The negation of artistic standards is a dominant theme throughout Hellmouth and leads to the success of the group. In our contemporary society, the underground clings to ideals of destruction and negation. Pantheistic ideals allow for people to view themselves as a part of a greater whole. When organized religion is replaced with a more individual concept, the community becomes driven to stake claims on self. Here is where Hellmouth and other hardcore groups become extremely important to the individual. Hellmouth makes the community wake up and attempt to reclaim the notions of the past. This reclamation is where the band gets its motivation, drive, and success within all forms of music. Through using the past movements of Detroit hardcore as a focus, the group reconfigures contemporary aggressive music into a harsh sound representing the past. Community ideals and giving back to the scene broaden this aggression into a positive outlook within a society that views the underground participants as offensive to the masses. Vulgarity connects the participants through music, dance, and the overall outlook of Hellmouth. "The True Cult Ov Hellmouth never sleeps" and drives the underground into fits of community and reflection. Without the vulgarity and negation of standards, our world will continue to fall into oblivion.

Notes

1. "Jay Navarro — Hellmouth." Personal interview. 19 Nov. 2010.
2. Kruse, Holly. "Subcultural Identity in Alternative Music Culture." *Popular Music*, vol. 12, no. 1 (Cambridge, UK: Cambridge University Press, Jan 1993), 33–41.
3. Kruse, "Subcultural," 34.
4. Hellmouth."Myspace."*Myspace|SocialEntertainment*, www.myspace.com / hellmouth666(accessed August 28, 2010).
5. Hellmouth. *The True Cult Ov Hellmouth: Apocalypse and Blasphemy Issue*. Detroit: Hellmouth, 2009.
6. Navarro, interview
7. Callwood, Brett. "Hellmouth: Destroy Everything. Worship Nothing." Rev. of *Destroy Everything. Worship Nothing. Metro Times* [Detroit] 11 Mar. 2009.
8. Navarro, Jay. "The Calling, Part 2." *Gravestone Skylines*. Hellmouth. Paper and Plastick, 2010. Vinyl recording.
9. Pattison, Robert. *The Triumph of Vulgarity: Rock Music in the Mirror of Romanticism*. (New York: Oxford UP, 1987), 10–15.
10. Pattison, *Vulgarity*, 27.
11. Mander, William, "Pantheism", *The Stanford Encyclopedia of Philosophy* (Summer 2013 Edition), Edward N. Zalta (ed.), forthcoming URL = <http://plato. stanford.edu/archives/sum2013/entries/pantheism/>.
12. "Pantheism"
13. Navarro, interview
14. Moossavi, Ali. "Cold as Life." *Hardcore Times*. 8 Oct. 2006. Web. 31 July 2009. <http://hardcoretimes.net/content/view/54/63/>.
15. Toms, Dougie. *Hardcore Times*.
16. "Larry Cole." E-mail interview. 5 Aug. 2009.
17. "CTYC — Vinnie "Enzo" Dufour." Personal interview. 20 Aug. 2009.
18. "CTYC — Roy Bates." Personal interview. 20 Aug. 2009.
19. "Tony Vegas — the A– Gang." Personal interview. 3 Dec. 2010.
20. Rettman, Tony. *Why Be Something That You're Not: Detroit Hardcore 1979–1985*. (Huntington Beach, CA: Revelation Records, 2010), 85.
21. Peterson, Brian. *Burning Fight: the Nineties Hardcore Revolution in Ethics, Politics, Spirit, and Sound* (Huntington Beach, CA: Revelation Records, 2009), 243.
22. Rettman, *Why Be Something You're Not*, 87.
23. Tsitsos, William. "Rules of Rebellion: Slamdancing, Moshing, and the American Alternative Scene," *Popular Music*, vol. 18, no. 3 (Cambridge, UK: Cambridge University Press, OCT 1999), 399.
24. Tsitsos, "Rules of Rebellion," 399.

25. Navarro, Jay. "Amen, Assholes." *Gravestone Skylines*. Hellmouth. Paper and Plastick, 2010. Vinyl recording.

26. Pattison, *Vulgarity*, 188.

27. Fornas, Johan. "Moving Rock: Youth and Pop in Late Modernity."*Popular Music*, vol 9., no. 3 (Cambridge, UK: Cambridge University Press, Oct 1990), 296.

All lyrics used with permission courtesy of Jay Navarro and Hellmouth.

Afterword
Colin Helb

The chapters contained in this collection represent a varied and interdisciplinary approach to the study of musics, both related and seemingly unrelated. While much of the music discussed in the chapters have stylistic and aesthetic similarities—distorted guitars, shouted and screamed vocals, and aggressive drumbeats—cultural and social variants, often extra-musical in nature, present subcultural identities potentially un(der)recognized by laypersons and observers outside their respective subcultures. Heavy metal, punk, hardcore, thrash, and industrial music may potentially seem like different names for the same animal to some, but to those who have pledged allegiances to these genres of music, and to the cultures surrounding these genres, there are clear and distinct markers that create the identifiers, cues, and badges of identity. That, which is acceptable to one culture, is grounds for dis-identification to another. Leather jackets, Mohawks, red or white laces, tattoos, and/or a healthy dose of distrust of the establishment may be accepted or rejected at a specific time, in a specific location, and amongst the internally and externally defined subcultural surroundings, yet may seem as alien as the overarching mainstream years later, in a different location, and while listening to a slightly different style of music. Similarly, for those of us who study popular music, we hold these potentially miniscule variants—the small and possibly dismissible cultural nuance that makes one band punk and another hardcore—to be the cornerstones of our respective studies. Whether it is musical or extra-musical, the path a scholar chooses to follow in his or her analysis of a genre, an artist, a scene, or a subculture informs and is informed by personal experience, disciplinary education, and culture, itself thereby simultaneously splintering the paths of research and collecting them into a single pool of knowledge.

Granted, when studying *aggressive music* of any genre, there is *inherently* a common ground, in fact, as illustrated in the chapters of this book, there are a lot of common grounds. Now, we could spend umpteen *more* pages attempting to do what has already been done: explore common and distinct subjects and foci of study. We could draw correlations between approaches, explore instances in which similar subjects are understood in different manners, and formulate theses to canonize the study as a whole. We could speak *back* to the chapters that, if you are anything like me, are now, at this stage in your absorption of the previous contributors' work, dog-eared, highlighted, underlined, and penciled full of other questions, ideas for personal research, and even outright rejections writ large with multiple explanation points.

Good. Go with it. Begin your research today.

Though I will not spend more time doing this, I *will* take this opportunity to briefly pay homage to a few important works of scholarship in an attempt to create the coda for our book. These pieces of scholarship have been personally important to my development as a young scholar, but are also suggestions I now make to other nascent scholars just beginning their journey. If for no other reason, they present important stepping-stones (albeit not the only ones) in the understanding that this music truly is worthy of study; that the easily dismissible, loud, and aggressive is not only worthy of study, but is important to study.

Early on in my graduate education, it was conveyed to me that academia is perpetually about ten years late when it comes to the humanities. This is particularly important to those who study popular culture, and is not necessarily a bad thing. We need time to process, right? When I was introduced to *The Aesthetics of Rock*, a book written by Richard Meltzer in his early twenties and at a time when rock music was barely a decade old, I was simultaneously enamored with its approach to taking rock music seriously, befuddled that such a battle needed to be waged, amazed by Meltzer's youth, and angered by what I saw as gross misinterpretations of rock music. With decades between Meltzer's youth and my own, I was, as Meltzer was before being, invigorated by youthful skepticism toward the establishment. And, although Meltzer was clearly on the outside at the time of his writing, he was, at the time of my consumption and in my naïve opinion, part of the establishment at the time of my reading. Strange how time changes cultural position.

When I was introduced to Dick Hebdige's *Subculture: The Meaning of Style*, I again went through a barrage of emotional, intellectual, and cultural reactions to this groundbreaking study. At the time, I was taken with the concepts of high and low culture, big "C" Culture versus little "c" culture, and punk as a serious subject of study. From the beginning of his 1979 book, Hebdige also wrestles with these concepts. "Culture," he states in the first chapter, "is a notoriously ambiguous concept." It is both process and product, and, as an area of study, "rather uncomfortably on the fence between [. . .] a standard of excellence and a 'whole way of life.'" These concepts, these "often contradictory" concepts, became, and have continued to be, personal mantras for me and have continued to guide the way many of us approach the study of popular culture, music, and the media associated with such areas of study.

Subculture is as much a textbook on the approach of popular culture studies as it is an inspirational focused study on the *style* of punk. And that is quite important to the worth of Hebdige's book: it is on the *style* of punk, not necessarily on punk *music*. In fact, throughout the pages of *Subculture*, there is relatively very little on music despite the fact that it is indisputably a "music book."

Like *Subculture*, Donna Gaines's *Teenage Wasteland: Suburbia's Dead End Kids* found its way to me years after its initial publishing. Focusing on the fans, the culture, and the extra-musical, Gaines's study was, and remains, enlightening to the reader and inspiring to the scholar in that it presents not only a justification that the "burnouts" of the "children of ZOSO" are worthy of critical analysis, but that doing so can speak to a wide variety of subcultural studies. And while Gaines does make mention of the "heavy hitters" of the time—Judas Priest, Ozzy Osborne, etc.—she is far more interested and focused upon fans otherwise identified as burnouts and "dead end kids" in and around Bergenfield, New Jersey. While this study, like *Subculture*, does not analyze the music on a musicological level, instead focusing on the culture *surrounding* and *built upon* the music on an ethnomusicological level, it does so on such an academic and intellectual level that the fact that the music is not discussed is never present as a "missing element."

Finally, Robert Walser's *Running with the Devil: Power, Gender, and Madness in Heavy Metal Music* sets a high bar for the rest of us to live up to. Whereas Gaines's and Hebdige's respective approaches are clearly entering the conversation(s) from a social/cultural doorway, Walser is trained in musicology and enters the conversation by way of a more "conventional" manner in his analysis of chord structures, patterns, and tonality on par with some of the finest studies of music theory and performance. Yet, despite this "highbrow" approach, his foci on elements of power, gender, and madness — as suggested by the book's subtitle — are more in keeping with growing popular culture methods of study. Thereby, Walser, in an approachable and applicable manner, bridges a gap between the purely qualitative and quantitative, the highbrow and the lowbrow, and the aggressive and beautiful.

While, as the chapters in this book suggest, there are numerous other worthy established scholars to look toward, other entrances to join the conversation(s), and subtle splinterings yet to be studied and explored, these few examples hopefully lead the reader to not find in the closing pages of this book an end, but a beginning. This beginning, this continuation of the conversation(s) on the study of aggression in popular music and the popular culture of and around aggressive music, is important.

Bibliography

Adorno, Theodor W. 1953 (reprinted 2003). "Zeitlose Mode: Zum Jazz." In *Gesammelte Schriften: Kulturkritik und Gesellschaft I*, edited by Rolf Tiedemann, 123–37. Frankfurt on the Main: Suhrkamp.

American Technology Corporation. "LRAD / Product Overview," http://www.atcsd.com/site/content/view/15/110/.

Anderson, Benedict. *Imagined Communities: Reflections on the Origin and Spread of Nationalism*. New York: Verso, 2006.

Ang, Ien, *On Not Speaking Chinese: Living Between Asia and the West* (London; New York: Routledge, 2001), 34.

Aparicio, Frances. *Listening to Salsa: Gender, Latin Popular Music, and Puerto Rican Cultures*. Music/Culture. Hanover, NH: Wesleyan University Press/University Press of New England, 1998.

Asesino, Susana. "The Nortec Edge: Border Traditions and 'Electronica' in Tijuana." In *Rockin' Las Americas*. Edited by Deborah Pacini Hernandez, Héctor Fernández L'Hoeste, and Eric Zolov, 312–31. Pittsburgh: University of Pittsburgh Press, 2004.

Atkinson, Paul *Handbook of Ethnography*. London; Thousand Oaks, Calif.: SAGE, 2001.

Attali, Jacques. *Noise: The Political Economy of Music*. Minneapolis, MN: University of Minnesota Press, 1985.

Atton, Chris. "Fan Discourse and the Construction of Noise as a Genre," *Journal of Popular Music Studies* 23, Issue 3 (2011): 324–342.

Auhagen, Wolfgang, Chen-Gia Tsai, Li-Ching Wang, Shwu-Fen Wang, Yio-Wha Shau, and Tzu-Yu Hsiao. 2009. "Aggressiveness of the Growl-Like Timbre: Acoustic Characteristics, Musical Implications, and Biomechanical Mechanisms." *Music Perception* 27.3: 209–21.

Bailes, Sara Jane. *Performance Theatre and the Politics of Failure: Forced Entertainment, Goat Island, Elevator Repair Service*. New York: Routledge, 2011.

Barootes, Ben. 2007. "Nobody's Meat: Freedom through Monstrosity in Contemporary British Fiction." In *Monsters and the Monstrous: Myths and Metaphors of Enduring Evil*, edited by Niall Scott, 187–99. Amsterdam: Editions Rodopi.

Barron, Lee, and Ian Inglis. 2009. "Scary Movies, Scary Music: Uses and Unities of Heavy Metal in the Contemporary Horror Film." In *Terror Tracks: Music, Sound and Horror Cinema*, edited by Philip Hayward, 186–97. London: Equinox.

Barthes, Roland. 1977. "The Grain of the Voice." In *Image—Music—Text*, translated by Stephen Heath, 179–89. London: Fontana.

Bartz, Christina. 2006. "Außergewöhnliche Geschichten von normaler Mediennutzung." *Transkriptionen* 7: 15–19. Beggy, Carol and March Shanahan, "The Adams Family, revisited," *The Adams Family, Revisited—The Boston Globe*, April 23, 2008, http://www.boston.com /lifestyle/food/articles/2008/04/23/the_adams_family_revisited/.

Berland, Jody. "Postmusics." In *Sonic Synergies: Music, Technology and Community, Identity*. Edited by Gerry Bloustien, Margaret Peters, and Susan Luckman, 27–38. Burlington, VT: Ashgate, 2008.

Bey, Hakim. *T. A. Z.: The Temporary Autonomous Zone, Ontological Anarchy, Poetic Terrorism*. Brooklyn, NY: Autonomedia, 1985.

Bigelow, Bruce V. "Device Helped Thwart Pirates." *San Diego Union-Tribune*, November 9, 2005, http://legacy.signonsandiego.com/uniontrib/20051109/news_1b9cruise. html.

Blanchard, J.M. "Of Cannibalism and Autobiography," *MLN* 93, no. 4 (May 1, 1978).

Blush, Stephen. *American Hardcore: A Tribal History*. Los Angeles: Feral House, 2001.

Bogue, Ronald. 2004. "Violence in Three Shades of Metal: Death, Doom and Black." In *Deleuze and Music*, edited by Ian Buchanan and Marcel Swiboda, 95–117. Edinburgh: Edinburgh University Press.

Brannon, Norman. *The Anti-Matter Anthology: A 1990s Post-Punk & Hardcore Reader*. Huntington Beach, CA: Revelation Books, 2007.

Bromley, David G., and Larry D. Shinn, Eds. *Krishna Consciousness in the West*. Lewisburg: Bucknell UP, 1989

Bugs, Tom. "Weevils: BugBrand, Audio Electronics." Bugbrand.co.uk, http://www.bugbrand.co.uk/index.php?main_page=index&cPath=1_4& zenid=2e33e55d3d6f95cfe8487f883c27f8e9.

Cage, John. *Silence: Lectures and Writings by John Cage*. Middletown, CT: Wesleyan University Press, 1973.

Cascone, Kim. "The Aesthetics of Failure: 'Post-Digital' Tendencies in Contemporary Computer Music." *Computer Music Journal* 24, no. 4 (Winter 2002): 12–18.

Chion, Michel. 1999. *The Voice in Cinema*. Translated by Claudia Gorbman. New York: Columbia University Press.

———. 2009. *Film, a Sound Art*. Translated by Claudia Gorbman. New York: Columbia University Press.

Christe, Ian. 2003. *Sound of the Beast: The Complete Headbanging History of Heavy Metal*. New York: HarperCollins.

Clendinning, Elizabeth A., and Kathleen McAuley. 2010. "The Call of Cthulhu: Narrativity of the Cult in Metal." In *The Metal Void: First Gatherings*, edited by Niall Scott and Imke Von Helden, 245–56. Oxford: Inter-Disciplinary Press.

Cogan, Brian "Do they owe us a living? Of Course they do!" Crass, throbbing Gristle and Anarchy and radicalism in Early English Punk rock" *The Journal for the Study of Radicalism*, Vol 1, No. 2 2007, 77–90.

Cogan, Brian *The Punk Encyclopedia* New York: (New York: Sterling, 2008).

Cohen, Jeffrey Jerome. 1996. "Monster Culture (Seven Theses)." In *Monster Theory: Reading Culture*, edited by Jeffrey Jerome Cohen, 3–25. Minneapolis: University of Minnesota Press.

Cone, Edward T. *The Composer's Voice.* Berkeley: University of California Press, 1974.

Cornelius, Adam. *People Who Do Noise,* DVD. Directed by Adam Cornelius. Portland OR: Cold Hands Video, 2007.

Cusick, Suzanne. "'You are in a place that is out of the world . . .': Music in the Detention Camps of the Global War on Terror." *Journal of the Society for American Music* 2 (2008): 1–26.

Dasa, Madhumangala. "From Punk to Monk." *Back to Godhead.* Vol. 24, No. 10. October 1st, 1989. http://backtogodhead.in/from-punk-to-monk-by-madhumangala-dasa/ Accessed 6 Mar 2013.

Demers, Joanna. *Listening Through the Noise: The Aesthetics of Experimental Electronic Music,* New York: Oxford, 2010.

Daniel, Drew *33 $^{1}_{3}$ 20 Jazz Funk Greats* (New York: Continuum, 2008).

Daynes, Sarah. "The musical construction of diaspora: the case of reggae and Rastafari." *Music, Space and Place: Popular Music and Cultural Identity*, Ashgate Popular and Folk Music Series (Aldershot; Burlington, VT: Ashgate, 2004), 25–27.

de Certeau, Michel. *The Practice of Everyday Life* (Berkeley: University of California Press, 1984): xviii-xix.

Doyle, Peter, *Echo and Reverb: Fabricating Space in Popular Music, 1900-1960*, 1st ed, Music/culture (Middletown, Conn: Wesleyan University Press, 2005), 176–177.

Dunn, Sam, and Scot McFadyen. *Global Metal.* USA: Warner Home Video, 2009.

Dyer, Simon "Throbbing Gristle Biography" in *RE/Search #4/5,* V. Vale ed. (San Francisco: Re/Search Publications, 2007)

Eckers, Cornelia, Diana Hütz, Malte Kob, Peter Murphy, Diana Houben, and Bernhard Lehnert. 2009. "Voice Production in Death Metal Singers." *Proceedings NAG/DAGA2009* http://www.eti.hfmetmold.de/forschun g/Publications/media/voiceproductiondeathmetalsingers.pdf.

Erbe, Marcus. 2009. "Elektroakustische Musik = kybernetische Musik? Versuch einer Ortsbestimmung." In *Ordnung undKontingenz: Das kybernetische Modell in den Künsten*, edited by Hans Esselborn, 188–99. Würzburg: Königshausen und Neumann.

Fanon, Frantz. *The Wretched of the Earth*. New York,: Grove Press, 1965.

Fernández, Ronald. *The Disenchanted Island: Puerto Rico and the United States in the Twentieth Centur.y* Florida: Praeger, 1996.

Forster, Jason. 2008. *Commodified Evil's Wayward Children: Black Metal and Death Metal as Purveyors of an Alternative Form of Modern Escapism.* Saarbrücken: VDM.

Frith, Simon, *Sound Effects: Youth, Leisure, and the Politics of Rock'n'roll*, 1st American ed (New York: Pantheon Books, 1981), 37–38.

Frith, Simon, *Performing Rites: On the Value of Popular Music* (Cambridge, Mass: Harvard University Press, 1996), 152–157.

Ford, Simon *Wreckers of Civilization: The Story of COUM Transmissions and Throbbing Gristle* (England: Black Dog Publishing 1999).

Fornas, Johan. "Moving Rock: Youth and Pop in Late Modernity." *Popular Music*, Vol 9., No. 3, (Cambridge, UK: Cambridge University Press, Oct 1990), 296.

Ghazala, Reed. *Circuit Bending: Build Your Own Alien Instruments.* Indianapolis: Wiley Publishing, 2005.

GinSatoh. "Hanatarashi Hanatarashi part 2." http://www5a.biglobe.ne.jp/~gin/rock/japan/hanatarasi/hanatarashi2/hanatarashi2.html

Goc, Nicola. 2007. "'Monstrous Mothers' and the Media." In *Monsters and the Monstrous: Myths and Metaphors of Enduring Evil*, edited by Niall Scott, 149–65. Amsterdam: Editions Rodopi.

Goodman, Steve. *Sonic Warfare: Sound, Affect, and the Ecology of Fear.* Cambridge, Mass. and London: MIT Press, 2010.

Gosling, Tim. "'Not For Sale': The Underground Network of Anarcho-Punk." In *Music Scenes :Local, Translocal, and Virtual.* Edited by Andy Bennett and Richard A. Peterson, 168–86 Nashville, TN: Vanderbilt University Press, 2004.

Grawunder, Sven. 1999. *Obertongesang versus Kehlgesang: Die Erforschung eines besonderen Stimmgebrauchs.* Unpublished diploma thesis, Martin-Luther-University Halle-Wittenberg http://email.eva.mpg.de/~grawunde/KehlgesangversObertongesang.pdf.

Grosz, Elizabeth. "Embodied Utopias: The Time of Architecture." Chap. 8 in *Architecture from the Outside: Essays on Virtual and Real Space,* 131–150. Cambridge, Mass: The MIT Press, 2001.

Haenfler, Ross. *Straight Edge: Hardcore Punk, Clean-Living Youth, and Social Change.* New Brunswick, NJ: Rutgers UP, 2006.

Hagen, Ross. "Fandom: Participatory Music Behavior in the Age of Postmodern Media." PhD diss., University of Colorado–Boulder, 2010.

Hall, Stuart. "Encoding and Decoding." *Media and Cultural Studies: Keyworks*, Rev. ed., Keyworks in Cultural Studies 2 (Malden, MA: Blackwell, 2006), 165–166.

Hanley, Jason J. "'The Land of Rape and Honey': The Use of World War II Propaganda in the Music Videos of Ministry and Laibach." *American Music* 22/1 (Spring 2004): 158-74.

Hansen, Christine Hall and Ranald D. Hansen R, "Schematic Information Processing of Heavy Metal Lyrics." *Communication Research* 18 (1991): 373-411.

Hebdige, Dick. *Subculture: The Meaning of Style.* New York and London: Methuen and Co.,1979.

Hecker, Pierre. 2012. *Turkish Metal: Music, Meaning, and Morality in a Muslim Society.* Farnham: Ashgate.

Heesch, Florian. 2011. "Extreme Metal und Gender: Zur Vokalpraxis der Death-Metal-Vokalistin Angela Gossow." In *Musik und Popularität: Aspekte zur Kulturgeschichte zwischen 1500 und heute,* edited by Nina Noeske and Sabine Meine, 167–86. Münster: Waxmann.

Hegarty, Paul. *Noise/Music: A History.* New York: Continuum Publishing, 2007.

Hesmondhalgh, David. "Post-Punk's Attempt to Democratise the Music Industry: TheSuccess and Failure of Rough Trade." *Popular Music* 16, no. 3 (1997): 255–74.

Holt, Fabian. *Genre in Popular Music.* Chicago: University of Chicago Press, 2007.

Johnson, Bruce, and Martin Cloonan. *Dark Side of the Tune: Popular Music and Violence.* Burlington, VT and Aldershot,Hampshire: Ashgate, 2008.

Joseffer, Jordan. 2010. Stone Vengeance. *Thrasher*, March.

Joseph, John. *The Evolution of a Cro-Magnon.* Brooklyn: Punkhouse Publishing Company, 2007.

Judah, J. Stillson. *Hare Krishna and the Counterculture.* New York: John Wiley & Sons, 1974

Kahn-Harris, Keith. *Extreme Metal.* New York: Berg, 2007.

Kittler, Friederich. *Gramophone, Film, Typewriter.* Translated by Geoffrey Winthrop-Young and Michael Wutz. Stanford, CA: Stanford University Press, 1999.

Krämer, Sybille. 2003. "Negative Semiologie der Stimme." In *Medien/Stimmen,* edited by Cornelia Epping-Jäger and Erika Linz, 65–82. Cologne: DuMont.

Krautkrämer, Florian, and Jörg Petri. 2011. "Horrormetaltypo– HeavyMetal als Gestaltungsmittel: Zum Verhältnis von Typografie, Metal und Horrorfilm." In *Metal Matters: Heavy Metal als Kultur und Welt,* edited by Rolf F. Nohr and Herbert Schwaab, 87–108. Münster: Lit.

Kristiansen, Jon. 2011. *Metalion: The Slayer Mag Diaries.* New York: Bazillion Points.

Kromhout, Melle Jan. "'Over the Ruined Factory There's a Funny Noise': Throbbing Gristle and the Mediatized Roots of Noise in/as Music." *Popular Music and Society* 34, no. 1 (February 2011): 23–34.

Kruse, Holly. "Subcultural Identity in Alternative Music Culture." *Popular Music*, vol. 12, no. 1 (Cambridge, UK: Cambridge University Press, Jan 1993), 33-41.

Kuhn, Gabriel, ed. *Sober for the Revolution: Hardcore Punk, Straight Edge, and Radical Politics.* Oakland, CA: PM Press, 2010.

Lahickey, Beth. *All Ages: Reflections on Straight Edge.* Huntington Beach, CA: Revelation Books, 1997.

Lincoln, Yvonna, and Egon Guba. *Naturalistic Inquiry.* Beverly Hills, CA: Sage, 1985.

Lindenbaum, Shirley "Thinking About Cannibalism," *Annual Review of Anthropology* 33 (January 1, 2004)

Lindow, John "Kidnapping, Infanticide, Cannibalism: A Legend from Swedish Finland," *Western Folklore* 57, no. 2/3 (April 1, 1998)

Lucas, Caroline, Mark Deeks, and Karl Spracklen. Grim up North: Northern England, Northern Europe and Black Metal. *Journal for Cultural Research* 15, no. 3 (2011): 279–95.

Mahon, Maureen. 2004. *Right to Rock: The Black Rock Coalition and the Cultural Politics of Race.* Durham: Duke University Press.

Mander, William, "Pantheism", *The Stanford Encyclopedia of Philosophy* (Summer 2013 Edition), Edward N. Zalta (ed.), forthcoming URL = <http://plato.stanford.edu/archives/sum2013/entries/pantheism/>. "Pantheism"

Marcus, Greil "Martian Genes," *The Threepenny Review*, no. 26 (July 1, 1986).

Maus, Fred. "The Disciplined Subject of Musical Analysis." In *Beyond Structural Listening?: Postmodern Modes of Hearing*, 13–43. Berkeley: University of California Press, 2004.

McDermott, Kathleen, "'All Dressed Up And Nowhere To Go': Youth Unemployment And State Policy In Britain," *Urban Anthropology and Studies of Cultural Systems and World Economic Development* 14, no. 1/3 (April 1, 1985)

McIntyre, Alice. *Participatory Action Research.* Qualitative Research Methods Series. Los Angeles: Sage Publications, 2008.

McLaughlin, Noel, and Martin McLoone. "Hybridity and National Musics: the Case of Irish Rock Music." *Popular Music* 19, no. 2 (April 1, 2000): 191.

Meléndez, Edwin, and Edgardo Meléndez. *Colonial Dilemma:Critical Perspectives on Comtemporary Puerto Rico.* USA: South End Press, 1999.

Memmi, Albert. *The Colonizer and the Colonized.* 1st American ed. New York,: Orion Press, 1965.

Montero, Maritza. "Community Action and Research as Citizenship Construction." [In eng]. *American Journal of Community Psychology* 43, no. 1–2 (Mar 2009): 149–61.

Mosser, Kurt, "'Cover Songs': Ambiguity, Multivalence, Polysemy," Popular Musicology Online 2008, http://www.popular-musicology-online.com/issues/02/mosser.html. (Accessed on 1 August 2012).

Mudrian, Albert (ed.). 2009. *Precious Metal: Decibel Presents the Stories Behind 25 Extreme Metal Masterpieces.* Cambridge: Da Capo.

Muster, Nori J. *Betrayal of the Spirit: My Life behind the Headlines of the Hare Krishna Movement.* Urbana, IL: U Illinois P, 1997.

Nehring, Neil, "Rock Around the Academy," American Literary History 5, no. 4 (December 1, 1993): 785.

———. "NOISE — THREE MUSICAL GESTURES: Expressionist, Introvert and Minimal Noise." *Journal of Music and Meaning* 2 (Spring 2004), http://www.musicandmeaning.net/issues/showArticle.php?artID=2.4.

Nessi, Federico, "Throbbing Gristle" Artlurker.com Accessed on August 28, 2010 from http://www.artlurker.com/2008/09/throbbing-gristle-by-federico-nessi/

Novak, David. "2.5x6 Metres of Space: Japanese Music Coffeehouses and Experimental Practices of Listening." *Popular Music* 27, no. 1 (2003): 15–34.

Novak, Jelena. 2010. "Monsterization of Singing: Politics of Vocal Existance." *New Sound* 36: 101–19.

Ohi, Kevin, "Devouring Creation: Cannibalism, Sodomy, and the Scene of Analysis in 'Suddenly, Last Summer'," *Cinema Journal* 38, no. 3 (April 1, 1999): 39.

O'Meara, Catherine. "New York Noise: Music in the Post-industrial City, 1978–1985." PhD diss., UCLA, 2006.

Oren, Michel. "Anti-Art as the End of Cultural History." *Performing Arts Journal* 15, no. 2 (May, 1993): 1–30.

Overthun, Rasmus. 2009. "Das Monströse und das Normale: Konstellationen einer Ästhetik des Monströsen." In *Monströse Ordnungen: Zur Typologie und Ästhetik des Anormalen,* edited by Achim Geisenhanslüke and Georg Mein, 43–79. Bielefeld: Transcript.

Pattison, Robert. *The Triumph of Vulgarity: Rock Music in the Mirror of Romanticism.* (New York: Oxford UP, 1987), 10–15.

Phillipov, Michelle. *Death Metal and Music Criticism: Analysis at the Limits.* New York: Lexington Books, 2012.

Pieslak, Jonathan. *Sound Targets: American Soldiers and Music in the Iraq War.* Bloomington and Indianapolis: Indiana University Press, 2009.

Pillsbury, Glenn T. 2006. *Damage Incorporated: Metallica and the Production of Musical Identity.* New York and London: Routledge.

Pinto, Vito. 2012. *Stimmen auf der Spur: Zur technischen Realisierung der Stimme in Theater, Hörspiel und Film.* Bielefeld: Transcript.

Pittam, Jeff. 1994. *Voice in Social Interaction: An Interdisciplinary Approach.* Thousand Oaks: Sage.

Plasketes, George, "Further Re-flections on 'The Cover Age': A Collage Chronicle," in *Play It Again: Cover Songs in Popular Music*, George Plasketes, ed., (Burlington, VT: Ashgate, 2010): 29.

Prabhupada, A.C. Bhaktivedanta Swami. *Bhagavad Gita As It Is.* 2nd ed. Mumbai: Bhaktivedanta Book Trust, 1986.

Purcell, Natalie J. 2003. *Death Metal Music: The Passion and Politics of a Subculture*. Jefferson: McFarland.

Reiko "Throbbing Gristle Interview" in *RE/Search #4/5*, V. Vale ed. (San Francisco: Re/Search Publications, 2007)

Rettman, Tony. *Why Be Something That You're Not: Detroit Hardcore 1979–1985* (Huntington Beach, CA: Revelation Records, 2010).

Reynolds, Simon. *Rip it Up and Start Again: Postpunk 1978–1984* (England: Penguin 2005).

Rhodes, Eric Bryant, "The Filth and the Fury," *Film Quarterly* 54, no. 3 (March 1, 2001): 58.

Rivera, José Ortiz "Cifra Récord De 1,135 Asesinatos En El 2011." *El Nuevo Día*, December 31, 2011 2011.

Rodgers, Tara. *Pink Noises: Women on Electronic Music and Sound.* Durham: NC: Duke University Press, 2010.

Rondón, César Miguel, Frances R. Aparicio, and Jackie White. *The Book of Salsa: A Chronicle of Urban Music from the Caribbean to New York City*. Latin America in Translation/En Traducción/Em Tradução. Chapel Hill: University of North Carolina Press, 2008.

Rushkoff, Douglas *Media Virus: Hidden Agendas in Popular Culture* (New York: Ballantine Books, 1994)

Russolo, Luigi. *Art Of Noises.* Translated by Barclay Brown. New York: Pendragon Press, 1986.

Saarig, Roni *The Secret History of Rock: The Most Influential Bands You've Never Heard* (New York: Billboard 1998)

Sakakibara, Ken-Ichi, Leonardo Fuks, Hiroshi Imagawa, and Niro Tayama. 2004. "Growl Voice in Ethnic and Pop Styles." In *Proceedings of the International Symposium on Musical Acoustics (ISMA2004)* http://www.hoku-iryo-u.ac.jp/~kis/paper/isma04.pdf.

Sangild, Torben. "Aesthetics of Noise." Copenhagen: Datanom, 2002. http://www.ubu.com/papers/noise.html.

Savage, Jon. *England's Dreaming: Anarchy, Sex Pistols, Punk and Beyond* (New York: St. Martin's Press, 1991).

Scheller, Jörg. 2011. "Vom Schrei zur Schreischule: Heavy Metal als Paradessenz." In *Metal Matters: Heavy Metal als Kultur und Welt*, edited by Rolf F. Nohr and Herbert Schwaab, 279–89. Münster: Lit.

Schiffer, Sheldon "The Cover Song as Historiography, Marker of Ideological Transformation," *Play It Again: Cover Songs in Popular Music*, George Plasketes, ed. (Burlington, VT: Ashgate, 2010)

Schwandt, Thomas. *Dictionary of Qualitative Inquiry*. Thousand Oaks, CA: Sage, 2001.

Serres, Michel. *Genesis.* Translated by Geneviève James and James Nielson. Ann Arbor: University of Michigan Press, 1995.

Sheinbaum, John. 2002. "'Think About What You're Trying To Do To Me': Rock Historiography and the Construction of a Race-based Dialectic." Ed. Roger Beebe, et al. *Rock Over the Edge: Transformations in Popular Music Cultures.* Durham and London: Duke University Press.

Shuker, Roy. *Understanding Popular Music* (New York, NY: Taylor & Francis 2008), 127.

Singel, Ryan. "Report: Teens Using Digital Drugs to Get High." *Wired*, July 14, 2010, http://www.wired.com/threatlevel/2010/07/digital-drugs/.

Smith, Nick. "The Splinter in Your Ear: Noise as the Semblance of Critique."*Culture, Theory and Critique* 46/1 (2005): 43–59.

Snell, Dave, and Darrin Hodgetts. "Heavy Metal, Identity and the Social Negotiation of a Community of Practice." *Journal of Community & Applied Social Psychology* 17, no. 6 (2007): 430–45.

Spracklen, Karl, Andy R. Brown, and Keith Kahn-Harris. "Metal Studies? Cultural Research in the Heavy Metal Scene." *Journal for Cultural Research* 15, no. 3 (2011): 209–12.

Sundberg, Johan. 1987. *The Science of the Singing Voice.* DeKalb: Northern Illinois University Press.

Thacker, Eugene. 2010. "Three Questions on Demonology." In *Hideous Gnosis: Black Metal Theory Symposium 1*, edited by Nicola Masciandaro, 179–219. Leipzig: Amazon Distribution.

Théberge, Paul. *Any Sound You Can Imagine.* Hanover, NH: University Press of New England, 1997.

———. *The Parasite.* Translated by Lawrence R. Schehr. Baltimore and London: The Johns Hopkins University Press, 1982.

Tirado, F. "Lamb of God: "No Somos Satánicos." *El Nuevo Día*, October 7, 2010.

Tsitsos, William. "Rules of Rebellion: Slamdancing, Moshing, and the American Alternative Scene," *Popular Music*, vol. 18, no. 3 (Cambridge, UK: Cambridge University Press, OCT 1999), 399.

Toshiharu, Mikawa. "Noise in Japan (Part 2)," http://japanoise.net/j/ incapal 5.htm.

Trogotronic. "Trogotronic Information." http://trogotronic.com.

Vale, V. "Genesis and Paula P-Orridge" *RE/Search Modern Primitives* (San Francisco: Re/Search Publications 1989).

Vale, V. "Throbbing Gristle on KPFA" in *RE/Search #4/5*, V. Vale ed. (San Francisco: Re/Search Publications, 2007)

Vale, V. "Genesis P-Orridge Interview" in *RE/Search #4/5*, V. Vale ed. (San Francisco: Re/Search Publications, 2007)

Varas-Diaz, Nelson and Irma Serrano-Garcia. "The Challenge of a Positive Self-Image in a Colonial Context: A Psychology of Liberation for the Puerto

Rican Experience." [In eng]. *Am J Community Psychol* 31, no. 1–2 (Mar 2003): 103–15.
Viano, Maurizio "Sid and Nancy," *Film Quarterly* 40, no. 3 (Spring 1987)
Waksman, Steve. 2009. *This Ain't the Summer of Love: Conflict and Crossover in Heavy Metal and Punk.* Berkeley: University of California Press.
Waldenfels, Bernhard. 2003. "Stimme am Leitfaden des Leibes." In *Medien/Stimmen*, edited by Cornelia Epping-Jäger and Erika Linz, 19–35. Cologne: DuMont.
Wallach, Jeremy, Harris M. Berger, and Paul D. Greene. *Metal Rules the Globe: Heavy Metal Music around the World.* Durham, NC: Duke University Press, 2012.
Walser, Robert. *Running with the Devil: Power, Gender, and Madness in Heavy Metal Music.* Middletown, CT: Wesleyan University Press, 1993.
Weinstein, Deena. 2011. "The Globalization of Metal." In *Metal Rules the Globe: Heavy Metal Music around the World*, edited by Jeremy Wallach, Harris M. Berger, and Paul D. Greene, 34–59. Durham: Duke University Press.
Weinstein, Deena. 2000. *Heavy Metal: Its Music and Its Culture.* NY: Da Capo.
Weinstein, Deena, "Appreciating Covers," *Play It Again: Cover Songs in Popular Music.* George Plasketes, ed. (Burlington, VT: Ashgate, 2010): 246.
Weinstein, Deena. *Heavy Metal – A Cultural Sociology* (New York, NY: Lexington 1991).
Wenger, Etienne *Communities of Practice : Learning, Meaning, and Identity.* Cambridge, England: Cambridge University Press, 1998.
Wenger, Etienne, Richard A. McDermott, William Snyder, and NetLibrary Inc. *Cultivating Communities of Practice a Guide to Managing Knowledge.* Boston, Mass.: Harvard Business School Press, 2002. http://www.col umbia.edu/cgi-bin/cul/resolve?clio4241520.
Wessinger, Catherine. "Deaths in the Fire at the Branch Davidians' Mount Carmel: Who Bears Responsibility?." *Nova Religio: The Journal of Alternative and Emergent Religions* 13, no. 2 (2009): 25–60.
Whittington, William. 2007. *Sound Design and Science Fiction.* Austin: University of Texas Press.
Winegarner, Beth. 2013. "An Unusual Heavy-Metal Love Story." *Newyorker.com* http://www.newyorker.com/online/ blogs/culture e/201 3/03/an-unusual-heavy-metal-love-story.html.
Wood, Robert. T. *Straightedge: Complexity and Contradictions of a Subculture.* Syracuse, NY: Syracuse UP, 2006.
Zumthor, Paul. 1994. "Body and Performance." In *Materialities of Communication*, edited by Hans Ulrich Gumbrecht and K. Ludwig Pfeiffer, translated by William Whobrey, 217–26. Stanford: Stanford University Press

About the Contributors

Eric Abbey is a professor of English and Literature at Oakland Community College in Michigan. He is the author of *Garage Rock and Its Roots: Musical Rebels and the Drive for Individuality* (McFarland, 2006). Eric also plays keyboards and sings with Michigan-based dub reggae band 1592.

Sean Ahern is a graduate student in the American Studies program at The University at Buffalo in New York. Sean's research interests include music scenes, punk studies, sports fandom, and geek culture. A graduate of the Communication Studies program at Colby-Sawyer College and the Popular Culture Studies graduate program at Bowling Green State University, Ahern's master's thesis looked at mass-media images within the music of The Clash. Sean has presented his work at the National Communication Association Annual Convention, the Popular Culture Association/American Culture Association National Conference, and the National University of Ireland at Galway. Sean's work on geek culture and the Scott Pilgrim series has been published online by O13Media (Oltremedia) at Roma Tre University. Sean serves on the editorial board for the *Journal of Fandom Studies*.

Brian Cogan, PhD is an Associate Professor in the Department of Communications at Molloy College in Long Island, New York. He is the author, coauthor, and coeditor of numerous books, articles, and anthologies on popular culture, music, and the media. His specific areas of research interest are media studies, music, fandom, punk rock, popular culture, comic books, graphic novels, and the intersection of politics and popular culture. He is best known as the author of *The Encyclopedia of Punk* (Sterling 2008). He is currently co-writing the autobiography of legendary punk drummer Marky Ramone.

Mika Elovaara, PhD is an author, teacher, coach, a former professional athlete, and a lifelong fan of punk and metal. He has presented numerous articles on punk and metal at regional, national and international conferences; written a variety of publications from encyclopedia articles for *The Encyclopedia of American Music and Culture* to ESL textbooks and research monographs, and is currently working on an extensive book on the meaning of metal, based on his five years of empirical research. Dr. Elovaara's courses include "The Political Voice of Punk," "(Mis)Understanding Music: Hip-Hop, Punk and Metal," and "Cultural Studies in Music: The Legacy of Legends" for graduate students. Mika is also a board member and reviewer for the *Journal of American Culture*.

Marcus Erbe, PhD is a Research Associate (Wissenschaftlicher Mitarbeiter) for Contemporary Music Studies at the University of Cologne, Germany. His PhD dissertation on the problem of transcribing electroacoustic music was awarded the 2011 prize by the Offermann-Hergarten Foundation. Dr. Erbe's research includes metal culture, contemporary music history, as well as media and art theory. He also writes for *Ox Fanzine*. A recent article titled "'This Isn't Over Till I Say It's Over': Narratives of Male Frustration in Deathcore and Beyond" is available online.

Kevin Fellezs, PhD is an Assistant Professor of Music at Columbia University, where he shares a joint appointment in the Institute for Research in African-American Studies. He is the author of *Birds of Fire: Jazz, Rock, Funk and the Creation of Fusion* (Duke University Press), a study of fusion (jazz-rock-funk) music of the 1970s. Fellezs has published articles in *Jazz Perspectives*, *Journal of Popular Music Studies*, *Popular Music History*, and the *Institute for Studies in American Music Newsletter*. He has also published essays in a number of edited anthologies including *Heavy Metal: Controversies and Countercultures* (Equinox).

Ross Hagen, PhD is a lecturer in Music History at Utah Valley University in Orem, UT. He received his B.A. in Music at Davidson College, N.C. in 2001, and his masters (2005) and PhD (2010) degrees in Musicology from the University of Colorado at Boulder. Hagen's research deals primarily with music fandom and intersections between popular music and the artistic avant-garde. Publications include a chapter in the book *Metal Rules the Globe* (Duke University Press, 2012) and entries in the *Grove Encyclopedia of American Music and the Encyclopedia of American Music and Culture*. Hagen has also presented papers at national conferences for the Society for Ethnomusicology, the International Association for the Study of Popular Music, and the Popular Culture Society. In addition to his academic work, Hagen has composed music and sound cues for several UVU theatrical productions and has released around a dozen albums on various independent record labels. Hagen is a decent bassist, an "okay" guitarist, and a recovering oboist.

Colin Helb, PhD is an assistant professor of communications at Elizabethtown College in Pennsylvania. His research focuses on issues of identity and culture in semiprofessional and localized music scenes. Colin runs the net.label Cornslaw Industries and records and performs under a variety of names.

Eliut R. Rivera-Segarra is a clinical psychology student at the Ponce School of Medicine and Health Sciences in Puerto Rico. His research interests include stigma theory, religion and heavy metal studies. Rivera-Segarra has presented his work on heavy metal studies at the Convention of the Puerto Rican Psychological Association and the EMP Pop Conference.

Nelson Varas-Díaz, PhD is a social psychologist and an Associate Professor at the University of Puerto Rico. Varas-Díaz's work on social stigma and communal identities has appeared in the *Interamerican Journal of Psychology, Qualitative Health Research, American Journal of Community Psychology, AIDS Education & Prevention, Qualitative Report,* and *Global Public Health.* He has engaged his previous research experience in the field of heavy metal studies and published a chapter on the contributions of progressive metal of social stigma theory in *Can I Play with Madness? Metal, Dissonance, Madness and Alienation,* edited by Colin A. McKinnon, Niall Scott and Kristen Sollee. Dr. Varas-Díaz is currently the principal investigator for the first systematic study of the heavy metal subculture in the Caribbean island of Puerto Rico.

Jeremy Wallach, PhD is an ethnomusicologist and anthropologist specializing in popular music, Dr. Wallach is Associate Professor in the Department of Popular Culture at Bowling Green State University, author of *Modern Noise, Fluid Genres: Popular Music in Indonesia, 1997–2001* (Wisconsin, 2008) and co-editor of *Metal Rules the Globe: Heavy Metal around the World* (Duke, 2011). His research interests include music and technology, Southeast Asia, world beat, punk, hardcore, and metal.

Evan Ware is a composer, music theorist, and doctoral candidate in the Music Theory and Composition program at University of Michigan working with Bright Sheng, Kristin Kuster, Karen Fournier, Walter Everett, and Joseph Lam. Evan is currently working on a dissertation about how the various covers of "My

Way" shed light on the ways in which meaning arises in the creation, performance, and reception of music. In addition to his academic studies, he devotes his time to studying Zen through meditation and kendo.

INDEX

Dionysian, 38, 40, 44, 46, 91
Discharge, 172
Disposed to Mirth, 61, 62
Do-it-Yourself (DIY), 95, 102, 112,
    117, 133, 172
domination, 13, 89, 97, 98, 99, 100,
    101
Doyles, Peter
    Echo and Reverb, 23
Dropkick Murphys, 21, 22, 23, 24, 25,
    26, 27, 28, 30, 31
    "(F)lanagans Ball", 24
    "10 Years of Service", 25
    "Cadence to Arms", 25
    "Caps and Bottles", 25, 27
    "Caught in a Jar", 25
    "Courtin' in The Kitchen", 23
    "Far Away Coast", 25
    "Johnny, I Hardly Knew Ya", 24
    "Kiss me I'm Shitfaced", 25
    "Tessie", 26
    "The Fields of Athenry", 23, 24, 25,
        26
    "The Irish Rover", 24
    "The Legend of Finn MacCumhail",
        25
    "The Rocky Road to Dubin", 23
    "The Rocky Road to Dublin", 25
    "The Wild Rover", 23, 25
    "Time to Go", 26
    "Famous For Nothing", 27
    "Going Out in Style", 21, 29, 30
    "Time to Go", 21, 26
    "Which Side are You on?", 25
    Blackout (2003), 21, 23, 28
    Do or Die (1998), 25
    Goin Out in Style (2011), 24
    Going Out in Style (2011), 21, 28,
        29
    Sing Loud, Sing Proud!, (2001), 25,
        27, 28
    The Meanest of Times (2007), 24,
        27
    The Warrior's Code (2005), 24
drugs, 142, 143, 144 146, 147, 148,
    151, 156, 158, 161
drum, 30, 122, 130, 140, 153, 156, 161,
    171
drummer, 123, 145, 157
Dubliners, 21

Duchamp, Marcel
    Bicyle Wheel, 94
    Fountain, 94
DVA Clock, 108, 115

E

Earth. *See* Black Sabbath
Earth Crisis, 176
egalitarian, 92, 97, 102
electronic music, 95
Elektra, 132
Ellwood, Robert S., 144
    on ISKCON, 143
Eluveitie, 42
    "Omnos", 42
empower. *See* power individual
Equal Vision Records, 139, 141, 150,
    153, 157, 159, 160
Eugenics Council, 96
Every Time I Die, 176
Exodus, 131, 132
Exploding Plastic Inevitable, 110
extreme music, 67, 91, 98, 99, 100,
    107, 109, 110, 115, 118, *See also*
    metal, extreme metal
extreme volume, 91, 99

F

Facebook, 78, 83, 85, 152
Factory Records, 114
Fairbain, Nicholas
    on Throbbing Gristle use of grant
        money, 112
Fanon, Frantz
    on colonialism, 79
fanzine, 61, 94, 133, 158
fascism, 99, 107, 108, 114
Feisty Cadavers, 174
Ferret Records, 171
Finntroll, 41, 42
    Tundra (band member), 41
Fish, Rob. *See* 108
Flannigan, Harley. *See* Cro-Mags
Flogging Molly, 22
Fluxus, 94, 110, 111
Foley, Maurice
    Madhumangala Dasa, 148

Negative Approach, 169, 174, 175,
177, 178
Nehring, Neil, 1
Nessi, Federico
on Throbbing Gristle importance,
107
Neubaten, 117
Neurosis, 172
New Wave of British Heavy Metal
(NWOBHM), 128
Nick Smith
on noise concerts as commercial
events, 102
Nightwish, 56
Nine Inch Nails, 108, 117
Nitsch, Herman, 110
No Doubt, 159, 161, 170
No Fun Festival, 91, 101
noise music, 90
aesthetic, 89, 90, 91, 92, 93, 95, 96,
98, 99, 100, 101
industrial, 92, 108, 109, 110, 113,
114, 116, 117, 118
Japanoise, 95
mechanical, 92
military, 92
movement/genre, 95
movement/scene, 89, 90, 91, 92, 93,
94, 95, 96, 99, 101
music genre, 89, 90, 91, 92, 93, 94,
96, 100, 101
Novak, David, 94
Novak, Jelena, 66
on contemporary opera, 59
Novasak, 93
Novosad, Todd. *See also* Novasak and
Zoologist
on noise music artistic failure, 97
Nurse with Wound, 108, 115, 116
Nyby, Christian
The Thing from Another World
(1951), 59

O

Oceano, 176
Ochoa, Napoleón, 52, 53

cover of "Mother North", 51
O'Conner, Sinead, 23
Ohi, Kevin
film criticism, 14
O'Meara, Catherine
on comparing noise music, 94
Ortiz, Ramón
Ankla. *See also* Puya
Osbourne, Ozzy
"Suicide Solution", 38
othering, 13, 14, 15, 145
dehumanization, 14, 114
self-othering, 21, 23
Overthun, Rasmus, 58
typology of monster, 57

P

Paganfest, 36
Painjerk, 100
Pantera
5 Minutes Alone (1993) with Phil
Anselmo, 60
Paradise, Mike. *See* 108
Parents' Music Resource Center
"Parental Advisory
Explicit Lyrics", 37, 39
Parents' Music Resource Center, 37, 38
Parker, Charlie, 145
Pattison, Robert, 178
*The Triumph of Vulgarity, Rock
Music in the Mirror of
Romanticism*, 173
Patton, Charley, 121
Peter Christopherson
aka Sleazy. *See* Dropkick Murphys
Phillipov, Michelle, 66
Death Metal and Music Criticism
(2012), 66
Phillips, Sam, 126
Pink Floyd, 111
Pinto, Vito, 66
on voice, 59
plainchant, 55
Plant, Robert, 56, 129
Plasketes, George, 1
Pogues, The, 21, 23, 25, 30